M000290867

Research Design

SAGE has been part of the global academic community since 1965, supporting high quality research and learning that transforms society and our understanding of individuals, groups, and cultures. SAGE is the independent, innovative, natural home for authors, editors and societies who share our commitment and passion for the social sciences.

Find out more at: **www.sagepublications.com**

Connect, Debate, Engage on Methodspace

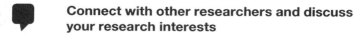 **Connect with other researchers and discuss your research interests**

 **Keep up with announcements in the field, for example calls for papers and jobs**

 **Discover and review resources**

Engage with featured content such as key articles, podcasts and videos

Find out about relevant conferences and events

Methodspace

Connecting the Research Community

www.methodspace.com

brought to you by

⑤SAGE

STEPHEN GORARD

Research Design

Creating Robust Approaches for the Social Sciences

SAGE

Los Angeles | London | New Delhi
Singapore | Washington DC

Los Angeles | London | New Delhi
Singapore | Washington DC

SAGE Publications Ltd
1 Oliver's Yard
55 City Road
London EC1Y 1SP

SAGE Publications Inc.
2455 Teller Road
Thousand Oaks, California 91320

SAGE Publications India Pvt Ltd
B 1/I 1 Mohan Cooperative Industrial Area
Mathura Road
New Delhi 110 044

SAGE Publications Asia-Pacific Pte Ltd
3 Church Street
#10-04 Samsung Hub
Singapore 049483

Editor: Katie Metzler
Assistant editor: Anna Horvai
Production editor: Ian Antcliff
Copyeditor: Jennifer Hinchliffe
Proofreader: Kate Harrison
Marketing manager: Ben Griffin-Sherwood
Cover design: Francis Kenney
Typeset by: C&M Digitals (P) Ltd, Chennai, India
Printed by: MPG Books Group, Bodmin, Cornwall

© Stephen Gorard 2013

First published 2013

Apart from any fair dealing for the purposes of
research or private study, or criticism or review, as
permitted under the Copyright, Designs and Patents
Act, 1988, this publication may be reproduced, stored
or transmitted in any form, or by any means, only with
the prior permission in writing of the publishers, or in
the case of reprographic reproduction, in accordance
with the terms of licences issued by the Copyright
Licensing Agency. Enquiries concerning reproduction
outside those terms should be sent to the publishers.

Library of Congress Control Number: 2012944072

British Library Cataloguing in Publication data

A catalogue record for this book is available from the
British Library

ISBN 978-1-4462-4901-7
ISBN 978-1-4462-4902-4 (pbk)

Contents

List of Tables

List of Figures

About the Author

Stephen Gorard is Professor of Education and Well-being at the University of Durham, a Methods Expert for the US government Institute of Education Science, member of the ESRC Grants Awarding Panel, and Academician of the Academy of Social Sciences. His work concerns the robust evaluation of education as a lifelong process, focused on issues of equity and effectiveness. He is a widely read and cited methodologist, involved in international and regional capacity-building activities, and used regularly as an adviser on the design of evaluations by central and local governments, NGOs and charities. He is currently an evaluator for the European Commission Directorate-General for Education and Culture, the Department of Work and Pensions, the Food Standards Agency, the Learning and Skills Information Service, and the Educational Endowment Foundation. He is working on identifying the causal link between attitudes, behaviour and school attainment for the Joseph Rowntree Foundation, patterns of school intakes for the British Academy, enhancing parental involvement for the Nuffield Foundation, multiple randomised controlled trials of policy and practice for the Educational Endowment Foundation, and improving social science research for the ESRC RDI. He is author of nearly 1,000 books and papers.

Preface

This new book is based on my own experiences of all the approaches described herein. It is for those who want to design their own research, or make critical judgements about the designs of others. It is suitable for new researchers, easy to read, simple in style, with little terminology, and intended for a wide audience. The book includes the elements of research designs, a description of the common existing designs, and even advice on sampling, analysis, ethics, and writing your first research proposal. It contains a large number of craft tips. Yet, it is not simply a cookbook or a set of off-the-shelf designs, and does not offer push-button solutions. Rather, it is about strategies for research, the logic of research, and how to make convincing research-based claims. It empowers readers to make judgements by focusing on why the elements of design matter, and how they can be used to generate an almost infinite variety of study designs. This book is also highly innovative, introducing new ideas for research design. Some readers will find some content contentious, but I have tried to provide a reasoned argument for all steps throughout. Even so, writing a book of this ambition is a tough task. I would urge readers to think carefully about the material in the book, and to pursue the examples and references cited within it.

Writing a book about research design for social scientists is a special challenge, because social science is so varied, ranging from approaches like cultural studies, through applied fields like business studies, to disciplines like psychology. Design is the 'Cinderella' of methods training. A typical training course for social scientists might move from epistemological considerations to methods of data collection and analysis, without any consideration of study design. There are plenty of books about instrument or sample design, and even more about methodology. Design tends to be confused with paradigm, data collection, or analysis. As a consequence, many researchers do not consider design as a separate issue when planning their own research. Many may not even know what design is, or feel that it is something reserved for those conducting factorial experiments or analysing cohort studies. Writing about research design is also a challenge because there is quite strong resistance to it. When people say that something is a Cinderella, they usually mean that it is ignored or forgotten. But in the fairy story, if you recall, Cinderella is deliberately repressed by her 'ugly' sisters. That is what I mean also about design. There is some unaccountable hostility to it, perhaps by those who have the most to lose if research improves. As this book illustrates, design leads to better social science research, just like any form of serious planning ahead would.

This book stems partly from preparing for a new project, funded by the UK Economic and Social Research Council (ESRC) as part of its Researcher Development Initiative, about the use of design in helping to explain techniques of analysis for new researchers. Thanks go to all involved, particularly Carole Torgerson, to Patrick Brindle for reminding me to write this book, to the reviewers for their helpful comments, to Patrick White especially for reading the first draft so carefully, and to my family for putting up with me while I wrote it.

Glossary and Key to Symbols

Action research – applied research, iteratively modifying and testing interventions in real-life settings, but the term is now sometimes restricted to reflective participatory studies.

Blind – where a research participant is not aware of their allocated group in a trial, thereby protecting against internal bias and subversion.

Case – the unit of analysis in a study, such as a sample or population member.

Case study – a study of one case, containing none of the elements of design, and sometimes used incorrectly to refer to in-depth work.

Causal model – link between cause and effect, usually consisting of an association, sequence of events, explanation, and intervention.

Cohort study – a longitudinal design, following a group of cases, often people born in the same short period of time.

Cross-sectional design – a snapshot study taking place in one time period, often involving a comparison of sub-groups.

Design effect – an estimated figure used to inflate the minimum sample size required for a cluster randomised design.

Design-based study – an iterative, developmental approach to creating an idea or artefact.

Design notation – a formal way of expressing the outline design of a study, using the following symbols to represent elements, arranged across the page to represent time, and down the page to represent sub-groups of cases:

O   This is an episode of data collection (unspecified type)

X   This is an intervention or treatment applied to the cases

N   This is a group of cases allocated to the group non-randomly

R   This is a group of cases allocated to the group randomly

M   This is a group of cases allocated to the group via matching

C   This is a group of cases allocated to the group either side of a cut-off value

[ ] These brackets suggest that the element is non-standard in some way. For example, [X] represents a naturally occurring intervention.

Double-blind – where neither the participants nor the researcher knows which group the participant is in (until later).

Effect size – a scaled measure of the difference between two groups, or their association. Commonly the difference between two means divided by their standard deviation.

Equipoise – a state of the existing knowledge about an intervention where there is some indication that it will work but there has not been a definitive test.

Experimental design – evaluation of a manipulated intervention where at least one randomly allocated sub-group receives the treatment and at least one does not. Includes laboratory experiments and field trials.

Fidelity to treatment – in an intervention study, an assessment of how well or faithfully the intervention is implemented by participants.

Granger causation – weak form of natural experiment in which predictors are removed from a regression model to see if this leads to a change in the outcome variable.

Intention to treat – a form of analysis for pragmatic evaluations in which cases are analysed as part of the groups to which they were initially allocated even though they have dropped out or changed groups.

Interrupted time series – graphical approach to a natural experiment, looking for sudden differences in an ongoing trend, after an intervention.

Longitudinal design – study involving a sequence of data collection episodes taking place with the same cases, such as a cohort study.

Natural experiment – evaluation of an intervention not manipulated by the researcher, meaning that cases cannot be randomly allocated to control and treatment groups.

Meta-analysis – type of evidence synthesis in which the effect sizes of prior studies are combined arithmetically.

Placebo – false treatment given to sub-groups in a trial, to help preserve a blind situation.

Population – all possible cases of interest to a study, from which a sample may be selected.

Power – an indication of the strength of a study in terms of sample size, showing how small or variable an 'effect' size the study could detect.

Process evaluation – usually in-depth field work conducted as part of a trial to check how well the intervention is implemented (fidelity to treatment) and how participants react to it.

Propensity score – used for matching control cases in a natural experiment, based on identifying characteristics most likely to be linked to participation in the intervention arm.

Randomised controlled trial or RCT – evaluation of an intervention which is manipulated so that at least one randomly allocated sub-group receives the treatment and at least one does not.

Regression discontinuity – method for generating an unbiased comparator group in a natural experiment by looking at cases either side of an important threshold.

Researcher effect – unconscious impact the researcher can have on the nature of the findings, including demand characteristics in interviews, and differential awareness of some findings.

Sample – cases involved in a study, deliberately selected to represent a wider population.

Synthesis – process of summarising existing evidence on a topic, including systematic review, secondary analysis, and meta-analysis.

Warrant – the logical argument leading from research findings to the conclusions drawn.

1

Introduction – 'Design' as Distinct from Methods

ONE
What is research design?

SUMMARY

- Attention to research design at an early stage is necessary for rigorous social research.
- Many areas of social science do not pay enough attention to design.
- Many existing resources for new researchers over-emphasise research methods at the expense of design.
- The elements of a research design include the cases studied, their allocation to sub-groups, the timing and sequence of data collection, and any interventions.
- These elements can be portrayed in a simple design notation to represent new or existing designs.
- An important part of research design involves thinking beforehand about the kinds of conclusions that you might want to draw.

1.1 ▏▎ Introduction to design

This is a book about research design for social scientists. It argues that research design has been largely ignored in the development of new researchers, at the expense of a focus on methods of data collection and analysis. Perhaps this is because so many people generally care so little about their social science. To understand what I mean by this, consider areas of innovation where research design is strong. These might include the development of transport such as cars or elevators, of consumables such as medicines or packaged foods, and of gadgets from toasters to internet-capable televisions. In all of these areas, and many more, all of the products are tested before use. In many countries it is illegal to market such a product without rigorous testing. Even if it were not illegal, a strong pressure to test all products would come from the consumer. People want their aircraft to fly rather than crash, and their medicines to work rather than to poison them inadvertently. So, the research to test these things must be designed with a robust approach. Of course medicines and aircraft still fail, despite testing. This regrettable fact is not an argument against testing; it is an argument for more and better designed testing.

People should also care about the quality of studies in economics – witness the worldwide economic downturn in 2007/08 that was almost entirely un-predicted by the thousands of professional economic researchers in each country. The public should care about the billions of public money spent on school 'improvement' schemes that have no discernible impacts on the desired outcomes. Similar concerns should arise in research relevant to housing, crime, social services, business leadership, politics, international development, well-being, social inequalities, marketing, and a host of other fields. Perhaps people do not care as much as they might because, even where research in social science has serious public implications, the 'result' could be a long way off in the future, or hard to discern in the present. People rarely fall ill or die as a direct result of poor social science research. Now, this should not mean that they do not want improvements in public services like housing, education, or criminal justice. But perhaps their concern is less immediate than the fear that a badly designed plane might crash, because the consequences of poor design in social science could be less visually dramatic.

Two other reasons may be that social science research is often ignored by its potential users such as politicians, and practitioners in the public services, and that its research findings are often of very poor quality anyway. None of these reasons is an excuse, but in combination they might form an explanation for how and why social science research gets away with ignoring research design. What this book does is to imagine that more people genuinely care about the quality of social science research, in the way that they care about the effectiveness and safety of aircraft and medicines. The book imagines that when a child is taken into care, or a government changes the sentencing guidelines for criminal courts, then the public would demand that these decisions are made using the best possible evidence.

Design is not chiefly about techniques or procedures. It is more about care and attention to detail, motivated by a passion for the safety of our research-based conclusions. At its simplest, research design is about convincing a wider audience of sceptical people that the conclusions of the research underlying important decisions are as safe as possible. This is perhaps the major difference between the objects of design in medicine and engineering, where things can be seen to work or fail quickly, and in most social sciences, where we can only seek to be convincing. If something works, that is convincing in itself, but where we do not know whether something works, we can at least demand to be convinced that it *ought* to work. We should want to be convinced that it is worth risking the happiness of a family by removing a child from its parents, risking public safety by releasing prisoners early, or spending public money on almost any intervention. Such decisions might be correct, or they might be a wasted opportunity or worse. It is the task of social scientists to help make such decisions as foolproof as possible. At present, despite a small amount of excellent work in every field, this is just not happening sufficiently.

New researchers largely complete their development lacking any understanding of research designs, and this is reflected in the inadequate work of many areas of public policy research. There are many examples of public policy interventions, some covered in this book, that have been well-intended and rolled out into practice on the basis that they seem plausible and unlikely to do any harm. Yet when they have been rigorously evaluated, they have been found to be ineffective or even harmful. This means that ineffective and even harmful initiatives can divert scarce resources away from effective ones – a particular problem in the current economic downturn, when decisions are being made to abandon programmes on a whim rather than in terms of genuine cost-effectiveness. So, policy-makers and public auditors are increasingly calling for good research evidence on the development of cost-effective and efficient policy and practice solutions, establishing causal-type relationships between innovative changes and their desired effects. This is a key ethical issue for publicly-funded research.

In an attempt to improve the situation, this book is for a range of audiences. These suggested readers include newer researchers in those areas of social science where design is already important – including health promotion studies, for example. For them, the purpose of the book is to provide a relatively gentle introduction that can lead to more advanced templates for rigorous research design. The book is also for newer researchers in areas where research design is present only in a limited fashion. It should encourage them to go beyond focusing almost exclusively on longitudinal designs in sociology, or merely laboratory experiments in psychology. For them, the purpose of the book is to set the common design(s) within their disciplines into a wider context, and to suggest that a mature social science requires a greater variety of designs. Perhaps, most urgently, this book is for newer researchers in those many areas of social science where design is almost completely absent, where methods resources do not even address design, or it is confused with instrument design, *post hoc* statistical procedures, or bizarre issues like 'paradigm wars' (Gorard 2004a). This is probably the situation in most fields, including economics – the supposed 'queen' of the social sciences.

This is most definitely a book for readers who do not know what research design is, did not take a course on it as a doctoral researcher, who would otherwise feel content to continue with their existing approach to generating evidence for public consumption, and whose mentors, supervisors and colleagues feel the same. As this book argues, such complacency is unethical and unwarranted. In the example areas listed so far there are key issues of safety, efficiency and equality. People have lost their jobs as a result of an economic downturn caused partly by untested financial products, for example. The public should care about such things, but the researchers who work in such areas often claim to care about them even more. If they do care, they will want to ensure that they design their research to be as rigorous as possible. Ignoring design is one way of saying openly to the world – 'I don't care about the quality of my research, the wasted opportunities it represents, the waste of peoples' time participating in or reading it, or the dangers to the very people that the research is meant to help'.

1.2 ⫶ Design and methods

An important point for readers to understand is that research design is <u>not</u> about methods of data collection and analysis. What all rigorous research designs, and variants of them, have in common is that they do not specify the kind of data to be used or collected. No kinds of data, and no particular philosophical predicates, are entailed by common existing design structures such as longitudinal, case study, randomised controlled trial or action research. A good intervention study, for example, could and should use a variety of data collection techniques to understand whether something works, how to improve it, or why it does not work. Case studies involve immersion in one real-life scenario, collecting data of any kind ranging from existing records to *ad hoc* observations. The infamous 'Q'-words of qualitative and quantitative, and mixed methods approaches are therefore not kinds of research design; nor do they entail or privilege a particular design. Of course, all stages in research can be said to involve elements of 'design'. The design of instruments for data collection is one example. But research design, as usually defined in social science research, and as discussed throughout this book, is a prior stage to each of these. Thinking about methods before design is similar to an architect ordering building materials or setting deadlines for construction before settling on what the building will be (de Vaus 2001).

This point is quite commonly confused in the literature, where randomised controlled trial designs are seen as tied to 'quantitative' methods of data collection and analysis (Ceglowski et al. 2011), or it is assumed that a life-course research design must be 'qualitative' (Fehring and Bessant 2009). This point is also confused in some research methods resources, even those purportedly about design, including Creswell and Plano Clark (2007) who are really writing about methods issues not about research design. These writers and many like them contribute to the widespread misunderstanding of design issues. Do not be misled. Otherwise, judgement about what should be a design issue, such as how well the research will cater for rival explanations of the evidence, will be confused with judgement about the perceived merits of a method, such as whether to use a survey or interviews.

A study that followed infants from birth to adolescence, weighing them on 1 January every year, would be longitudinal in design. A study that followed infants from birth to adolescence, interviewing their parents about their happiness every year, would also be longitudinal. A study that did both of these would still be longitudinal, even though some commentators would distractingly and pointlessly categorise the first study as 'quantitative', the second as 'qualitative', and the third as 'mixed methods'. In each example, the design – 'longitudinal', or collecting data from the same cases repeatedly over a period of time – is the same. This illustrates that the design of a study does not entail a specific form of data to be collected, nor does it entail any specific method of analysis; nor does any method require a specific research design.

Almost all existing research resources for newer researchers concern methods of data collection and analysis, and almost all of the rest concern red herrings about paradigms, or treating serious subjects like epistemology as though they were fashion items to be tried on and rejected on a whim. This is true even of many texts that claim to be about research design. This book is very different. Methods of investigation and the philosophy of social science are important, and aspects of both appear throughout the book. But they are not its starting point or its focus.

1.3 ᛁᚨᛁ The elements of design

The elements of design covered in this book include the cases (participants) involved, the ways in which cases can be allocated to sub-groups, the time sequence of data collection episodes, and any manipulated interventions. These elements are the same, except perhaps for some terminology, as those presented by de Vaus (2001) and Shadish et al. (2002). The book presents these elements of design using a shorthand notation, as a convenient way of expressing more complex designs, and the differences between them. The notation is very simple, and all designs will also always be fully described and illustrated with examples where they first appear in a chapter. Do not be alarmed. What follows here is a brief introduction to the notation.

In a design, the cases are the participants in a study or the objects of a study. The letters R, C, M and N are used to denote groups of cases, allocated to their groups randomly (R), by using a cut-off point (C), through matching (M) or none of these (N). The letter O is used to represent an episode of data collection, which could be observation, measurements, conversations, text or indeed any form of data. If it is necessary to distinguish two or more different types of data collection, a sub-script will be added to the standard notation O. Thus, O_1 and O_2 might represent two different kinds of data taken from the same cases (such as a standard test and an interview). This vagueness about what the methods of data collection are is deliberate (see above). The letter X is used to represent an intervention or change of some sort that might influence the cases to which it is applied. Again, if it is necessary to distinguish two or more different types of intervention, a sub-script will be added to the standard notation X. Thus, X_1 and X_2 might represent two different kinds of treatments given to the same cases. I also use a square bracket, as in [X], to denote an intervention that occurs naturally rather than created by the research. Time is represented by a flow of events from left to right, and different groups of cases are denoted by different lines on the page. A simple example could be:

(→Time→)

N	X	O		(Group 1)
N		O		(Group 2)

This shows a study of an unknown number of cases, sub-divided into two groups (two lines on the page), and divided naturally or non-randomly (N for each). The first group of cases is given a treatment or intervention (X) and the second group is not (blank). Both groups then have the same unspecified data collected from them (each have an O without any sub-scripts). The diagram shows that the data collection (O) occurs after the intervention (X), and the intervention occurs after the allocation to groups (N) because of their order in the line representing time from left to right. There are varieties of design notations, and more complex issues involved, but this shorthand will do for the present. It will enable me to present the designs in this book as an easy picture, once you get the hang of the notation, and should allow you to make notes on any research you are reading and to communicate designs to colleagues.

1.4 ▐ The structure of this book

Research design in the social sciences is a way of organising a research project or programme from its inception in order to maximise the likelihood of generating evidence that provides a convincing answer to the research questions for a given level of resource. Chapter Two presents a simplified cycle for a field or programme of research and how this relates to the elements of design. The next section of the book looks at the rationale for research designs. It provides grounds for deciding on which design is most appropriate for a given study. Chapter Three looks at research questions, how we might generate them, and best express them in order to achieve useful and meaningful answers. Chapter Four introduces the idea of a warrant for research claims, as the part of an argument that could convince a sceptical person to believe the answers to the research questions. Chapter Five is all about the nature of causal claims, which have a special place in explanatory social science research.

The third section of the book concerns the various elements of a design. There are many elements to consider in a research design, but they commonly include the selection of cases of interest to be used in the research (Chapter Six), the appropriate allocation of cases to sub-groups and their subsequent comparison (Chapter Seven), what happens over time (Chapter Eight), and any intervention to be evaluated (Chapter Nine). A specific design or project may have only some of these elements, but some well-known designs involve all of them. These elements of a research design can be combined and varied in many ways, so that each new project might devise a completely new kind of design. On the other hand, there is a variety of standard designs that it is worth being familiar with, both to assist when reading the research of others, and to give some idea of the range available for your own research.

The next section moves to slightly more advanced issues relating to design. A range of further and currently less common research designs is presented in Chapter Ten. Chapter Eleven discusses traditional and generic threats to the validity of research conclusions, and introduces some important new ones. The key issue of how to differentiate between patterns or simply 'noise' in the data is addressed in Chapter Twelve. Chapter Thirteen looks at the ethics of research design, and conflicts of interest in the conduct of research.

Finally, Chapter Fourteen sums up the argument that a robust approach to social science research design is necessary, and offers a few guidelines for choosing a design and developing a grant application, using the principles and ideas in this book.

Each chapter also ends with three 'exercises' that readers might like to consider while reading. These exercises will tend to get more complex and involve greater judgement as the book progresses. They are followed by my notes and suggestions for discussion, which are an important part of the argument and narrative of the book. They often introduce material in a different way, or even suggest ideas not covered elsewhere, and so should be treated as an integral part of the text. Each chapter ends with a suggestion for further reading on the same topic.

⇌ Initial exercises on research design

1 Using the simple design notation described in this chapter, a piece of research might be presented as:

N	O	X	O	(Group 1)
N			O	(Group 2)

Assume that this design represents an evaluation of a new training course for social workers. The intervention (X) is the training course. In one region, a group of volunteers (Group 1) take the training course, and their remaining colleagues (Group 2) do not. The volunteer group are initially given a test of the skills that the training is intended to improve. After training, the volunteers and their colleagues (Group 2) are given the same test.

 a How many groups of cases are there in this research design?
 b How have the cases been allocated to groups – and have they been allocated by chance or not?

c How can we tell from the design notation that Group 1 was given a test before the training?

d If the volunteers score better on the test after the training than they did before, suggest a few reasons why this is not necessarily evidence that the training is the cause of the improvement.

e If the volunteers also score better on the final test than their colleagues, suggest a few further reasons why this is not necessarily evidence that the training is the cause of the difference between Groups 1 and 2.

f Finally, if the colleagues do as well as the volunteers in the skills test, suggest at least one reason why this is not necessarily evidence that the training is ineffective.

2 Imagine designing a new piece of research that tries to follow a group of all men leaving a specific prison after their custodial sentence, in a specific month. The researcher will interview each person once as soon as possible after they leave prison, and then monitor them a year later to see if they have a job, have re-offended, and so on. What would the simplest version of this research look like in design notation?

3 Select a journal article reporting new research in your own area of interest. Try to present the design of this research using the simple notation introduced in this chapter.

⇐ Notes on initial exercises

1 a There are two groups in this design because there are two lines of notation, with each line representing the research process as experienced by one group.

b The cases have not been allocated to groups by chance. We know this because each line begins with **N**, denoting a non-random division between them. In the example, the first group consists of volunteers, and the second of everyone else in the study.

c We know from this design that Group 1 is given the skills test before the training, because the first episode of data collection (O) appears to the left of the treatment (X). Time is assumed to flow from left to right.

d The volunteers might score better on the test after the training than they did before simply by chance, especially if the difference is small. They might also do better through practice, because they have already taken the same test before the training. Or something else might have happened between the two tests, such as formative experiences at work. Any of these explanations and a host of others could show that the difference between the before-and-after tests is not related to the training. This is why it is important to have a comparable group that are also tested but do not receive the training.

e The volunteers might score better on the test than their colleagues, by chance or as a result of practice, or due to some other experience that is unique to the volunteers. But the simplest explanation could be that the two groups are clearly not comparable. By volunteering, the group that receives the training has perhaps shown itself to be more enthusiastic, better motivated and keener to improve their skills than the other group. They might therefore have performed better in the test than their colleagues even without the training. We do not know from this design.

f It is possible that the training is effective, even if the colleagues do as well as the volunteers in the skills test. Again, there are many possible reasons for this, including chance, or that the effect of the training is too small to be detected, or even that the volunteers were those who felt most in need of training, having a lower level of skill initially. Another quite common problem is termed 'contamination'. Where volunteers who receive the training and other colleagues work together in the same offices or departments, the colleagues may learn about the training second-hand via inadvertent cascading in conversation. The volunteers might show their friends materials from the training course to help them as well. So, the training could be effective but the results not show up as a difference in the scores because, in reality, the training has affected both groups. These ideas begin to give some idea of the complexities of design and the difficulties of designing a study whose results will convince a sceptical audience.

2 The simplest notation that matches the design for the prison leaver study could be:

$$N \qquad O_1 \qquad O_2$$

There is only one group (one line). The group is a natural cluster in one prison (not random), and there are two different episodes of data collection (not a repetition of the same data collection, as in question 1). There is no intervention – the prisoners have already left prison at the outset.

3 A surprising number of articles report research without specifying a design. In many cases this is because so few of the elements of a design are included in the study that it is not worth discussing. For example, a simple survey of business leaders might have this design:

$$N \qquad O$$

It does not matter how complex the subsequent analysis is, nor how sophisticated the questionnaire is. There is only one designed group. This is so even if the analysis later divides the cases temporarily into sub-groups like male/female or by the size of their businesses. As there is only one group, there is no pre-specified method of allocating cases to groups. There is no intervention and no time sequence. It is a snapshot study. The same design notation would be used if individual interviews replaced the survey, because the design is independent of the precise methods of data collection. And the same notation would be used if a series of focus groups replaced individual interviews. The 'groups' in a research design, represented by different lines in the notation, are those for whom the research process is different. If research involves six focus groups all doing the same thing, there is only one 'group' for design purposes. The same applies to 100 interviewees, or 1,000 survey respondents.

⇶ Suggested reading

Chapters One and Two in de Vaus (2001) *Research Design in Social Research*. London: SAGE.

TWO

Introducing designs in the cycle of research

SUMMARY

- Different types of research have different purposes, from synthesising what we already know about a topic, through developing a new theory, to monitoring how well a new approach works in practice.
- Different research designs will be particularly suitable for these different types of research. No one design is always applicable or best suited for an entire programme of study.
- Designs can be classified in a number of ways, such as whether they involve a pre-specified comparison or not, whether there is a sequence of data collection episodes, and whether they involve a deliberate intervention or not.
- Research findings are intrinsically more convincing when the research design uses the 'better' or positive half of such classifications. For example, a comparative claim is intrinsically more convincing with a pre-specified set of comparator sub-groups.
- Such consideration reveals that, all other things being equal, something like a case study will always tend to be the least convincing design, while something like a randomised controlled trial will tend to be the most convincing.

2.1 ❚❙❚ Introduction

This chapter starts by looking at the concept of an over-arching research cycle, and suggests that different designs might be more or less appropriate at different phases in that cycle. Each design covered in this book, and many others, has a place in social science. This section tries to show how they fit together in a programme working towards the solution of a social science puzzle.

2.2 |ıl Research cycle

Whatever area of social science you work in, it is likely that the field as a whole will look something like Figure 2.1. This is a simplified description of a full cycle for a research programme. It is based on a number of sources, including the genesis of a design study (Gorard with Taylor 2004), the UK Medical Research Council model for undertaking complex medical interventions (MRC 2000) and one OECD conception of what useful policy research looks like (Cook and Gorard 2007). The cycle is more properly a spiral which has no clear beginning or end, in which phases overlap, can take place simultaneously, and could iterate almost endlessly.

The various phases illustrated should be recognisable to anyone working in areas of applied social science, like public policy. I discuss each of these steps in slightly more detail below, and then in succeeding chapters. Any one study or researcher might contribute to only some of these steps, but the field as a whole ought to progress in something like this fashion. Unfortunately, some fields seem

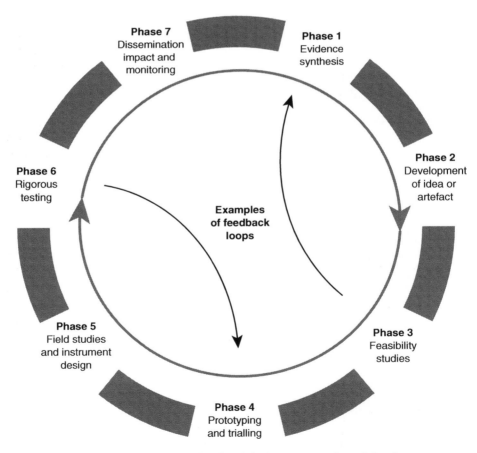

Figure 2.1 An outline of the full cycle of social science research and development

to have got stuck in a limited range of phases (Gorard et al. 2011). Of course not all ideas come to fruition. There should be questions that are answered by a synthesis alone. Then some ideas should halt at a pilot stage where they show no promise. But equally, this should not always happen. Some ideas ought to be developed all of the way to become tested 'products' engineered into use for other researchers, policy-makers or practitioners. These products could be theories, practical protocols, policy interventions or genuine artefacts like software or training manuals. The key point for this book is that different designs will be more appropriate at different phases in the cycle. So a healthy field, as a whole, will use a wide range of research designs – which means of course that everyone needs to know something about all designs, even if only to be able to conduct an appropriately critical literature review in their field.

Evidence synthesis

The cycle might start with an evidence synthesis, which should use existing data-sets and previously published literature in an unbiased way to produce a summary of what is already known in relation to the research question(s). The cycle might also end there, if existing evidence answers the question satisfactorily. In practice it tends not to, partly because the external funding structure for research discourages such honesty (Chapter Thirteen), and partly because researchers are generally so poor at conducting a synthesis of existing evidence. The characteristics of a good synthesis are discussed in Chapter Three. Once the existing evidence synthesis is complete, it should be clear what remains unanswered in the area of interest, and this can lead to a definition of the problem to be solved, the research purpose, and research questions.

Development and preparation

A high proportion of existing published work in social sciences seems to be in Phases 2 to 3 of the cycle. This is what may be envisaged as the research development phase. However, very little of this work currently starts with a serious attempt at research synthesis, offering instead only partial literature reviews and confusing conceptual frameworks. Even less of it moves on from this development work towards the preparation of a definitive large-scale study, or to creating something useful from the knowledge gained. Some of the reasons why this may be so were touched on in Chapter One.

Proto-typing and trialling of any new idea is vital, if resource is not to be wasted on a large-scale definitive study that has no chance of success. Trying ideas out at this development stage will tend to be done via small scale work, to minimise the risk and cost in case the idea does not work. With minimal risk and cost, several alternative ideas can be tried out in parallel. Feasibility studies can be as cheap as thought experiments (Chapter Nine), as simple as case studies, or they can be complex designs for multi-method data collection. Their purpose in the cycle is to assess the likelihood of success of the idea, and so to assist with the decision whether to proceed further in the cycle, or not. The decision can also be influenced by the potential gain from the idea, the resources required, and ethical issues.

Evaluation

Each prior phase might lead to a realisation that little more can be learnt and that the study is over, or that the programme needs radical revision and iteration to an earlier phase, or progression to a subsequent phase. However, the overall cycle can be envisaged as tending towards an artefact or 'product' of some kind. This product might be a theory (if the desired outcome is simply knowledge), a proposed improvement for public policy, or a tool/resource for a practitioner. In order for any of these outcomes to be promoted and disseminated in an ethical manner they must have been tested. A theory, by definition, will generate testable propositions. A proposed public policy intervention can be tested realistically and then monitored *in situ* for the predicted benefits, and for any unwanted and undesirable side effects. It is no good knowing that an intervention works if we do not also know that it is unpopular and likely to be ignored or subverted in practice. Similarly, it would be a waste of resource, and therefore unethical, simply to discover that an intervention did not work in Phase 6 and so return to a new programme of study in Phase 1. We would want to know why it did not work, or perhaps how to improve it, and whether it was effective for some regular pattern of cases but not for others. So in Phase 6, like Phase 1, the researcher or team who genuinely wants to find something out will naturally use a range of methods and approaches including measurement, narrative and observation. Methods really are independent of design.

2.3 ⋮ A simple design typology

The basic elements of research design introduced in Chapter One can be combined to form a wide variety of study designs. Most of these combinations would not have a well-known name but are as valid as any other combination nevertheless. The value of a design can only be judged in relation to the research questions it is intended to answer (Chapter Three). This in turn depends upon where the research programme is currently focused in terms of Figure 2.1. Some combinations of design elements have well-known names like 'case study' or 'longitudinal'.

One way of classifying such standard designs is in terms of whether they are active or passive. An active design would include a controlled intervention, introduced as part of the study. Examples of active designs that you may already have heard of include randomised controlled trials (RCTs), and laboratory experiments. Quasi-experiments, action research, interrupted time series, regression discontinuity, and design studies may also involve a specific intervention. All of these are intrinsically more convincing in testing a causal claim than completely passive designs (Chapter Nine). A passive design may consider changes over time but these changes do not occur as part of the research itself, because there is no specific or controlled intervention. Examples include standard cohort research, other longitudinal designs, case studies, and comparative or cross-sectional approaches.

Another way of classifying designs could be in terms of whether they involve a pre-specified comparator group, or not (Chapter Seven). Obviously, comparative studies are intrinsically more convincing in testing a comparative claim than non-comparative ones. Examples include RCTs, natural experiments, and comparative research. Non-comparative designs include standard longitudinal approaches and case studies.

A third way of classifying designs could be in terms of whether they involve repeated measures or some other planned elapse of time between the start and a final measure, or not. Such longitudinal designs are intrinsically more convincing in demonstrating a before-and-after claim than cross-sectional ones (Chapter Eight). Examples of designs with an automatic longitudinal element include standard cohort research, other longitudinal designs, RCTs, and natural experiments. Those usually without a longitudinal element include case studies, and comparative and cross-sectional approaches.

It is interesting that only RCTs and other experiments appear in the 'better' or positive half of each of these classifications. They are better for causal, comparative *and* time-dependent claims. In addition, RCTs have the advantage over quasi-experiments of having cases allocated to comparator groups at random. As shown in the rest of the book this means that given the right conditions and questions, an RCT or equivalent laboratory experiment is the best and most convincing design to use. Much of the rest of research, as in the full cycle, can be envisaged as working towards such a trial.

It is also notable that case studies are always in the worse half of each of these classifications. In themselves, they have no comparator, no intervention and no longitudinal element. As a design they are simply an episode of (possibly extended) data collection:

N   O

This notation represents observations (O) or data collected at one point in time with no intervention, no pre-defined comparator groups, and so no rule about how cases were allocated to comparator groups. With so few of the elements of research design present here, there is little that such research can do beyond exploratory initial descriptive preparation for subsequent studies. Such work might be useful in generating ideas and possible explanations for a causal model perhaps. However, the authors of such work rarely seem to generate such ideas. Even where the authors of such work describe it as exploratory, they do not then progress with it to a later phase of the cycle. Instead they seem merely to move to another exploratory study (see Gorard et al. 2011 for examples).

✹ A case study, in isolation, will never be the preferred design for any study that aims to be convincing or definitive. Case studies can be valuable, especially towards the start of the research cycle, largely because they are simple and quick to set up. I realise that some commentators would say that case studies are to be preferred because they allow a researcher to study a case in-depth. But you must recall the point from Chapter One. Designs are independent of the methods of data collection. It is as feasible that a case study was an examination of the financial accounts of one company as that a longitudinal study involved an in-depth observation of someone's adjustment to a new job over the first six months. No design has a monopoly on depth or breadth of data.

The need for warranted conclusions requires the researcher to identify the kind of claims to be made – such as descriptive, associative, or causal – and then ensure that the most appropriate possible design is used. A comparative claim *must* have an explicit and suitable comparator, although it is truly shocking how often this is not found. The warranting principle in Chapter Four is based on this consideration – if the claim to be drawn from the evidence is not actually true then how else could the evidence be explained? The research-based claim should be the simplest explanation for the available evidence. What the research design should do is eliminate (or at least test or allow for) the greatest possible number of alternative explanations before the final claim to knowledge is made. In this way, the design eases the analysis process, and provides part of the warrant for the research claim. Design makes research better.

There are a host of already known designs other than those mentioned so far, and presumably many more waiting to be combined from the elements of research. Which design is used for any study should depend largely on the kind of claims and conclusions to be drawn. And these in turn depend on the research questions to be answered, which are the subject of the next chapter.

⇶ Exercises on designs

1 Two doctoral researchers at a social science conference describe their research projects. The first researcher is a social historian, looking at the impact on the diet of agricultural labourers of the enclosure of common land in England. The researcher examines records and other sources relating to meals for the labourers in one area, from around 25 years before the recorded start of land enclosure, and then from around 50 years later. The second is an education researcher who has persuaded their own institution

to schedule their adult education classes more flexibly, in order to encourage a wider range of participants. This researcher has conducted a survey of people taking adult education classes in the year before the change took place, and in the year after. The survey asked people about their occupational and educational backgrounds.

a What is the simplest design notation for each study?
b How would the design look different if the second researcher had used interviews with the adult learners, rather than a survey?
c Both researchers want to argue that there was a change from the first to the second episode of data collection, and that this change was due to enclosure in the first study and the rescheduling of classes in the second. What is the biggest problem for their argument?
d How would you advise them to re-design each study to try and overcome this problem?

2 A third researcher at the same conference has used quite a complex research design, involving multiple groups and episodes of data collection. A member of the audience asks what the design is called, and then mocks the presenter for not knowing. Is it reasonable for a researcher to describe a design but not know what it is called?
3 Why might an intervention that was found to be reasonably effective in Phase 6 of a research cycle turn out to be much less effective when rolled out into widespread practice? Come up with a range of suggestions, perhaps through discussion in a group.

Notes on exercises on designs

1 a The simplest design notation for the first study could be:

N   O

N   [X]   O

Different lines are used here because the cases are different before and after the intervention of interest. Of course, the first researcher did not really intervene to create the mediaeval land enclosure system in England (how could they?). This is why I put the X in square brackets. But this limitation is the same for all history, retrospective accounts, archaeology, palaeontology and so on, and so I think it is reasonable to represent the design like this. The first researcher is looking at evidence from one time period and then looking at evidence from a later period, with an important intervening change. In some respects it does not matter whether this change has already happened or not, or quite how long ago it happened.

The simplest design notation for the second researcher could also be:

N   O

N   [X]   O

They have gathered evidence from one cohort of adult learners, waited until their institution altered something important, and then gathered evidence from a later cohort. In essence, the design is very similar to the first despite the surface differences in the topics.

b If the second researcher used interviews rather than a survey, this would make no difference to the design. Data collection is only about what goes on within each O episode, and this is traditionally unspecified at the level of research design.

c Both researchers face the same problem. They cannot tell whether any difference between the two time periods is due to the intervening specified change; whether it would have happened anyway; is due to differences between the people; or whether it is just natural variation caused by incompleteness of records or the vagaries of data collection. Their argument would be unconvincing, as it stands.

d Probably the simplest thing both researchers could do is to add a relevant comparison group to their design, to combine with the before-and-after element. The second researcher could look at the before-and-after participation rates in another institution that did not reschedule classes, or they could have rescheduled only some of their classes in the first year to see what happened. Therefore, the design could be:

```
N       O
N              [X]      O
N       O
N                       O
```

This design is discussed further as a difference-in-difference, in Chapter Ten. It is harder for the first researcher, but they could pick any of a variety of slightly weaker comparisons. For example, they could have looked at diets 50 years before the start of the study, or 50 years after it, and so tried to judge if the change specifically during the onset of land enclosure was remarkable in any way. Therefore, the design could be:

```
N       O
N               O
N                   [X]      O
```

As you see, passive designs for causal questions can get complicated very quickly. This kind of design is discussed further, as an interrupted time series, in Chapter Ten.

2 It might be a little embarrassing for the third researcher if they were using what was clearly a simple and well-known design like a cohort study but had not learnt the name. Names are a useful shorthand as long as both the researcher and the audience mean the same thing by it. Not knowing the name would not affect the validity of the research of course. However, the implication here is that the design is not well-known. Perhaps it is some combination of two or more off-the-shelf designs. In this case it does not matter at all if it has no name. Even if the researcher gave it a name this would be useless for the presentation because it is then almost certain that the audience would not know what the name meant. Given that the design will have to be explained anyway the name might just be confusing. In general, knowing the names of designs is over-rated. Where the design is simple, such as a case study, there is often considerable confusion and disagreement between experts about what it means. It is therefore ambiguous and needs spelling out. Where the design is unfamiliar and complicated then the name will not lead to recognition and could be ambiguous. So, it will still need spelling out. Design notation, or similar, is more likely to clarify the design, and is safer than just using a name.

3 There are many reasons why an intervention that was found to be effective in Phase 6 of a research cycle might turn out to be much less effective when rolled out into

widespread practice. The results of the evaluation might have been faked or inadvertently misunderstood by the researchers involved (Chapter Four), perhaps because of a conflict of interest (Chapter Thirteen). Did you consider that? The intervention might have been better resourced as an experiment than when it was rolled out. This often happens. The evaluation might have involved only volunteers, whereas the rollout might be imposed on all, leading to sullen participation. The context for the evaluation might have been more suitable for success than the greater variety of settings encountered on rollout. The general training to use the intervention might be worse than it was during the experimental phase. And so on.

Suggested reading

Gorard, S. (2010) 'Research design, as independent of methods'. In C. Teddlie and A. Tashakkori (eds) *Handbook of Mixed Methods*. Los Angeles: SAGE.

2

The Preliminaries of Research Design

THREE

Identifying researchable questions

SUMMARY

- Research questions and designs are clearly related, and the merits of any design are judged in terms of the questions it can help to answer.
- Questions arise from a variety of sources, sometimes set down by external agencies and sometimes stemming from deep personal interest.
- The formulation of questions can be assisted by reviewing the relevant literature, re-analysing existing data, and consideration of theory.
- Literature searches must be systematic and comprehensive, to minimise bias.
- Literature can help determine what needs to be done in order to move a field of research forward.
- Secondary data can establish a pattern, trend or issue to be investigated in more depth. It helps to avoid investigating something that does not exist!
- Theory can generate predictions to be tested by further research. Questions can be devised to help decide between two competing theories.
- Questions must be feasible, usually addressing a research 'puzzle'.
- Questions work well in small clusters ranging from descriptive to prescriptive.
- Above all, questions must be genuine. The researcher must be curious and willing to be surprised by the answers.

3.1 ‖ Introduction

This chapter is about research questions. The reason that this comes so early in a book on design is simple. As discussed in Chapter Two, there are no intrinsically good or bad research designs. The emphasis in research design is less on how to conduct a type of research than on which type is appropriate in the circumstances, given the research questions (Hakim 2000). It does not make sense, for example, to argue that a randomised controlled trial is always superior as a design to a comparative study, or a comparative study to a longitudinal one. A design can only be judged as more or less appropriate for the precise research question it is intended to answer. The design should provide the most convincing answer to the research question being asked. So, if the question is whether an intervention in public policy is effective or not then a randomised controlled trial may well be the most appropriate design. But if the question is whether boys report enjoying school more than girls then a randomised controlled trial would certainly not be an appropriate design. Forming and refining the questions to be answered by a new piece of research is an essential step in designing a study that will be convincing to a sceptical audience.

Research questions can stem from a number of different sources. Sometimes they are simply handed to the researcher as a contract. Someone wants a research question answered and is prepared to fund others to answer it. In this situation the key thing is to determine as precisely as possible what the funder wants answered. At the same time it is essential that the researcher remains independent. The funder can only specify the question. They must not control what the answer is (Chapter Thirteen). Sometimes research questions arise slightly less directly from current or future concerns in policy or practice. An example might be a completely independent evaluation of a new government policy. Sometimes the questions stem from the interest or autobiography of the researcher. Questions can also be generated by consideration of theory, by a review of existing research, or by a re-analysis of existing data. This chapter considers in turn the existing published literature, secondary analysis and theory as the bases for generating answerable research questions. It then suggests how literature, existing data and theory can be successfully synthesised. The chapter ends with some craft tips about creating research questions.

3.2 ▮▮ Reviewing the literature

One obvious way to generate research questions is to look at what has been published in a research area already. A review of existing published evidence can help determine the nature of a problem, what is currently not known about it, how people have generally researched it before, and whether there is widespread interest in it. It can identify completely unanswered questions. However, White (2009) points out that using existing work like this could also constrain your thinking, and the way you address the problem. This is not an argument against reviewing the literature. It is a suggestion to be careful, to think 'out of the box', and to allow other influences as well. Sometimes a topical issue, or slant on an issue, can be suggested via news reports or social media. It is even possible that media or political mis-representation of an issue is what sparks off a new research question.

A review of the literature must be done properly. It must be comprehensive and systematic in order to reduce partiality and bias. It must involve the full range of designs and methods of data collection and analysis for the same reason. Therefore, all researchers must be aware of the power and relative merits of different designs, and they must be capable of appreciating work using any available method. A review must be an overview of all relevant evidence. Suggesting that evidence is irrelevant simply because of its nature is obviously a cop-out. When someone says, as they frequently do, that they are only this or that kind of researcher ('qualitative' is one example), what they really mean is that they choose bias and partiality because they are too idle or too incompetent to understand or use a fuller range of research.

Existing knowledge and the expertise of others are both good places to start. It is also a good idea to advertise for evidence relevant to a topic, perhaps posting a request via a website or social media links for experts to suggest sources. Keeping up to date with journals in your area is also essential. Most publishers have a free contents alerting procedure, sending you an email with the contents pages for any new journal issue you are registered for. I also still find it useful to hand search some key journals, often using the hard copy as a break from reading electronically. Nevertheless, most material is likely to come from electronic searching of bespoke databases. There are a growing number of such repositories of evidence. CSA Sociological Abstracts at http://www.csa.com.ezproxyd.bham.ac.uk/factsheets/socioabs-set-c.php indexes and abstracts the international literature in sociology and the social and behavioural sciences. PsycINFO at http://www.apa.org/pubs/databases/psycinfo/index.aspx includes records for peer-reviewed journals, books, and dissertations relevant to psychology and related disciplines. ERIC, the Education Resources Information Centre, at http://www.eric.ed.gov/ provides unlimited access to more than 1.4 million bibliographic records of journal articles and other education-related materials, often with full-text, and it includes the 'What Works Clearinghouse'. In fact, each policy field or social science discipline will have at least one database like this, and often a search of one involves a search of several at the same time. There are 'Research Papers in Economics (RePEc)' for economists and 'Social Services Abstracts' for researchers in social work, and many more. You must use one or more of these for your literature search, else you are not really looking for evidence at all. You can then 'daisy-chain' by following up the references cited within any report that you review. A key advantage of using such databases is that they contain a considerable amount of grey literature, officially unpublished. This includes research reports to funders, conference papers, and Masters and Doctoral theses. Of course, a lot of this grey literature is not very good, but then peer-review is no real guarantee of quality either. Using grey literature appropriately can help to overcome the inbuilt bias towards publishing exciting, positive or innovative results at the expense of the dull and the worthy. This is known sometimes as the 'file-drawer' problem.

The bias or file-drawer issue works like this. Imagine 20 doctoral researchers trying to find a way of reducing criminal re-offending rates. Unknowingly they all try something very similar. For 19 of them the approach does not work. They just pass their PhD and do not pursue the topic. The 20th finds that the approach works, and then publishes the findings in a mainstream journal. What happens now in any future literature review? Some 'reviewers' will not search the journals properly, or will not keep up to date, and so will miss this key study. Some 'reviewers' will come across the study but ignore it as it uses what they think of as the wrong conceptual framework or paradigm! Both of these types of reviewers will have a serious bias in any review they undertake. Some reviewers will use the published result. They will, unfortunately and unintentionally, also have a bias in their review because they have not picked up the 19 occasions when the approach did not work. But a reviewer who searches the databases will find the other 19 studies, and realise that this approach has been tried many times but only worked on one occasion. They have minimised the bias by putting the success into context with all of the times the intervention failed. The result of the synthesis would be the exact opposite depending on whether all studies were included or only those that were easiest to find. This is a simple example of a much bigger problem. It is avoided by searching properly for as much existing evidence as possible, both published and unpublished, and retaining as much of it as possible in your review.

Searching an electronic database is fairly simple. You select some search terms – words that you would expect to appear in a research report relevant to your area of interest. You will need to include synonyms, and to consider different spellings and terms used in different parts of the globe. These terms can usually be combined with logical operators (OR, AND, NOT). See Gorard et al. (2011) for more detail. Getting the search right requires care and several iterations. It is usually worth checking that some pieces you know to be relevant do turn up as a result. If not, you need to widen the search. Often the problem is that the number of reports found is huge and unwieldy, perhaps 100,000 or even 1,000,000. This gives an indication of how much research exists. Limits can be set, such as the earliest date or the language of the report. Most database search results can be copied to Endnote or similar reference software. The results will include the reference and title, almost always an abstract, a link to the report, and increasingly the full report itself.

The next step is to clean and sort the results of the search. There will be some duplication. Different databases will have some of the same pieces as each other. Some projects will produce several very similar reports of what is essentially the same evidence. It is important that this material is not double-counted. However careful the search was, there will be reports that do not contain any research evidence, ones that are unclear about what was done and found, and some that are actually irrelevant to your area of interest. These can be eliminated from further consideration by skimming the abstract. The remaining reports can be read in full and their evidence summarised.

It is important to summarise the evidence actually presented in the report, not the author's impression of any evidence that is not presented, nor the author's interpretations or conclusions. As Chapter Four demonstrates, these conclusions can often be in error. A review of literature which presents a summary of what a previous author presented about an analysis of data, can be distant and distorting (Hakim 1982). The evidence has to be assessed for quality in terms of the methods as described. An uncritical synthesis of poor quality work would be a poor quality synthesis (Pawson 2006). If the methods are not appropriately described in the report then the evidence cannot be used. This is not a very stringent requirement, yet it is surprising how little survives this test. For any review, the likelihood is that the majority of the material found in the search is not actually research, or does not present any evidence, or does not present the methods used to gather the evidence. Of the remainder, a high proportion will contain obvious design flaws.

3.3 ‖ Secondary analysis

In any area of research you are interested in, large relevant high quality datasets will already exist (Gorard 2012a). Note that examining data directly is different to and much more powerful than simply using reports from the literature. The accumulation of evidence is important in social science, and so the consideration of existing data is essential for at least the early part of an empirical investigation – if only to ensure that any new data proposed does not already exist. Official public datasets are likely to be larger in scope and scale, and higher quality in terms of completeness and validity, than anything a researcher could generate through primary fieldwork. Creating new and primary evidence can be costly and inefficient. Funding bodies allocating publicly-funded grants or commissioning research, such as the UK Economic and Social Research Council, require applicants to show that they have looked to see if the data they require already exists, and to present a case that it does not. In addition, once a publicly-funded project is completed, the datasets generated must be lodged with a public data archive, thereby increasing the chance for each new proposal that something similar already exists.

Sometimes, the use of existing records is inevitable, such as for historians considering respondents who no longer exist, and for whom new recall and recollection are no longer possible. Otherwise, speed and cost are probably the most obvious advantages of using secondary data. Secondary data might be used to help select the sample for a further in-depth study (Chapter Six). It can provide the appropriate figures for each stratum in a stratified sample. It can be used to assess the quality of an achieved sample by providing some background figures for the population.

Contextual secondary data can also be used to show that a problem exists which needs to be addressed using other techniques, and to begin to describe the nature of that problem. When investigating the causes of increasing crime in city centres, for example, the researcher needs to show via secondary data that this problem is actually getting worse. Many 'moral panics' are based on misreading the situation. Secondary data can also show something about the nature of the problem being investigated. Is the increase in all categories of crime, and is it manifested differently in different cities? It only makes sense to move to the primary phase of an investigation once the study has been justified, the sample has been planned, and the existing data examined for patterns – all via secondary data. A good synthesis of evidence will consider existing datasets as well as what has been published in the literature. The result can transform what we think we know about an area. But perhaps more importantly, a secondary analysis can help ensure that the research questions are the right ones.

3.4 ▮▮ Theory

Is an underlying theory necessary for a piece of research? In some ways, the answer must be 'yes'. A theory can help us to decide what and how we research, and to measure and explain. It can be useful in the transfer of research findings to new settings, and as an end-product of research. Above all, a theory is cheap. Theories allow us to consider alternative positions simultaneously, and to accept failure without great cost. Theory and research are usually inseparable complements, since a piece of research tests ideas stemming from a theoretical model, leading to modification of the theory (Dubin 1978). Theories lead via logical deduction to hypotheses, thence to observation, empirical generalisation, and so to further theories. It is also true to some extent that every concept used in research is a theory. Even such an apparently basic operation as the measurement of a length involves acceptance of a series of theories about the nature of length and the isomorphic behaviour of numbers (Gorard 2010a).

However, a bigger overarching theory is not always necessary for good research. These are several fairly straightforward situations where we are ignorant of the consequences of important decisions we are forced to make in practice. In my own area of education this is distressingly true despite the hundreds of billions that have been spent on research in the UK alone. For example, we do not really know the relative benefits of single-sex teaching, decreased class sizes, homework, group work, rote learning and many other basic issues in education. Of course, work on any of these areas depends on the understanding of ideas like single-sex teaching, or homework. And some progress can be made by re-considering what they mean. But, in general, the people who fund public research (the taxpayers) and the people who will be affected by it (just about everyone) know what these things mean. The role of theory is severely limited in the ensuing research. There are so many practical problems to deal with, and so many policy and practice interventions already taking place that it is easy to see how a new study might well have no major theoretical element at all.

Another limitation for theory is that it is *always* possible to find some kind of explanation for any set of observations (Gorard et al. 2011). So, the existence of a theory, in itself, should never be considered convincing, or be mistaken for evidence. Theories will always be under-determined by the evidence on which they rest, since any finite number of observations can be explained by a potentially infinite number of theories. This suggests that the theory is very much the junior partner in the research process. If it is clear that altering how a phenomenon works to improve outcomes with no damaging unintended consequences and at reasonable cost, then it matters less if the mechanism by which this happens is not understood. On the other hand, even the most convincing explanation possible is of little consequence if the phenomenon has no discernible effect on outcomes. For example, all potential aviators around the 1900s followed the same Newtonian theories of physics, but some of their ensuing planes flew and some did not. It was only the testing that sorted the one from the other. The theory alone was not sufficient. Nor is the theory even necessary, for if, on the other hand, someone had managed to fly in some way that contradicted the prevailing theory then it would be the theory that would have to change. The mere act of flying would be far more powerful than the most plausible theory could ever be. Science and technology, therefore, often advance through instrumentation rather than theory, with the theoreticians playing continuous 'catch-up' with their potential explanations (Davis 1994).

A theory is a tentative explanation. A reasonable theory is one that provides a simple, plausible explanation of what has been observed via research. A better theory is one that explains observations like this, but also survives being tested out further. An even better theory is one that does all of this and also correctly predicts something that is totally unexpected. But all theories will eventually be found to be false. Meantime, some of them can be useful, mostly to generate research questions. As Hume (1962) and others have observed, there is little point in accumulating supportive evidence for any theory. Such evidence tends to be easy to find even when the theory is totally wrong. Therefore, we need to look for evidence which should not exist according to the theory. We try to show that the theory is wrong. If we fail to show that it is wrong, then that is the best test for the present. This is so obvious that it should not need much explanation. Suppose we wish to show that phenomenon A always has characteristic B, then finding more and more examples of A with characteristic B does not advance our ideas. There may still be examples of A without B. It is these disconfirming instances that our research should seek instead (Chapter Five). Another, allied, way of envisaging the use of theory in the development of research is to try and rule out any sensible alternative explanations (de Vaus 2001). This is one of the major purposes of research design.

However, there is a lot of misunderstanding about theory in social science. Blumer (1954) asked 'what is wrong with social theory?' His answer was that social theory was inward-looking, largely divorced from the empirical world, and often merely creating new vocabulary for old ideas. Theory was used to 'interpret' the facts and 'not a studious cultivation of empirical facts to see if the theory fits' (p. 3). Unfortunately, a lot of these comments could still be made today (Gorard 2004b). Many people working in social sciences treat theory as some kind of fashion item, as something that they can 'adopt' and presumably discard on a whim. Yet they also seem to treat it is a kind of religion, with belief, adulation, and schisms (Tooley and Darby 1998). I think the key problem is that there are really two things – theory as described so far in this chapter, and something else confusingly also called 'theory' that is designed to be un-testable, and so an unchangeable article of faith.

It is acceptable for people to use untestable 'theory' as a framework, lens or tool to help generate ideas and questions for research. It is as acceptable as using their own experience, or the sometimes arbitrary wishes of a funder, for example. But it is not acceptable that such ideas are allowed to predetermine or even influence the outcomes of research. The need to make new explanations consistent with some already established body of theory tends to stifle progress (Feyerabend 1993). Rather than specifying in advance the conditions under which a theory would be deemed to be false (however unlikely that might appear in prospect), adherents of stable theories often defend their position in advance by arguing against logic itself (Hollis 1994). Such non-productive work starts from a premise that social experience is confounding, contradictory and paradoxical, because that is how it often appears to new researchers. This tradition, therefore, preserves its prior theories for much longer because, for its researchers, a theory does not fail when it is contradicted by experience. As soon as theory itself becomes such an obstacle to what or how research is conducted, it becomes worse than useless. I generally ignore this second kind of theory. Stick to productive theory, and remember that, by itself, theory rarely leads us to new inventions or the creation of useful artefacts.

3.5 ╻╻╻ Synthesising what we know

Having considered the literature, existing evidence and theoretical explanations relevant to the research topic, a researcher needs to sort out all of this information to generate the most appropriate research questions. This can be done as a narrative, which is a good method when used with care. Different kinds of pre-existing evidence can be put together to draw useful conclusions. This can be done even though none of the studies in isolation may be sufficient, and all may have noticeable flaws as research in their own right. And the results can be used to derive further questions that are so far unanswered. For example, Gorard et al. (2011) conducted a narrative synthesis of 166,441 research reports from eight major social science databases, excluding studies only on the basis of relevance and readability. The topic included children's aspirations and expectations, and whether these are a cause of higher attainment at school. The evidence was structured around the four elements of a causal model (Chapter Four) – association, sequence, theory and intervention. Most notably the review found no rigorous evaluations of interventions explicitly concerned with raising or lowering aspirations and so influencing educational outcomes. Therefore, no study was found that shows how altering aspirations actually leads to difference in outcomes. In conclusion, there was not enough evidence to establish a causal link between aspirations/expectations and educational outcomes.

Having completed a simple synthesis like this, what further research questions does it raise? An obvious way forward would be to fill the void of rigorously evaluated interventions. There is a huge industry in the UK dedicated to raising aspirations in the belief that this will be efficacious in improving educational or occupational outcomes. Someone needs to test this before too much money and effort is wasted. This is the ethical way forward (Chapter Thirteen). The new research question could be something like:

> Does artificially raising the aspirations of [age group of children] using [existing intervention] lead to higher than expected scores in [phase of statutory testing]?

This would make a relatively simple project for a new researcher. Interventions to raise aspirations and metrics to measure aspiration are already in use by their advocates, so do not need to be developed from scratch. They could simply be used and tested as they are. The research might need around 30 schools (Chapter Six), and a minimum of around a year of elapsed time between intervention and test of attainment. Such a study could be easily completed as a PhD or similar. If the study was convincing enough, it could change the entire field either by putting a nail in the coffin of an industry built on nothing more than belief, or it could demonstrate that, despite lack of clarity about the strength of association and the sequence of events, the approach of raising aspirations really does work. My guess is that in almost any area of social science a good review of evidence, one that is comprehensive and unbiased, will always answer some questions and crystallise what the really important next questions are.

A disadvantage of the narrative approach is that it can lead to an unstructured and complex account, especially where there is a considerable amount and range of evidence. Alternatively, as long as a number of studies are genuinely addressing the same research question then their numeric results can be combined into one overall answer. This is possible using a range of more formal approaches, including meta-analysis (Glass et al. 1981). In meta-analysis, the search phase would be similar to a narrative review, with exclusion on the basis of relevance and clarity (as above). All reports that have tested what is essentially the same hypothesis can be converted to a common measure of 'effect' size (Chapter Twelve). These effect sizes are then weighted, usually for sample size (Chapter Six), and their weighted average is calculated. In this way, a number of smaller studies are presented as though they were one big study. This increases the statistical power, and so reduces the chances of being misled by volatility or an aberrant result (Wilson and Lipsey 2001).

If there are two studies each with a sample of 100 cases, and both find a noteworthy difference between two sub-groups in their samples (men and women perhaps) then a meta-analysis calculates the overall results as though for a sample of 200 cases. Here there would be no weighting of results as both studies are of the same size. Thus, the overall result could be the simple average of the effect sizes in both studies. If both studies had produced equal and opposite results – such as a difference in favour of men in one and women in the other – then the overall result would be of no difference. Presumably the difference appearing between the studies was due to volatility of small numbers, bias or similar. If both studies had produced equal and opposite results but the first had a sample of 1,000 and the second a sample of 100, then the overall result of a difference in favour of men for the first study would be less likely to be true, since it has been modified by the smaller opposite result in the second study. The second study cannot be ignored, but it also cannot be allowed to over-rule or cancel out the larger first study.

What are the downsides of such an approach? There are good guidelines on how to conduct a meta-analysis for almost every stage except the eventual calculation. For example, it is advised that all studies should be read and assessed by more than one person, that the methods and results are recorded in a standard format, that the common effect sizes are drawn as a graph before analysis, and ideally that research is judged without knowledge of the author or publication outlet (Egger et al. 1997). The drawing of a graph is a good idea because it can show abrupt cut-offs in the distribution of effect sizes that might indicate publication bias or even censorship of results – known as the 'file-drawer problem' (see above, and Cooper and Hedges 1994). The problem itself is best avoided by ensuring that grey literature, theses and unpublished research reports are included in the search from the outset. A meta-analysis, like a narrative review, can only ever be as good as your search of evidence allows it to be.

From this stage on, there are a number of ways of synthesising the effect sizes, and no single method is the correct one. One way forward is to use the results of all relevant studies. This is what I tend to favour, and what Glass et al. (1981) proposed. Otherwise, selecting studies other than on relevance or incomprehensibility could be a further source of bias. On the other hand, it seems questionable that a synthesis should include poorly-designed and conducted studies. Why should they have equal footing with good research? So, some commentators prefer to weight studies by quality as well as scale, and some prefer to exclude studies altogether if they do not meet specific quality criteria. But this leads to the issue of what the criteria are and how we judge quality. Perhaps constraining or editing studies so that they fit with your rules for a meta-analysis is itself a source of bias. Anyway, how many studies will there be that genuinely have the same research question (Pawson 2006)? As ever, your choice here must be reasoned and explicit to be convincing to a sceptical reader.

One obvious problem with meta-analysis in all of its traditional forms is that it is selective in the evidence used. It is only applied to numeric data, meaning that things like in-depth data, observations, and professional judgements are generally excluded. Therefore, some more innovative approaches have been developed that attempt to be as inclusive as a narrative synthesis and as straightforward as a meta-analysis. One is a Bayesian synthesis, probably developed first in a medical context (Dixon-Woods et al. 1999). For example, one study attempted to identify the most important factors determining the uptake of the MMR vaccine by parents (Roberts et al. 2002). The evidence consisted, as usual, of existing expert knowledge, in-depth studies (such as those based on interviews with parents), and measurement studies including the outcomes of attempts to increase MMR uptake. A narrative account could be messy. A meta-analysis would only involve the third kind of evidence.

Instead, each expert reviewer first used their expertise to list and rank the factors that they believed would affect the uptake of childhood vaccines (such as parents' belief about the vaccine's efficacy). They were then asked to read a series of studies not susceptible to numeric analysis in a randomised order, and to adjust their initial lists of factors and their rankings accordingly. The resulting lists from all reviewers were then combined to yield a probability for each factor being responsible for vaccine uptake or not. This probability can be quite precise, but it is based on a ranking task that involves judgement by experts moderated by reading further evidence. It is, of course, subjective but it is also pooled or shared between experts. This probability for each factor was then treated as a 'prior probability' for a kind of meta-analysis based on any remaining studies with a numeric outcome relating to that factor. This meant that the meta-analysis did not start from a position of feigned ignorance, as is standard, but worked from a prior probability which it could then only adjust. This means that all elements of evidence contributed to the final result. The results showed that inclusion of the prior probabilities makes a considerable difference, and that excluding non-numeric evidence from reviews runs the risk of losing valuable evidence for evidence-based practices. The study also showed that wrong decisions would be made, both in research and clinical terms, if the review had used only one kind of data. Such bias matters in reviews. This approach, while still facing developmental problems, can easily be adapted for use in social science (Gorard and Roberts 2004, Gorard et al. 2007). It would be absurd to endanger practical progress by claiming, as many of those claiming to do research currently do, that we cannot combine qualitative and quantitative approaches because they emerge from different paradigms, which are 'incommensurable'.

At present, the kinds of comprehensive syntheses outlined here are rare. If more took place, one consequence might be that a research programme ended more often at Phase 1 in the cycle (see Chapter Two), where the answers to the research questions are already as well established as social science answers can be. Another consequence might be that researchers more often revised their initial questions suitably, before continuing to other phases of the cycle. For example, there is little point in continuing to investigate why the incidence of crime is increasing in cities if initial work shows that it is actually decreasing. The eclectic re-use of existing evidence would be more ethical than standard practice (a patchy literature review), making better and more efficient use of taxpayer and charitable money spent on the subsequent research (Erzberger and Prein 1997).

3.6 |ǀ A few tips for writing questions formally

It is important that research starts with at least a draft of its research questions, partly because only then can an appropriate design be created. Otherwise the research is not really research at all, it is just data gathering. The questions leading to the design give the data gathering a necessary structure. They help us decide what data to collect, where, when and how to analyse it. Of course the initial questions may be revised in light of experience, and new ones may be added. But having a draft set of questions from as early as possible saves a great deal of trouble and confusion later.

Kuhn (1970) and others have drawn a distinction between a scientific problem and a puzzle. A problem might be something we do not understand or cannot control, like the number of people dying from an infectious disease. Asking how we can solve this problem is not a good research question, as it is too broad and undirected. A puzzle, on the other hand, is based on a question that there must be an answer to. All that is required to solve a puzzle is talent, time and effort. 'What is the nature of the infectious organism?' might be a research question for a scientific puzzle. Using existing well-tried techniques, it should be possible to characterise the infection. Another puzzle might be – what are the observable characteristics of those people who have been infected? The answers to such puzzles combine within a research programme or cycle (Chapter Two) in a way that works towards a solution to the overall problem itself. Converting a new problem into a series of puzzles is a major and immensely valuable undertaking. It is literally a paradigm shift. For someone attempting this kind of scientific revolution (using Kuhn's term), their question is not the substantive one of solving the problem. Instead it would be: how can we convert the problem into a series of puzzles each of which can be addressed using existing or feasible techniques? Solving a puzzle can be just as valuable. It is what Kuhn called 'normal science'. Most new researchers will work with a puzzle, inside an existing field. It is important for them that the questions they pose, while substantive, are genuinely puzzle questions. Unfortunately, too much time and resource is currently being wasted chasing social science questions that could not possibly be answered with our existing approaches in social science.

Some new researchers worry about novelty and originality, and wonder whether there is anything really new when working within a field. Perhaps this is a special concern for masters and doctoral dissertations where 'originality' is one of the requirements. However, as the examples above show, every field is likely to have important unanswered questions. Novelty can come from combining work in two areas, such as aspiration and attainment, or well-being and climate. Or the topic itself could be already studied but you could transfer it to a new place, a new time period, a new age-group, or a new sub-group of the population, using a new dataset, or a method imported from another discipline. A project can even set out to replicate an important prior finding directly. This, in itself, would be quite novel in the social sciences. Originality is not really an issue. Perhaps it is better to think of it as being important to use your time and resource investigating something that matters, and that could be useful in some way to some audience.

It is best to be interested in the research questions you set out to answer. This will help sustain motivation when things go wrong, as they inevitably will. It is important to want to know the answer, and so to be genuinely curious. It is perfectly proper, therefore, that a research question arises from your passion, or from your life and the lives of those around you. You might be interested in the operation of council services, hospitals, housing associations, or in the experience of job loss, violence, shop-lifting, marriage, or retirement, precisely because you have some experience of them yourself.

However, the curiosity that underlies such research demands that it is possible for the findings to surprise you. Your interest must be in finding the most convincing answer, not in finding a pre-determined answer. The latter would not be research. It would simply pretend to be research, and is unethical. It is important to have some idea of the kinds of answers that are possible, because this is part of the warrant (Chapter Four), and it is perfectly proper to have a 'favoured' or most likely answer. But there is a danger of favouring one answer too much. If I watch the Olympics on television and wish that a particular athlete will win an event, it makes the viewing more entertaining, even though there is nothing that I can think, do or say that will influence the outcome. In social science, on the other hand, there is a considerable danger that my desire for a specific result may influence my responses to individuals in interview, my reading of data, the kinds of analysis I select, and even the kinds of mistakes I make when entering columns of figures. Guard against this (Chapter Eleven).

It is usually wise to have a short series of research questions rather than just one, or a long laundry list. These could generally be something like:

What is the problem, pattern, or trend?

What produces this?

What could or should be done to improve it?

This suggested grammar is not intended to constrain more innovative approaches, but something like this can help unpack the various elements in a larger question. For example, suppose you were concerned about the growth of gun crime in the US. You might start with a descriptive question:

What is the trend for gun crime in the US between 2000 and 2012?

If you discover that gun crime has increased since 2000, the next question might be a causal or explanatory one:

Why has gun crime risen between 2000 and 2012? Or what has caused the increase?

And if you can come up with a convincing explanation, this would lead to a prescriptive question:

How can this trend be stopped or even reversed?

Each question will lead to further sub-questions, such as what the definition of gun crime is, or whether there have been changes in the way crimes have been recorded. And each question can be addressed by different approaches, sometimes in combination. The first might involve secondary analysis (see above). It is important to be sure of the pattern that the next two questions are trying to deal with. The second might involve both a review of existing evidence and new empirical research. The third might be legitimate speculation – legitimate as long as the reader of the research is made aware that the suggestions are speculative. Or it could be the first step in Phase 6 of the research cycle in Chapter Two – developing and trialling an intervention to address the problem of gun crime.

⚌ Exercises on research questions

1   One of the examples above suggested the following outline research question:

   Does artificially raising the aspirations of [age group of children] using [existing intervention] lead to higher than expected scores in [phase of statutory testing]?

   Given what you know so far, can you suggest the elements of a research design to provide a convincing answer?

2   A colleague of yours comes to you for advice about a new research project. They want to investigate the property rental market. Their draft research questions are:

   Are renters finding it more difficult to pay the rent?

   How are renters handling this increased difficulty?

   Being appropriately critical, what advice could you offer your colleague about these draft questions?

3   Find an empirical research report in your own area of interest. Try to identify the research questions. Does it have explicit research questions? Are they good questions, answerable like a puzzle with the kind of techniques actually used? Do they match the conclusions drawn by the research report?

☰ Notes to exercises on research questions

1 There are a number of ways of approaching this question, but all approaches will have some common elements. There must be a time sequence so that raising aspiration comes before the attainment scores. So we could have:

N O_1 X O_1 O_2

Here O_1 is the measurement of aspiration conducted both before and after an intervention to raise aspirations, and O_2 is the eventual attainment score. We can then look at whether aspiration rises over time and is linked to the final attainment score. It might be preferable also to have a prior attainment score so that we can better judge whether the eventual scores are 'higher than expected'. Thus:

N O_1 O_2 X O_1 O_2

This is a longitudinal design (Chapter Eight). It could be improved by comparing this group with another group who do not receive the aspiration-raising intervention, and by creating the groups by random allocation:

R O_1 O_2 X O_1 O_2
R O_1 O_2 O_1 O_2

This is a randomised controlled trial design (Chapter Nine).

2 You may find this topic interesting, or you may not. This is irrelevant, and your advice must be set within the terms of your colleague's interest. I have two major problems with these questions. There are probably further issues, but the two I worry about are so important that I would have to advise any colleague of mine not to proceed without radically re-drafting the questions. My first problem is the lack of comparator in the first question. Are renters finding it more difficult than *what*? Are they being compared to another group, another place, another time period, or something else entirely? The question is ambiguous. My second problem is that I suspect this is not a research question at all. If it were a real question then the colleague would be aware that one of the answers could be 'no'. If renters do not find paying rent more difficult than whatever it is, then the second question does not make sense. The second question suggests that the researcher either already knows the answer to the first, or is not genuinely curious. The first question is therefore a 'fake' one. You might be surprised how common this scenario is (Chapter Seven).

3 You may also be surprised to find that many research reports do not have explicit research questions. Others seem to have so many, buried within sections on aims, objectives and conceptual frameworks, that they are hard to pin down. You may also be surprised to find that neither the techniques used nor the conclusions drawn seem to follow from the questions, even if there are questions. Check this carefully.
For example, I recently read the abstract of a paper that said it looked at how effective a particular approach was in the education of people with special needs. The conclusion similarly made claims about how effective the approach was. But the published research question itself was about teachers' perceptions of how well the approach worked. The beauty of such a question for a lazy researcher is that the research then simply involves talking to teachers about their perceptions of an approach. The difficulty of such a question is that it ignores the rather more important question of

whether the approach is any good – for the students not the teachers. By pretending that the research was about the former but actually only doing the latter, the report author tried to have it both ways. This kind of thing, including a focus on perceptions rather than using perceptions as part of the evidence for effect, is distressingly common. Thinking more clearly about research is the subject of the next chapter.

⹀ Suggested reading

White, P. (2009) *Developing Research Questions: A Guide for Social Scientists.* London: Palgrave.

FOUR

Warranting research claims

SUMMARY

- A piece of research has to be comprehensible to its intended readers, in order for its account to be convincing.
- Good quality evidence relevant to a research conclusion is only a part of what is needed to be convincing.
- A warrant is the logical argument, with supporting evidence if needed, that shows why a specific research conclusion should be preferred over all others.
- Warrants are often missing or neglected in research reports. This makes the reports less, not more, believable to a sceptical reader.
- A good argument will highlight where it is weakest, or is especially open to challenge.
- In general, the best explanation of any evidence (for the time being) is the one that makes the fewest new assumptions.
- Writers should distinguish clearly between legitimate speculation about possible explanations, and any firm logically-entailed conclusions.
- Probabilistic conclusions should contain an indication of the extent to which the writer would be prepared to wager that the conclusion was valid.

4.1 ▮▮ Convincing arguments

A well-designed piece of research, and its report, is actually a kind of argument (Toulmin et al. 1979). The argument is such that a sceptical audience should be convinced by the conclusions of the research. The findings must be believable, and the implications drawn from the findings must be logical. The argument, as presented in any report of the research, must also be clear and comprehensible so that anyone interested in the study can follow it as easily as possible. Un-needed complexity of explanation in any research report should be treated as a sign of incompetence, laziness or trying to hide something – perhaps all three. It is only when we can understand a piece of writing describing research that we can begin to decide if it is convincing. Academics across all disciplines report widespread preference for expressing complex ideas succinctly, demonstrating care for their readers, avoiding jargon, and using concrete examples. But consideration of published articles in top journals shows that these characteristics are rarely exhibited (Sword 2009). The problem of incomprehensible writing is widespread in social science. As an extreme example, much-discussed on the internet, consider this extract from Bhaskar (1994, p.163):

> 'Indeed dialectical critical realism may be seen under the aspect of Foucauldian strategic reversal – of the unholy trinity of Parmenidean/Platonic/Aristotelian provenance; of the Cartesian-Lockean-Humean-Kantian paradigm, of foundationalisms (in practice, fideistic foundationalisms) and irrationalisms (in practice, capricious exercises of the will-to-power or some other ideologically and/or psychosomatically buried source) new and old alike; of the primordial failing of Western philosophy, ontological monovalence, and its close ally, the epistemic fallacy with its ontic dual; of the analytic problematic laid down by Plato, which Hegel served only to replicate in his actualist monovalent analytic reinstatement in transfigurative reconciling dialectical connection, while in his hubristic claims for absolute idealism he inaugurated the Comtean, Kierkegaardian and Nietzschean eclipses of reason, replicating the fundaments positivism through its transmutation route to the superidealism of a Baudrillard.'

Actually this sentence, while far too long, with too many parentheses, and misuse of the semi-colon, has a rather simple list structure. What makes it so hard for me to read is the name-dropping and neologisms. I get no sense that the author has made any effort to explain their points to me or any other reader. I pick this passage because its writer is otherwise famous, successful and influential, and because it won an annual award for the worst piece of writing in the English language in 1996. But actually I have seen worse, and I suspect readers will have come across their own favourites.

Writing has to be comprehensible to be convincing, and both the author and the reader are required to make an effort. Since writing inevitably comes before reading, if it is obvious that the author is not fulfilling their part of this contract, this then frees the reader to ignore or reject the writings. This is not to say that all research writing will be easy to read, or that it must be so. There are technical issues, terms and assumptions that might inhibit wide public readership. If I struggle to read an extract from a piece on gene-splicing research for example, it would not be fair for me to suggest that the author was not explaining it well merely because I had difficulty understanding. If it were a technical paper for a professional audience of peers, it is more likely that my considerable ignorance about such topics is the stumbling block. If it were a book to assist the public understanding of science however, I might have a point. And, even in areas like social science where I as a professor might be expected to understand it, it is just possible that under all of the obfuscation there are ideas of such importance that it is worth persevering. The work of David Hume (Chapter Five) is quite brilliant, but harder for us to read today because of its dated style, terminology and spelling.

A similar issue arises with the even more brilliant ideas of Isaac Newton in his 1687 Principia Mathematica. But here the obscurity was partly deliberate, since Newton apparently believed that some precious knowledge should not be widely known. Hopefully, no social scientist today believes the same, and anyway very few of us will ever write anything so important. It is, therefore, generally safe to assume that if an author wants you to read their material then they will make it as easy as possible. Conversely, if they do not do so it is reasonably safe to assume that they are not confident that what they are writing will stand up to sceptical scrutiny. They may not actually understand it themselves. Clarity and accuracy are essential in reporting research. Rhetorical flourishes can be part of a good argument, keeping a reader interested by enlivening the written words. Rhetoric, like clarity, makes it easier not harder to read or listen to an argument.

4.2 ⦀ Warranted conclusions

Once we can understand a research report, we can begin to decide whether we are convinced by its findings and conclusions. The general validity of research findings is well covered in existing methods resources. This chapter deals with the less well-known issue of whether the conclusions drawn by a researcher are 'warranted' by the evidence presented before them (Gorard 2002a). Rather than presenting a formal explanation of what a warrant is, it is probably easier to look at a couple of examples where there is a problem of warrant.

Imagine that I conducted a range of informal interviews with national politicians, trying to understand their views on why the proportion of the population voting in elections had declined, and what politicians proposed to do about it. Most politicians who were asked agreed to take part, and they were generally co-operative and helpful. The achieved sample was wide and reasonably representative. One of my findings might be that almost all participants in the study felt that politics and politicians themselves were not the main cause of a decline in voting. Instead, they felt that this decline was part of a wider social change, and several had interesting ideas about why that was and what could be done to interest people in voting more. I might then conclude from this finding that the level of annual bonuses paid to bankers should be reduced by legislation!

I hope that all readers can see that, while they might agree with doing what the conclusion says, the conclusion cannot be justified on the basis of the study as described. The study might well be a good one, within the real constraints faced in conducting social science. The finding might be valid, or as safe as we could reasonably expect (remember the finding is not that politicians are not to blame, but that most politicians report believing that they are not to blame). And the idea that bankers' bonuses should be reduced might even be justified by evidence from other studies. But the key point is that the reduction in bankers' bonuses cannot be justified by the evidence presented by this imaginary research study. The conclusion is not 'warranted' by the evidence or findings. In fact, it is just irrelevant to them as far as I can see. I hope this is obvious. But this lack of relevance is a surprisingly common feature of research writing, perhaps occurring where research leads to no clear conclusion but the author feels that they have to say something to justify having done it.

The warrant, then, is the part of the argument that shows how the evidence and findings lead (or not) to the conclusion stated. It is a linking claim. Another obvious example of a problem in this link would be when the evidence is considered to be so poor that the conclusion, while relevant, was unwarranted. In the study above, imagine that I had asked 100 politicians to take part, and only three had agreed. Perhaps all three were males from the same party, and the interviews were only a few minutes long. In this situation, whatever substantive conclusion I drew, other than that I was not very successful at interviewing politicians, would be very questionable. Slightly less obvious, and so a more common problem, is where research writers misinterpret their evidence and provide a conclusion that could only have been warranted by their misinterpretation. This is perhaps a particular problem when researchers care too much about what their findings will be. Note that this problem can and does arise even when the research produces evidence that is ostensibly high quality. I have discussed many such examples previously (e.g. Gorard 2008a). Look for examples in the literature relevant to your own discipline.

Even less obvious is where the conclusion fits the evidence, and *vice versa*, but another competing conclusion would fit even better. In an imaginary example, Huck and Sandler (1979) describe an experimental psychologist who trains fleas to jump in response to hearing a noise. This is an example of conditioning. After conditioning, each flea jumps when the noise occurs. While the fleas remain conditioned to jump, the psychologist cuts the legs off some of the fleas. These fleas no longer jump when the noise occurs. The imaginary psychologist notes the finding, and concludes that cutting off their legs affects fleas' hearing in some way. Is this a reasoned conclusion? It is clearly safer than in the example about voting, where the conclusion was irrelevant to the evidence. Here the conclusion addresses the issues of not reacting to the noise, and provides a genuine attempt at explanation for the observed evidence. The conclusion does not rely on a misunderstanding or misrepresentation of the evidence presented. The conclusion that fleas somehow hear through their legs could, indeed, be true.

This leads to a key point about warranting claims from research evidence. The evidence must have validity, and the presentation of the findings must have integrity. But as the examples show, such qualities alone are not sufficient to warrant all or any conclusions drawn from them. The conclusions must be relevant, and what else? An inverse way of looking at a warrant is to ask of any conclusion – if this conclusion is not actually correct then how else could I explain the evidence presented for it? In the flea example, if it is not true that their hearing is affected by cutting off their legs then there are a number of other plausible explanations for them not jumping. It may be trauma or fatigue after the operation, but it is more likely that they cannot jump without legs whether they hear the noise or not. Legs may be essential to jumping, but not necessarily to hearing. I realise this seems a long-winded approach to this point, but it is generally easier to see the logic of a warrant for the first time in a rather silly and obvious example, rather than a more complex real one.

4.3 ⃦ More formally

It is time to turn to a more formal explanation of what a warrant for a research con-clusion is, and how this relates to the importance of research design. Remember, a warrant is the step in the research logic that connects a research finding to a conclusion. It is, if you like, why that conclusion is the conclusion to draw from that finding, or set of findings (Booth et al. 1995). A research finding could be that some phenomenon has been observed to have a certain characteristic. Examples might include that politicians do not generally believe low voter turnout to be their fault, or that ex-prisoners with jobs are less likely to re-offend. Perhaps it is that girls generally get better qualifications at school than boys do. Maybe there is an inter-generational correlation between the occupations of parents and their off-spring, or new companies in developing countries find it hard to compete in a globalised free-market. I am not saying these statements are true, but simply that they could be research findings.

We could summarise such findings as having the style of saying that phenom-enon A has characteristic B. Or put more simply:

A is B

The research conclusion could be that the same phenomenon A has some other characteristic (C). C could be a cause of A having the characteristic B, or C could be just another characteristic linked to A. The conclusion would be:

Therefore, A is also C

In this formal style (with 'Therefore' at the start), it is clear that the conclusion stems from a prior argument, and is always a consequence of the prior steps in that argument. However, the argument is obviously incomplete:

A is B

Therefore, A is also C

This would be like saying that politicians do not believe that voter disinterest is their fault, and therefore concluding that politicians are not to blame (in reality rather than just in their own reports). The conclusion 'A is also C' does not follow just from knowing or believing that 'A is B'. There is at least one missing step. The simplest additional step that would make this argument valid would be something like – everything with characteristic B also has characteristic C. The full argument is then:

A is B

All B are C

Therefore, A is also C

This argument works, and the conclusion is logically and validly drawn from the two prior steps. This simplest form, known to philosophers as a 'syllogism', has three components. In research terms, the first step (A is B) is the finding, and the last step (Therefore, A is also C) is the conclusion. The second step (All B are C) is the warrant. This second step should be made explicit in any research report, perhaps especially when it is itself contentious. The argument works as a structure, meaning that if we accept the first two steps then we must logically accept the conclusion. The first step will be convincing insofar as the research evidence is of high quality. The issues involved in making this judgement are the kind dealt with in standard methods texts and courses. Is the sample large and representative enough? How much non-response was there? What were the instruments like? Does the analysis make sense? Are the patterns clear, or the differences big enough to matter? The second step must be convincing on its own however. It is not usually a result of the new research being reported. It must be based on something already known and quite widely accepted, because it is the reason why the new findings in the first step must lead to the conclusion in the third step. In the politician example, the warrant for the conclusion that politicians are not to blame because they do not believe they are at fault could be the claim that politicians are always right. This would be a logical argument, but spelled out in full it is easily challenged on the basis that politicians are not always right. This is why it is important that such research-based claims are always spelt out in full.

For example, my research has found that some potentially disadvantaged students in schools in England are increasingly being allocated places in schools along with other potentially disadvantaged students (Gorard and Cheng 2011). The changes over time are not large but they are clear. I might conclude that the way in which places are allocated at schools therefore needs to be changed in order to halt or reverse this trend. You might accept my evidence and you might agree with my conclusion. But to be convincing to a sceptical reader I need to show that my evidence is as good as it can be in real-life. I also need to make my warrant explicit. In fact, the warrant here would involve two separate steps. First, I would need to explain that this clustering of students with others like them was a bad thing, and ought to be stopped or reversed. But readers may not be convinced. For example, there is a coherent argument that having disadvantaged students concentrated in fewer schools makes it easier to target them for extra help or funding. Clustering similar students together might be a good thing. I do not agree with this but I would have to explain why. My explanation why segregation is a bad thing might involve the results of previous studies about the damaging effects of social clustering between schools. This shows that warranting claims can be a complex and lengthy iterative business. But this stage is essential if research users are to have confidence that they can act on research conclusions. The second stage of the warrant in this example would involve explaining why the school allocation procedure is thought to be the cause of, and remedy for, the growth of segregation. As with the first stage of the warrant, this explanation could involve prior research evidence, and is itself disputable by a sceptical reader.

To return to some of the earlier examples, if it is shown that girls generally get better qualifications at school than boys, a researcher might want to conclude that the assessment system for these qualifications should be made more gender-neutral. To make this viable the researcher would have to warrant the conclusion by also showing that the higher level of qualifications by girls is not merited by their talent. The argument could be:

Girls do better

It is not fair that girls do better, because the assessments must be biased

Therefore, we need to alter the unfair assessment system

Expressed like this, it is clear that the middle stage of the argument would be very hard to establish.

As another example, if it is shown that ex-prisoners with jobs are less likely to re-offend, then a researcher might want to conclude that more ex-prisoners should be given jobs, to reduce re-offending rates. What is missing here is the warrant for the conclusion, which could be something like – having a job *causes* the reduction in re-offending. The argument would be:

Those with jobs re-offend less

They re-offend less because they have a job

Therefore, giving a job to other ex-prisoners will reduce their chances of re-offending as well

This form of argument is very common in public policy but, distressingly, in many real examples the middle stage of the argument is either assumed or simply ignored. Correlation becomes a kind of magic. Imagine the argument without the warrant, and apply the inverse warrant principle. If the conclusion here is wrong, how can we explain the evidence? One obvious alternative explanation could then be that those who get a job after prison are also those who are already less likely to re-offend anyway. There is an association between the two but it is not causal or it is in the wrong direction (Chapter Five). If this were so, then merely giving jobs to all, whatever its other merits, would not necessarily reduce future offending. This shows that the middle bit in the argument, the warrant, is absolutely essential. Always complete the argument in your own research reports, and always insist that others complete the argument in their reports.

Naturally, arguments can have a much more complex structure than any of those presented so far (Toulmin et al. 1979). As well as a claim or conclusion based on evidence via a warrant, an argument can legitimately include further backing for the claim, qualifier terms showing the relative strength of the evidence, reservations, exceptions, and pre-emptive rebuttal of potential counter-arguments. As this last point makes clear, it is good practice for the writer both to identify and comment on possible weaknesses in their own argument. When drawing conclusions from evidence, researchers should draw attention to those parts of their chain of reasoning that could be disputed by others. When reading the conclusions of others, consumers of research should consider the possible weaknesses in the warrant. When I am reading research I am reassured to find an author who helps me to find weaknesses or reservations, and suggests ways of dealing with them. I adopt the same practice, wherever space permits, in my own work, which is an idea I have referred to as the 'Seven Samurai' principle (Gorard 2003). As part of my study of between-school segregation, discussed above, Gorard et al. (2001b) presented a set of findings about changes over time in the social composition of UK secondary schools. I followed this in the paper with eight separate competing explanations for these findings, and spent the rest of the paper considering the relative merits of each.

On the other hand, many senior and experienced colleagues with whom I have worked have responded to this practice by expressing the fear that acting in this way will weaken rather than strengthen their argument. I found this secretive, and fundamentally dishonest, approach of so many senior academics perplexing for a long time because I was under a misapprehension that our objectives were the same. I have only rather belatedly realised that such writers do not care about the truth of what they write, wanting only that others will be impressed by it. It is as though they were marketing something or had some other vested interest (Chapter Thirteen). Do not be one of them, please. Research is about finding things out. How do we decide which explanation of any set of results is the 'best'?

4.4 |¦| Handling multiple explanations

If we draw two points on a piece of standard graph paper, how many equations exist that can join those two points? Or if you prefer geography, how many ways are there of linking any two points on a map? Since I do not specify straight lines, the answer is infinity, at least in theory. There is the straight line, then one that bends up and back down just above a straight line, and an equivalent line below the straight one. Then there are bendy ones both above and below, there are curly and loopy ones, ones that go off the map at one edge and come back somewhere else, in an infinite variety. It is the same with explanations for research evidence. How many possible ways are there of explaining the research evidence in any study? The answer is literally limitless. As well as all of the sensible explanations you can think of, you can simply add extra parts to each of these explanations forever, like the loops in the line on the map. If your first explanation for some evidence is that having a job makes a person more likely to vote, then your second could be that this is because having a job allows them to buy more cakes, and that it is the cakes that make the person more likely to vote. Or you could conclude that having a job allows them to buy more cakes, and they have to leave their house to buy the cakes so they may as well vote on the way back from the shop. And so on. There is no limit to how many absurd additions can be made. This problem is technically referred to as the 'under-determination of theory by data' (Glymour et al. 1987).

So, deciding on research conclusions involves a combination of great creativity coupled with pedantic logical analysis. The creativity is needed to envisage and construct as many plausible explanations of the observations as possible. This is a key skill for a researcher and for a reader of the research of others, and one that can probably be improved with practice (Huck and Sandler 1979). The logical part lies in sifting through the alternatives, and excluding some while retaining those explanations that fit the observations best. The warrant is part of how we can try to decide between these competing explanations, to demonstrate that the proposed explanation is the best we have at this point in time. Only when all plausible alternative explanations, both methodological and substantive, have been shown to be inferior should any research claim be allowed to stand.

This stage sounds like a big job. It is a big job, but it is made easier by two things. As this book will demonstrate, the main reason for considering research design is so that when the research is conducted it is done in a way that already excludes a large number of rival explanations automatically (Weiss 2002). It really is the smart way to conduct research. The second way of reducing the scale of rival explanations is to embrace simplicity. This principle has manifested itself in many ways over centuries, from William of Occam's 'razor' through to Morgan (1903) and his 'law of parsimony'. Pearl (2000) suggests that it is rational to eliminate from immediate consideration any theory for which there is a less elaborate, simpler, alternative that is consistent with the data. All of the forms of this principle can be summarised as urging us as social scientists not to make any unnecessary assumptions in our explanations. We therefore limit our potential explanations to those that employ in their chain of reasoning the fewest assumptions for which we have no direct evidence.

According to this tried and successful principle, in the example above we might eliminate all explanations for any links between having a job and voting behaviour that involve cake, because we have no evidence at all that cake is implicated. If we can explain what we found with what we already know, then we must not add anything redundant (like cake) to our simplest explanation. If we cannot find even one decent explanation of the link, without resorting to cake, then we are permitted to make that one assumption. This assumption could be that cake is involved, but it could be anything else – any *one* thing else. It forms a speculative theory that has not arisen directly from the research evidence and so must be tested as soon as possible. Simplicity is why we would prefer the explanation that the flea (also above) cannot jump rather than that they cannot hear once their legs are removed. Returning to the map analogy, simplicity is like saying when we want to travel between two points, we should use the straight line wherever possible because it is the shortest distance to travel. If an obstacle or express route means we want to deviate from the straight line we should do the least necessary in order to complete the journey efficiently. So, in research, we sometimes have to make assumptions in our explanations. But the assumptions must be necessary and they must be the fewest necessary. This principle of simplicity is practical and allows the most social scientific progress in a given time, by making it easy to see when an explanation is wrong – as all explanations will, I am afraid, be found to be in time.

Consider this real example. The evidence is that death rates due to cancer (of all types) increased over the course of the twentieth century in Europe, and they look set to continue to rise in the twenty-first century. One possible conclusion is that the 'modern' lifestyle is to blame, including perhaps additives in the food we eat or pollution and damage to our environment. Two sets of events, the growth of cancer and historical lifestyle changes, seem to occur together. Therefore, we might assume that they are causally related and, of course, they may be. If they are causally related the cause and effect sequence only makes sense in one direction. But we also need to be creative in considering other plausible explanations, and then we have to decide which of these is the simplest. The lifestyle explanation makes at least one assumption that the evidence does not provide. It assumes that the correlation is causation. Another very plausible alternative is based on the fact of mortality. We all die eventually. Therefore, a change in the probability of death by any one cause affects the probability of death by all other causes. As death rates due to typhoid, smallpox and war have declined so the death rates due to heart disease or cancer must be expected to rise. Sadly, the people who invented cures for the major infectious diseases of the Victorian era might actually be the ones who inadvertently increased death rates from cancer and heart disease. If we add some more evidence, that people now live longer, on average, than at the start of the twentieth century, then the lifestyle theory becomes a much poorer explanation for the rise in cancer than the simple reduction of other avoidable causes of death. If we are poisoning ourselves then we should not be living longer. The 'degree of freedom' explanation, that reducing one cause of death inevitably raises another, makes fewer assumptions for which we do not have direct evidence, and is therefore simpler. This explanation could be wrong, but because it is the simplest it is also the explanation with the soundest warrant at present. This is what we should always look for, in our own research and that of others.

4.5 ¦¦ Handling tentative explanations

There are at least three ways in which writers can rather easily, at first sight, strengthen their warrants by weakening their claims. One way would be to say simply that if the reader accepts what a report has shown in the way of evidence and argument so far, then the conclusion reported also follows. It is perfectly proper to say something like this in a conclusion, as long as the argument is correct. For example, to say that if it is true that poverty is linked to health risks, and that poverty is part of the cause of health risks, then it follows that reducing poverty can also reduce health risks. The conclusion is logical, and it is sustained if the two prior parts of the argument (the 'premises') are true. It is a clearer statement of the conclusion than just implying the argument, and simply concluding that reducing poverty reduces health risks without the middle step. But this also means that if the conclusion is later found to be false, then it follows that one of the premises, the evidence or the warrant, must also be untrue.

This logic is known as 'denying the consequence'. An argument that says if statement A is true then B must be true, also implies that if B is not true then A cannot be true. It cannot be any other way. An example might be to say if a duck has a broken wing it cannot fly, and here is a duck which can fly so the premise proves that this duck cannot have a broken wing. There is no other possible conclusion. Because, in this example at least, all ducks with broken wings are members of the set of all ducks that cannot fly, if a duck can fly it cannot have a broken wing. This is a very powerful point in logic that comes simply from looking at the negative or denial of something (Phillips 1999). A similar approach is used in the inverse warrant idea, and you may have met something like it in the criterion of falsifiability proposed by Popper (1959), and in the common practice of statistical null hypothesis testing. So, if you are really concerned with your area of social science making progress you might want to phrase your conclusions as conditions, which means that even if the conclusions turn out to be wrong we can still make progress by learning that one of the premises is also wrong.

However, beware of confusing this approach with 'affirming the consequence', which is a very common logical error. This fallacious version of the argument says if A is true then B must be true, and therefore if B is found to be true this means that A is also true. This is a very poor argument. An example of affirming the consequence might be to say if a duck has a broken wing it cannot fly, and here is a duck which cannot fly so the premise proves that this duck has a broken wing. But it proves nothing of the sort. There are many other reasons why a duck may not be able to fly. The set of all ducks includes all ducks who cannot fly and the set of all ducks who cannot fly includes all ducks with broken wings (for the sake of this example, at least). But at each level the set contains other possible members. There can and will be some ducks who can fly, and some ducks without broken wings who cannot fly.

Another way of strengthening warranting practice by weakening our claims is to make it clear that our claims are speculative. These claims could be plausible and potentially useful explanations of the evidence, but not necessarily true in terms of logic. Specifying these is fine, as long as any reader of the research is made aware of their speculative nature. An example might be that since ex-offenders with jobs are less likely to re-offend it is worth seeing if providing jobs for other ex-offenders will lead to less re-offending. This is a speculative proposal not a definitive causal claim (that would not be warranted), and it is perfectly valid as expressed.

A third useful way of strengthening warranting practice by weakening our claims is to make probabilistic claims. What I mean by this is that when we present research findings we need to give some indication, via caveats or similar, of the extent to which we would be prepared to bet on them being true, or the extent to which we would wish others to rely on them being true. A problem with this approach is that people are generally very poor at handling probabilities. There is much misuse and misunderstanding. A couple of important examples will illustrate what I mean here.

Forensic evidence such as a DNA profile is now routinely used in police and judicial proceedings to try and make a match with the DNA of a suspect. The analysis yields a probability of the match, and this can sound impressively small. It might be that the probability of the two samples of DNA not being from the same person is 1 in 10,000 or lower. This is a very small probability, and could be used in court as part of an evidence base for the prosecution. However, there is a danger that the prosecutors (at least until recently), the police, the jury and the media somehow suggest that this probability is the inverse of the probability of the guilt of the accused. In effect, the 1 in 10,000 chance of a match if two peoples' DNA were selected at random is conveyed as a 9,999 in 10,000 chance that the accused is guilty. This is what Gigerenzer (2002) describes as the 'prosecutor fallacy'. It can be seen to be a fallacy by asking someone who propounds this fallacy to lay out their warrant for the argument. The evidence is that there is an estimated 1 in 10,000 chance of the match found. The conclusion is that this makes it overwhelmingly likely that the accused is guilty. What is the warrant here? The prosecutor would also have to argue that there is no human error in the matching process, that the match signifies the presence of the suspect at the crime scene, that the presence at the scene necessarily entails guilt, and so on. This is so with almost any evidence. It does mean that the estimated probability of guilt comes down considerably, but the real problem is with the implied calculation of guilt in the first place. The prosecutor has to argue that the number of potential suspects is so small that a 1 in 10,000 chance is the equivalent of 'beyond reasonable doubt'. If the crime took place in a country of 100 million people, and if we make the favourable assumption that potential suspects are limited to residents only, then

1/10,000 means that 10,000 residents could have the same forensic match as the accused. Thus, the suspect, on this evidence alone, has a 1/10,000 probability of guilt (or even somewhat less, given the constraints above). This is much higher than for an average resident, and therefore germane to the case without being conclusive. But it is, of course, much, much lower than 9,999/10,000. The importance of the initial error is hard to overestimate in law, medicine and beyond. Yet, it can be easily sorted out by asking the person making the argument to lay out the complete steps explicitly. In this example, as in many others, once the warrant is made explicit the conclusion can be easily seen to be false or greatly exaggerated (Dawes 2001).

Perhaps even more important for the future of social science research is the argument that is merely implied in most reports of statistical significance testing. This argument is one that is always well worth insisting be spelled out explicitly. My prediction is that if such explicit warranting of statistical claims became anything like standard practice then statistics as currently envisaged would simply cease as a research activity. I illustrate the need for a warrant here with an extract from a real paper (Funk and Gathmann 2011). I selected it as the first in the current issue, at time of writing, of The Economics Journal. It is therefore peer-reviewed, and in a prestigious outlet. It is not unusual in what it does and says – the approach it describes is standard. I had to pick a paper to discuss, and this just happens to be it.

The paper presents historical data from the quasi-independent cantons of Switzerland, comparing the scale of local government with indicators of direct democratic control, such as whether there is a mandatory referendum on the budget. The evidence is that the group of cantons with greater voter control is associated with smaller budgets and so smaller government, compared to the rest of the cantons. In their Table 2, Funk and Gathmann (2011, p.1261) present t-test statistics and associated probabilities for differences in mean scores between two groups of cantons. The means scores are for a range of relevant measures, such as expenditure *per capita*, the percentage of the population in employment, and the percentage living in urban areas. Funk and Gathmann are trying to portray whether there are 'significant' differences between the two groups of cantons they are comparing. What does this mean?

The argument based on statistical significance is structured as follows, although almost no one ever expresses the argument. It starts with the structure of the valid logic of denying the consequence.

If the nil null hypothesis, that there is no difference between the two groups of cantons, is true, then we will find no difference between them in their expenditure (or whatever).

There is a measured difference between the two groups of cantons, in terms of their expenditure.

Therefore, the nil null hypothesis must be untrue. There is, in fact, a difference between the two groups, at least in terms of expenditure.

This is a rather long-winded way of saying that if we have good evidence of a difference between the two groups, then the two groups are patently not identical! The conclusion here follows logically, and must be accepted as long as we also accept the quality of the measurement of the difference. If the measurement of the difference between the two groups is dubious in any way, then the conclusion is not necessarily true. And this is the problem as soon as we move from an argument in symbolic logic to one which uses real-life evidence. The logic is now:

> If the nil null hypothesis is true, then we will find no difference between the expenditure in the two groups.
>
> However, there does appear to be a difference in expenditure between the two groups.
>
> Therefore, the nil null hypothesis may not be true.

This is a tentative or uncertain claim for the conclusion, and so how convincing we find the conclusion depends on how convincing we find the evidence of a difference, as expressed in step two of this argument. There are two broad categories of reasons why we might not accept the measured difference between the groups. The measurements might be in error, unreliable, entered into a spreadsheet incorrectly, or misinterpreted. The measurements might only be estimates, or they might even be fraudulent. Governments have been known not to tell the whole truth in their accounts. All of these measurement problems are important and need to be taken into account when warranting claims from this or any other study. Even if the measurements were perfect (or good enough), the apparent difference between the two groups could still be an illusion caused by discrepancies in the sampling of the two groups. Sampling bias and variation is the second of the broad group of reasons why we might not accept the measured difference between the groups.

However, the first category of measurement problems and biases are not addressed at all by the t-test probabilities used by Funk and Gathmann (2011, Table 2). The t-test is like all traditional statistical analysis, including all tests of significance, and the use of standard errors and confidence intervals. It is concerned only with random sampling variation. Such tests are, of course, irrelevant when the full population of cases is used since then there is no sampling variation. They cannot adjust for missing cases, whether from populations or samples, because these are non-random, and so t-tests are irrelevant to judgements about non-response and sample dropout. And they are irrelevant when the sample is not a randomly-selected one (Chapter Six). Significance tests are relevant only to making a judgement about sampling variation produced by the random selection of cases for a sample, and whether this variation is a good explanation of any manifested difference between the two groups.

The probability generated by a t-test (or any other test for statistical significance) is calculated on the assumption that the nil null hypothesis is true. The calculation shows how often a random sample of the size used by Funk and Gathmann (2011) would show a measured difference as large as the one they found, if expenditure *per capita* is equal in both groups. This probability is the figure used by researchers, like Funk and Gathmann, to help them decide if the measured difference between the two groups is 'significant'. What they mean by 'significant' is that the probability of the result they obtained is so low that the assumption of no difference between the groups must be incorrect.

The argument, when spelled out in full like this, is quite complex. It is also invalid in almost every respect. The calculation takes no account of any measurement problems or missing data, and so even if the rest of the argument were valid, the test of significance would be insufficient on its own. More crucially, Funk and Gathmann (2011) used population data with no random selection whatsoever. The data are for *all* Swiss cantons. Therefore, the calculation is not just insufficient – it is based on a false assumption (of a random sample). The probabilities that the calculation generates (because the software knows no better) are just nonsense. But even if we could ignore all of that, why would we or Funk and Gathmann (2011) want to know how often a difference as large as the one they found would emerge by chance if the two groups were actually equivalent in expenditure? They have calculated the probability of their data, assuming the nil null hypothesis is true. But what they really wanted was the probability of the nil null hypothesis being true, if the data they obtained was sound. These two probabilities are very different, and it is not possible to calculate one from the other without considerably more information (and the use of Bayes' theorem). As Cohen (1994) puts it, the probability of being a US citizen if one is a US Congress member (1) is very different from the probability of being a Congress member if one is a US citizen (much much less than 0.05). For more on this, see Chapter Twelve.

Forcing authors to lay out their warrant for statistical claims will force them to face the issue that even after all of their analysis, and making a number of unrealistic assumptions, they are no closer to knowing the probability that there is a real underlying difference in the population they are studying. The warrant for any conclusion of statistical significance, as traditionally envisaged, does not stand up to scrutiny. This approach to analysis survives, presumably, only because it is generally not made explicit. Indeed, experience as a reviewer suggests many of its users may not even be able to make it explicit. They do not understand at all what their analysis is about. As explained at the chapter start, serious lack of clarity in writing usually signifies lack of understanding by the writer. Two more general points emerge. It is hard to deal with probabilistic conclusions, because even valid logical structures like denying the consequence then let us down. Their logic is valid only when dealing with certainties, of a kind that are almost entirely absent from research in practice. And if spelling out the warrant for something as widely used and admired as statistical testing shows it to be illogical, just imagine how important it will be to clarify the warrant in other and even weaker areas as well.

4.6 ▎▎ Conclusion

In a research report, like an argument, presenting the warrant for the conclusions is essential. But in practice, the reporting of this step is often missed, as it is tacitly assumed by both the author and the reader. However, where the research is intended to change the views of others it is necessary to make the warrant explicit. This warrant can then be challenged, but unlike a challenge to the evidence this is not usually about quality or validity but rather about the relevance of the evidence to the conclusion.

Having conducted a considerable number of large-scale syntheses of research evidence, it is clear that a lot of research writing does not make its warrant explicit, and when I try to create a warrant for the research conclusion I am reading about, it often fails. That is one reason why, when synthesising or reviewing the evidence of others, I take no account of their conclusions and synthesise only their findings. Even where writers make an attempt at warranting their conclusions the result is often failure. Some illustrate standard fallacies, such as resting a conclusion on an appeal to popular sentiment, or to emotion, an *ad hominem* argument, irrelevant premises, the absence of contrary premises, or most often just a thinly disguised re-statement of their initial theories. Some refer, incorrectly, to the quality or range of their research methods. This lack of concern for warrants in the general literature may be a key factor explaining the lack of attention to research design in existing studies and in resources for researcher development (Chapter One). As succeeding chapters in this book illustrate, research design and warranting are intimately linked. One of the main reasons for getting the design of any new study right is that it then allows more rigorously warranted conclusions, of the kind that the researcher may want to draw after completing their study. For example, a warrant often contains a kind of causal claim, which states that if the research user (practitioner or policy-maker) does one thing then another will ensue. This kind of claim can be demonstrated by some designs but not by others. Causal claims are so important for design that they are the subject of the next chapter.

⫶ Exercises for warrants

1 Consider this argument in terms of the conclusion it draws.

> 'The number of social scientists has grown over past decades, but there have been widespread concerns about their quality and the relevance of much of their work. People should only consider becoming a social scientist if they look forward to the challenge of doing careful research, and are willing to work hard. Some people dispute the importance of social science. Social scientists all need to be very talented. Therefore, if you work hard and like a challenge you should become a social scientist.'

a   Try putting this argument into a simpler format. Ignore whether you think the prior statements are true or not.

b   Is the argument for the final sentence conclusion a good one?

c   Would the argument succeed if the conclusion had been 'Therefore, you should not become a social scientist unless you are talented and work hard'?

2   Brignell (2000) provides a nice example of a controversial warrant. Industry routinely uses a chemical called 'dihydrogen monoxide'. While tremendously useful, this chemical often leads to spillages, and finds its way into our food supply. It is a major component of acid rain, and a cause of soil erosion. As a vapour it is a major greenhouse gas. It is often fatal when inhaled, and is a primary cause of death in several UK accidents per year. It has routinely been found in the tumours of terminally ill patients. What should we do about this chemical? Should we ban it, severely restrict it, or let it be?

3   Select a journal article reporting new research in your own area of interest. List the conclusions or implications (not the findings) of this research.

a   Try to write out the formal steps in the argument from the findings to one of the conclusions.

b   Is the conclusion reported in the article warranted by the evidence presented for it?

⇌ Notes on exercises for warrants

1   a   It seems to me that the first and third sentences are not clearly relevant to the conclusion in the fifth sentence. Therefore the argument hinges on the second and fourth sentences. The argument is that social scientists need to be talented, hard-working and up for a challenge. Therefore, anyone who likes hard work and a challenge should be a social scientist.

b   This is not a good argument. There is something missing. All A might be B but that does not mean that all B are also A.

c   The argument would be better if the conclusion had been 'Therefore, you should not become a social scientist unless you are talented and work hard'? This ignores the issue of liking a challenge, but the conclusion is basically warranted if the two key prior statements (two and four) are true.

2   The chemical is water, of course – perhaps the most useful and vital chemical on earth. Yet in a survey, the clear majority of respondents, who did not know that it was water, believed that this chemical should either be banned or severely regulated. However, this is not a practical conclusion, or a logical one, even if the evidence (such that water appears in acid rain and in tumours) is valid. For example, an argument that water can be fatal and therefore must be banned is only convincing if it is also true that everything that could be fatal must be banned. The latter part of the argument is the 'warrant' for the conclusion that water must be banned. Since the warrant statement is not something that we would agree with it means that the argument is not a good one. Vaccinations, anaesthetics, aircraft, cars, stairs, lifts, peanuts and cats can all be fatal. Most people would not agree that all of these, and millions more examples like them, should be banned. So this means that nothing else substituted for water in this argument can make the argument work. The problem is not that we cannot ban water. It is that this structure is not a good argument for banning anything, including water.

Presumably, a better argument could involve laying out the costs and benefits of banning any substance. Water would then not be banned because its benefits so greatly outweigh its dangers.

3 a It is sometimes hard to distinguish between the research findings and the conclusions in an article, partly because a writer may make no attempt to separate them, and partly because any description will inevitably take certain things for granted. However, as a rule of thumb we can distinguish between those things known or taken for granted before the research was conducted, those things found out by the new research being reported, and the implications and suggested ways forward presented by the writer. The first might include our understanding of what a school, a family or a developing country was in the earlier examples in this chapter. And these understandings might change as a direct result of the research. The second are the factual or near-factual bits of evidence presented in the article – such as what a majority of politicians reported to be the cause of low voter turnout, or what official statistics show about who goes to school with who. These 'facts' might be wrong, but that is largely a methods question and not about the structure of the argument.

   b The implications and suggested ways forward presented by the writer are the 'so what?' In your chosen example, if we accept the first and the second things above, do we have to accept the third? Why? Again, use the inverse principle – if the conclusion is not correct how else can we explain the evidence presented for it? Is the writer making an implicit value judgement that not everyone will agree with? Is the conclusion even relevant? Is the conclusion merely a disguised re-statement of the first thing above – something known or taken for granted before the research was conducted? Even if the conclusion is valid, is there an obviously simpler explanation, like in the flea example?

⊒ Suggested reading

Huck, S. and Sandler, H. (1979) *Rival Hypotheses: Alternative Interpretations of Data Based Conclusions*. New York: Harper and Row.

FIVE

The nature of causal claims

SUMMARY

- An assertion that something causes something else is a strong explanatory claim.
- Yet there is limited value in having a research programme that is only descriptive and makes no attempt to identify or explain causes.
- Many researchers appear to be confused, making causal claims without the necessary evidence, or masking their causal claims by using softer synonyms.
- While hard to establish philosophically, the existence of causation is essential for social science research.
- The standard ingredients of a causal claim include: a correlation between cause and effect; the effect appearing after its cause; changes in the effect produced by varying the strength of the cause; and a plausible explanation of the process by which this happens.
- These 'ingredients' are complementary to the elements of research design, and lead directly to well-established designs such as cross-sectional, longitudinal and experimental.
- Causal models in social science can be envisaged as probabilistic in nature, wherein varying the strength of the cause will only *tend* to lead to changes in the effect.

5.1 ▌▎ Introduction

Some research is quite properly descriptive. It is useful to know how people feel about a new business, whether poverty is officially declining, or how many children were taken into care last year, for example. Such work is important, and long-established traditions such as political arithmetic have been based on simply laying bare the patterns of inequality and injustice (Gorard 2012a). But descriptive work is almost always turned into explanatory work very quickly.

Once we have laid bare an injustice, surely we will turn to thinking about how to overcome it. To follow the examples above, how can we make people feel better about that new business, why did poverty decline, and was it beneficial for those children taken into care? All of these questions follow on from the simple descriptive work, and all are causal in nature. They can all be re-written to include the words 'cause' or 'effect' in a way that descriptive questions cannot, such as: What would *cause* people to feel better about a new business? Even theoretical work is causal since a theory is, by definition, an attempt at explanation (Chapter Three).

Intriguingly, in presentations I often encounter researchers who claim that they are not interested in causal questions, and that their research is never explanatory in nature. A handful of examples, drawn from their own work will usually suffice to make them think again. In fact, I have never encountered a researcher not interested in causal issues, even when they say that they never use causal terms. Recent examples given to me by such researchers have included in their first two sentences of a description of their research the words 'impact', 'influence', 'improve', 'reduce', and 'cure'. One person even said that they wanted to understand the effect of something, using the exact word 'effect' in the first sentence of their description, but they still tried to argue that this did not betoken interest in causes.

Bizarrely, the opposite phenomenon is also common. In reviewing evidence from the literature it is common to find reports using strong causal terms to describe their findings, but without any justification in terms of the design or warrant involved in the study. Abbot (1998, p.149) complained that 'an unthinking causalism today pervades our journals', meaning that correlation, pattern or even opinion was incorrectly described in definitive causal terms. Some studies claiming causal inferences are really studies of associations, based on complex statistical analyses with passive or cross-sectional datasets. It is quite common for studies to interpret coefficients in regression models as effects and the explanatory variables as causes (Gorard et al. 2011). Studies using in-depth or small-scale datasets are, if anything, even worse in this kind of over-claiming. This unthinking causalism appears to be worsening, at least in some fields. Robinson et al. (2007) reviewed major education journal contents from 1994 to 2004, and reported a decline from 45% to 33% in the studies using evaluated interventions, but a growth in the use of causal statements in non-intervention studies from 34% to 43%. A particular culprit here was statistical modelling, including structural equation modelling and path analyses. All are routinely misunderstood by researchers as being some kind of test of causation, beyond association. The belief that statistical modelling and testing can demonstrate causation is 'circular thinking' (Morrison 2009, p.207); it assumes at the outset that which it purports to demonstrate. But the problem is more general than this. It pervades entire fields of social science. Hence this chapter is specifically about what it means to make the strong claim that something causes something else. The chapter starts by considering why we need the concept of causation at all.

5.2 ▮▮ Are there causes and effects?

Causes and effects are ideas used to encapsulate a firm impression we have about the way the world works. Many events and processes have a regularity and time sequence that offer both an explanation for why things occur, and a way of controlling them. However, causes cannot be deduced just from observing effects (Blalock 1964). Seeing a light bulb going off does not, by itself, allow the observer to deduce whether it has been switched off, there is a power failure or the bulb is broken, for example (Salmon 1998). Similarly, effects cannot be deduced simply by observing their possible causes. Who would have thought beforehand that striking a flint could create fire? Hume (1962) described cause and effect as an immutable habit of mind – we are pre-disposed to see regularities in our environment and ascribe something like causation to them. This may be a valuable evolutionary heuristic when time is short and a quick decision is needed. But it can also lead to mistakes and superstition in the longer term. We cannot prove that things are causally related. We cannot even prove that there are such things as causal relations. So what are the alternatives?

Perhaps everything is random

In both classical and operant conditioning, it has been shown that the association of two things leads the conditioned subject to behave in the presence of one thing as though it implied the presence of the other. Skinner's pigeons 'learnt' to pull a lever which had always accompanied the release of a pellet of food in the past. The conditioned subjects do this whether the lever is mechanically releasing the pellet or not. They behave as though the lever is a cause. In intermittent reinforcement schedules, where the pellet appears on only some occasions, this behaviour is even stronger – it will take more examples of no pellet after pulling the lever to un-condition the subject than it would if the pellet had previously always appeared. This means that probabilistic causation, of the kind commonly reported in social science, is paradoxically an even stronger habit of mind than Hume's constant conjunction idea. And this is so, even though it is more likely to be an erroneous association. Further, in accidental reinforcement schedules, providing pellets at random tends to reinforce whatever behaviour the subject was involved in at the time. This makes that behaviour more likely to be repeated by the subject, and so more likely to coincide with the next random arrival of a pellet. Eventually, the subject repeats an endless 'superstitious' ritual of one behaviour, only intermittently reinforced by the arrival of a pellet, so making the apparent association resistant to un-conditioning. This is a wonderful analogue for our unsafe causal beliefs in social science.

Could all of our purported causal models be similar? Imagine a very large table of random numbers using the digits 0 to 9. The probability of finding the sequence

'0 1 2 3 4 5 6 7 8 9' in this table depends on the probability of this sequence in itself (1/10^{10}) and on the size of the table (the bigger the table the more chance of finding this sequence somewhere in it). A table of random numbers can contain arithmetic sequences, and passages of repetition, without us denying its essential randomness. If the table is very large then the probability of such a sequence nears 100%. How unlikely this sequence is depends upon the number of chances it has to appear. If we do not know how many chances it has then we must not be impressed by its apparent regularity. But this impression is part of what Hume was cautioning about. For example, the sequence '3 2 7 5 8 8 4 5 1 9' has exactly the same probability of occurring as '0 1 2 3 4 5 6 7 8 9', but is much less likely to be noticed or acted upon than the apparently ordered sequence. Perhaps in a large (possibly infinitely large) universe all of the perceived regularities that create the impression of causation so forcefully in our minds are as illusory as this.

In fact, it is possible to imagine and describe events without reference to causes. Since this is so, and we cannot see, smell, hear, measure or register causes directly, it may be unwise to assume that they exist. An argument could be advanced that this is the most parsimonious, and therefore the most scientific, explanation of any set of observations. The practical problem with this view is that while it is intellectually coherent, it means the end of scientific endeavour. If everything is random then we can make no difference to anything because there are no 'becauses'! It would not be possible to predict or control any random events, by definition. So, anyone engaged in social science research is logically and ethically required to accept that causation is a possibility. Why would taxpayers or charity-givers or anyone support the funding of social science research that could never lead to any improvement in anything, if it were true that improvement is an illusion, resting as it does on a causal notion?

Perhaps causes and random events co-exist?

Most famously, quantum theory has suggested that causation and randomness are both needed to explain events at some level. Some events seem to be predictable and some not. A similar idea is accepted by economists and others who present evidence for rational choices as a causing agent. These choices, such as those involved in human capital theory, appear to work at aggregated levels but not for individuals. One interpretation is that individuals operate using idiosyncratic processes that only appear to be rational when grouped. Across the social sciences this same belief appears in models, in which the predictable components of behaviour are seen as causal in nature, and the unpredicted parts are seen as random error terms or individual whimsy (Pötter and Blossfeld 2001). Gambetta (1987) constructed a model that involves both causation and other competing explanations of a non-determinist nature, such as intentionality through personal choice (and choice cannot be a real choice if it is part of a determinist model).

There is, on the other hand, a principle of sufficient reason which suggests that all contingent facts must have explanations, or that all manifest events must have causes. It is possible to defend this principle, even against the claims of quantum theory, although there is no room to do so here (Pruss 2006). More simply, perhaps the severe problems of the co-existence of causal and non-causal events can be seen when considering how they might interact with each other. Assuming that chance and causation both exist and can interact, we are led to a contradiction and this proves that they cannot both co-exist and interact. For example, if some random events can be caused then they are not random – by definition. If the cause of some effects is randomness then the effects will appear randomly – necessarily. This is true whether we are discussing sub-atomic particles or the reason for selecting a candidate at a job interview.

On the other hand, if we assume that chance and causation both exist, but cannot interact as the contradiction suggests, then our explanation of the world is un-parsimonious (Chapter Four). We have no direct evidence for either causes or random events (Arjas 2001), so to use either one of them in an explanation involves making an assumption. To explain a set of observations using both involves making two assumptions, and is therefore un-parsimonious. We have enough trouble establishing whether causes exist or not. To allow them to exist alongside unrelated phenomena makes most social scientific propositions un-testable. The problem with causation is not that there are events that it cannot explain, but that it is invisible and elusive. Therefore, there is no value in mixing it up with a model of randomness which is also perfectly capable of explaining decisions by itself, but which is also not open to observation by social scientists. Given that there is no way of deciding between them empirically, either causation or non-causal events can be adopted, but there is no empirical justification for working with both at the same time. Rather, in a causal explanation, an intention or an individual choice can be an outcome (of family background, for example) as well as a cause. Most debate is actually about the nature of the cause (or effect), not about whether it is a cause. When psychologists argue the nature/nurture controversy, or sociologists debate the relative importance of structure and agency, they are basically arguing about what the relevant causes are.

5.3 ||| What is a causal model?

Having ruled out an explanation of social science events based solely on chance and an explanation that combines both chance and causation, we are left with causation itself. What is it? We know it is difficult to identify, and can be misleading. That is why we need research design. One of the main purposes of design is to try and prevent being convinced by superstition. Skinner's pigeons in an accidental reinforcement scenario could have tested the apparent association by not performing the behaviour and seeing whether the pellet still appeared (they could contrive a comparative element to their design, if you like). Unfortunately these pigeons do not do anything of the sort. They remain in their superstitious state. You can see films of them repeating increasingly absurd ritualistic behaviour, in the apparent belief that this was the reason for the appearance of food (I know Skinner himself foreswore explanations involving belief and other mental events, but I hope readers will see where I am going with this). Of course, humans do the same. Without careful temporal analysis, long-term records, useful comparators and willingness to intervene in different ways it is possible to be convinced of almost anything – that a dance makes rain appear, or that stroking rabbit fur affects the fall of a roulette ball. Note that such superstitious examples are firmly causal in nature. They are just wrong about their effectiveness. The majority of social science researchers who eschew research design and just collect data in an unsystematic way are like those pigeons. They create and pass on grand theories that are never tested, and perhaps cannot be tested. They never look for ways of trying to show their ideas to be wrong (falsification). And they try not to expose what they do to wider critique by inventing needless neologisms and writing very badly. Do not be a pigeon. Design is a large part of the remedy for this nonsense. In order to design research that does its best to identify causes, we need to be a little clearer on what a cause is.

Across his different writings Hume seemed to be ambivalent about causation (Coventry 2008). On the one hand, as a 'matter of fact', all we have to support the existence of causation is observed regularities of nature. We cannot use Hume's 'relation of ideas' (or more simply logic) to deduce causation from facts. And a reader can sense Hume's dissatisfaction with this (and with the more general problem of induction, as discussed in an exercise later in the chapter). Hume did suggest that cause was therefore only an observed regularity coupled with a belief or 'habit of mind'. But he also suggested that causal claims are, and must be, testable propositions about knowledge. They can be tested via *modus tollendo tollens* or falsifying the consequence (Chapter Four). We can say, if some thing is a cause of another thing then it follows that we should observe certain phenomena. What are these?

According to Mill (1882) a causal claim can be made if:

- the cause preceded the effect;
- the cause and the effect are related, and
- there are no plausible alternative explanations for the effect other than the cause.

These are all important elements, but Mill's criteria do not make clear what 'related' means. It might mean that a correlation alone is sufficient. Bradford-Hill (1966), and others working on the links between smoking and lung cancer, proposed another set of scientific conditions for the workable and ethical identification of a causal link. Put simply, we can talk of a cause:effect relationship between X and Y when most of the following descriptions apply:

- X and Y are associated in different studies, with different researchers, using different methods and differing populations.
- The frequency of association is substantial compared to the frequency of X or Y in isolation.
- There is exposure to, or experience of, X before the onset of Y in all cases.
- X can be used to predict onset of Y.
- There is a reduction in Y after the removal of X.
- There is an increase in Y after intervention X to increase Y.
- And there is a coherent, plausible, workable agreed mechanism for X to influence Y that is consistent with prior knowledge.

These ideas include and clarify two of Mill's criteria, and add a requirement that deliberate variation in the appearance or strength of the cause must yield a change in the effect. However, they omit a crucial element of Mill's ideas, which is the elimination of sensible alternative explanations. Cook and Campbell (1979) suggest that a cause can be identified where there: is co-variation of cause and effect when the cause changes; temporal precedence of the cause; and no plausible alternative explanation. I proposed a simplified model of causal evidence for social science that consists of four main criteria, clarifying and extending these ideas (Gorard 2002b).

1 For X (a possible cause) and Y (a possible effect) to be in a causal relationship, they must be repeatedly associated. This association must be strong and clearly observable. It must be replicable, and it must be specific to X and Y.
2 For X and Y to be in a causal relationship, they must proceed in sequence. X must always precede Y (where both appear), and the appearance of Y must be safely predictable from the appearance of X.
3 It must have been demonstrated repeatedly that an intervention to change the strength or appearance of X strongly and clearly changes the strength or appearance of Y.
4 There must a coherent mechanism to explain the causal link. This mechanism must be the simplest available without which the evidence cannot be explained. Put another way, if the proposed mechanism were not true then there must be no simpler or equally simple way of explaining the evidence for it.

If each criterion is seen as necessary (though not individually sufficient) for a causal model, then any research yielding evidence relevant to at least one of these criteria can contribute to the search for causal mechanisms. This is done through the falsification principle (Chapter Four). A cross-sectional study that finds no association between X and Y reduces the likelihood that there is a causal mechanism from X to Y, for example.

Association and design

One way of viewing causation is as a stable association between two phenomena. Where one is present or absent the other is also (Hume 1962). This view of causation has three main problems. It suggests that a singular event cannot have a cause.

We know that it opens us up to superstition, and it does not allow for intermittent association.

It is clearly wrong to suggest that a singular event cannot have a cause or causes. In a sense, all events are singular in time/place/context/actors. Mills' and others' criteria are best understood as describing how we can identify causes, and are not necessarily characteristics of all cause:effect sequences. Where we can observe or repeat very similar situations, such as striking a billiard ball in Hume's account, it is much easier to test a proposed causal model than when faced with a complex causal question about a one-off process, such as what caused the outbreak of the Second World War. Skinner's accidental reinforcement schedule is a powerful reminder of the dangers of allowing causal models to be based only on association. Something other than an association is needed before a causal explanation can be convincing. Skinner's intermittent reinforcement schedule shows us how difficult it might be to shake such causal models once they have been accepted. We can be easily fooled by association, especially where these associations involve large numbers and are backed by perceived expertise (Brighton 2000). Prediction, based on correlation alone, does not depend on a causal relationship, nor does it necessarily exhibit causation. This is true however impressive the prediction is – we may accurately predict the severity of a fire from the number of fire engines attending without attributing the cause of the fire to the engines (de Vaus 2001). Day always precedes night and so could predict night with 100% accuracy, but that would not make it the cause.

Time sequence and design

A second way of viewing causation is as a sequence of events with the cause preceding the effect. It is this sequence that allows us to identify which would be the cause and which the effect. An association of X and Y by itself could be X causing Y, Y causing X, or Z causing both X and Y. So a simple test involves the timing. If X precedes Y then Y cannot be the cause of X. Implicitly, this simple forward direction view of causation appears in much social science research. The assumption is that the predictors or independent variables are themselves unaffected by the outcomes or dependent variables (Berry 1984).

However, relationships between data which are seemingly in a temporal sequence can be reciprocal (Hagenaars 1990). We can accept causes simultaneous with their effects, such as where a ball rests on a cushion, and the cushion is 'causing the ball not to drop further' (Mackie 1974). Does greater investment in training lead to company growth, are richer companies more likely to spend money on training, or are both iteratively but causally related? If we drop two balls into a bowl, we can model the final resting places of both balls mathematically, but we cannot use this to decide which ball is 'causing' the other to be displaced from the centre of the bowl. The events are mutually determined (Garrison 1993). Wages and interest rates might be inversely related over time, but rather than deciding that one causes the other it might be more realistic to describe them as mutually determining. Mathematical statements or systems of equations can describe systems but they cannot express either intention or causality. They can be used to show that systems are, or are not, in equilibrium, and to predict the actual change in the value of one variable if another variable is changed. However, it is important to recall that this prediction works both ways. If y=f(x) then there will be a complementary function such that x=f(y). Which variable is the dependent one (on the left-hand, predicted side) is purely arbitrary. Nothing in mathematics or statistical analysis can overcome this limitation.

Again, research design can help however. It is obvious that there must be a time element in the design. A longitudinal design might be:

$$N \qquad O_a \qquad O_b$$

In this example, the potential cause A is observed to occur first (O_a), followed by the effect B (O_b). There are several limitations of this design. Recall the accidental reinforcement of pigeons. It may be that the order here in this limited section of time is illusory. It may be part of an ongoing and even alternating sequence like this:

$$N \ldots \qquad O_b \qquad O_a \qquad O_b \qquad O_a \qquad \ldots$$

Here, we cannot really say which of A or B comes first in sequence. So, even a valid association coupled with a valid sequence is not sufficient to establish a convincing cause. What else must we introduce before we are, or should be, convinced by a causal model?

Explanation and design

A possible contender for the magic ingredient, added to association and sequence to create a causal model, is the explanation or theoretical mechanism. Something must be added to the statistical association between an event and a later outcome for the model to be convincing. We need to describe a process that shows how the cause could generate the effect. A good example is the clear relationship between smoking and lung cancer. The statistical conjunctions and the observations from laboratory trials with animals were explained by the isolation of carcinogens in the smoke, and the pathological evidence from diseased lungs. These combined to create an explanatory theory. Chapter Three explained why any such theory should be as simple as possible. The explanation must be easy to test and make the fewest assumptions necessary to provide a mechanism linking cause and effect.

The theory needs to explain the co-variation between cause and effect and the time sequence. For this explanation to be plausible, the proposed effect must be capable of change (de Vaus 2001). While the sex of the student could affect the outcome of a job interview, the reverse could not usually be true. Sex would be unchanged by the interview process. In fact, we can go further than saying that the dependent variable must be capable of change. It must be able to be changed by the independent variable. If there is a relationship between the level of poverty among 16-year-olds and their examination results, then the only causal model that makes sense in the short-term is one where poverty leads to examination results, or where both are caused by something else. This kind of consideration can give a clue to the time sequence (as discussed in the previous section).

However, to extend the example used at the outset, it is possible to switch a light on and off without understanding how it works. The fact that it does work is part of what shows that the switch is the cause of the light going on and off. This suggests that the explanatory mechanism is the least important part of any causal model. If it is clear that altering the presence or strength of a potential cause 'works' in the sense of changing an effect, then it matters less if the mechanism is not understood. On the other hand, even the most convincing explanation possible is of little consequence if the potential cause has no discernible effect (see Chapter Three).

Interventions and design

The key therefore is not whether we can explain why a cause has an effect, but whether it can be demonstrated to have an effect at all. A final way of viewing causation is via the impact of an intervention. Does the proposed causal model work in practice, under controlled and rigorously evaluated conditions? Since causes are not susceptible to direct observation, but what they 'cause' is effects, then at least those effects must be observable (like the light coming on). We need evidence that controlled interventions have altered the level or presence of the potential cause and so produced changes in the purported effect that cannot be explained in any other way. Such evidence may be created in a number of robust ways, most notably via a randomised controlled trial (Chapter Nine).

5.4 ╟ Probability and causation

Potentially, causal models are very complex. Any event could be the effect of a large number of causes. All of these causes might be needed to create the effect, but insufficient in isolation. All causes work only within a given context (Emmet 1984). A fire needs oxygen, flammable material, and an ignition (flame). We can say that the flame causes the fire, but it does not do so alone. Also, any one or more of a variety of causes could be sufficient to create the effect. None of them might be strictly necessary. We might start a fire with a lighter, a match, a flint, or a magnifying glass. Also, any cause or combination of causes could have more than one effect. Starting a fire causes combustion of the flammable material, but it also causes heat and light. These kinds of causes are what Mackie (1974) named 'insufficient but non-redundant parts of an unnecessary but sufficient condition' or 'inus' conditions in brief. Because we may not need all of the possible inus conditions for any effect, there seems to be a lack of determinism, and this creates the appearance of probabilistic causes (Shadish et al. 2002). In this sense, a cause must merely raise the probability of its effect (Dowe and Noordhof 2004).

Another way of expressing this idea is to say that we may be unable to predict exactly what the effects of a set of causes might be, because of the complexity of their interaction. So, we predict effects in probabilistic terms, or after controlling for everything else. An example of a *ceteris paribus* causal model could be the erosion of a river bank caused by a meandering river (Corbi and Prades 2000). There is no doubt that the river bank will erode over time even though it is not possible to be precise about the exact pattern. This is reasonable, but makes it hard to test any causal model through attempted invalidation. The research therefore needs more rigour than a simple mechanical causal model, not less. Yet in social science, too many commentators seem to believe the opposite. They use complexity as an excuse to shun rigour. Do not be tempted to adopt this sloppy approach, or to accept it from others.

In some of the natural sciences we might clone cells, or find identical particles. Hume considered billiard balls, which are also similar to each other and may be envisaged as interchangeable. In social science, however, we cannot usually expose the same people or organisations both to a research process and not. This means that we must try to match our cases in order to make comparisons between treatments and processes (Chapter Seven). We may try to match two groups so that we can treat them differently and see what happens. This leads to several difficulties. For example, we might select two groups of very similar hospitals, change the management of one group, and see which group has the best results in terms of patient recovery. If we find after our research that one group has better results than another then this could mean that our 'intervention' has worked. Perhaps the new management of hospitals is superior, in terms of patient recovery. On the other hand, this result could just mean that our initial matching of the groups was not perfect. Either there was a minor initial difference that we ignored, but which developed over time into a more major difference in patient recovery, or there was an initial difference in terms of a variable or factor we did not measure, or were unaware of.

This means that the results of our experiments in social science are not generally clear-cut. We have to judge whether our findings are substantial enough to be worth taking note of. This judgement has to be at least partly probabilistic in nature. We can use statistical approaches to express the nature of these complex causal models, and this, of course, may be why probabilistic models of causation emerge (Goldthorpe 2001). They reflect, not the reality of the world or the study, but the limitation of our understanding. The probabilities are subjective in the sense that they express our limited ability to predict and explain. This does not make the events that they predict non-causal or random (Shafer 1996). Further, these same statistical procedures are now more widely used where an intervention has not even been attempted. There remains fundamental disagreement over the validity of doing this (McKim and Turner 1997), and the issue is discussed further in Chapter Twelve.

5.5 ▮▮ Conclusion

Explanatory work has an explicit or underlying causal model, which needs a warrant and a theory. To be really convincing, rather than just speculative, such work relies on an argument based on good research design. The elements of a convincing explanation include association in the form of cross-sections and comparators, a sequence in the form of longitudinal design, and controlled evaluated interventions. The result may appear as probabilistic rather than deterministic, and will have to be dealt with and analysed as such. These elements are the topics for much of the rest of this book. The elements and the designs they combine to make are not in any kind of opposition to each other; nor are they items to be selected on the basis of fashion or a personal preference. Evidence for *all* of these elements must be present in order to be confident that any relationship is causal, even though no one study would be expected to contribute relevant evidence on all of them.

⇶ Exercises on causation

1 You are appearing in a TV quiz, and are presented with three closed boxes. One box contains a desirable prize, and the other two are empty. You are allowed a free guess, to try and pick the box with the prize. You select one of the boxes (box A for example). The compere, who knows the contents of each box, then deliberately opens an empty box (box C for example) and shows it to you. The compere gives you a chance to change your mind. Do you now have any reason to pick another box (box B) or to stick with your original choice? Put another way, what have you learnt from the opening of box C?

2 Hume (1962) introduced the 'skeleton in the cupboard of philosophy' which is that the process of induction, or inductive reasoning, has no logical foundation. Yet it has been used as the chief criterion of demarcation between what is considered 'science' and what is not. Popper (1959) suggested a way around this, by highlighting the notion of falsification. This kind of testability, he said, was the true difference between science and all else. Using Popper's example, we cannot conclude with logical certainty that all swans are white merely from repeated observation of white swans (induction). But we can falsify the claim that all swans are white by just one observation of a non-white swan. Thus, progress comes from falsifying theories not from further confirmation of them. Was Popper correct? Has he created an approach which has a secure logical foundation and does not rely on induction?

3 Select a journal containing empirical research in your area of interest. Look at one complete issue, and examine each article for hidden causal claims and words. Do you think the authors realise how often they are making causal claims?

⇌ Notes on exercises on causation

1 Many people will argue that they have no reason to change their mind, but that they now have an improved chance of winning, whether they stick with A or pick box B. People tend to claim that whereas they had started with odds of 1 in 3, they now face odds of 1 in 2. But even being tempted by this 'analysis' displays a belief in backwards causation. Nothing that the compere has done in opening the box can change the position of the prize or, therefore, the odds of winning. When the game started you had odds of success of 1 in 3 (with box A). The prize was twice as likely to be in one of the other two boxes, even though one of the other two boxes must be empty. The fact that you now know *which* of the other two boxes is empty changes little. The prize is still one third likely to be in box A, and two thirds likely to be in one of the other two (which is simplified now to box B). Picking box B is twice as likely to be successful as picking box A. To consider otherwise implies that opening box C can have an effect on the actual position of the prize. The importance of this problem and others like them is that they illustrate our natural tendency to believe in backwards causation. Perhaps causation does not have to have the standard sequence (Mackie 1974)? In fact, in a full determinist model of events it makes as much sense for time to run backwards as forwards (it would, presumably, not be possible to tell the difference anyway).

2 I am not sure that it is as simple as this, and I can still hear the skeleton rattling in that cupboard. In formal logic, a contradiction such as 'A entails B' and 'Here is an A which is not B' cannot be explored further. The contradiction shows that there is a flaw somewhere in the prior logical chain, since both statements cannot be true. Logic does not help us find the flaw. Since A and B are ideal terms we do not attempt to tinker with them and overcome the contradiction. Contradiction is not the same as falsification. Neither statement is falsified in logic. They just cannot both be true. However, in the real world, where A and B become 'swans' and 'white', we can at least consider the possibility that only one of the propositions is falsified by the contradiction. This is what Popper does without making this step explicit. He then states that it is clear which proposition is wrong – so clear that the alternative is usually dismissed as merely 'playing with words' (Thouless 1974). But this supposed clarity is, like induction, actually only a habit of mind as well. In the example, Popper proposes that we change the definition of swan to include the possibility that some swans are not white, and does not even bother to argue against the alternative. Nevertheless, the other way out of the contradiction is equally logical. We could change the definition of black to exclude the possibility of being applied to swans. Thus the thing that looks like a black swan is actually not a swan because it is black. The choice is between changing our definition of swan or of black. In this example, we prefer changing the definition of the least familiar term, and black is a much more general term than swan. In fact, the same is true in every example of 'falsification' that I can think of. What seems like a logical argument for falsification is actually an appeal to the same non-logical phenomenon of familiarity that underlies induction, and therefore causation. When observation leads us to question a belief because it brings two beliefs into contradiction we tend to stick with the

most familiar of the two concepts, which suggests that Popper's notion of falsification does not actually eliminate inductive logic at all (see also Goodman 1973).

3 This is a skill that requires a little practice. So much research is dressed up not to look causal, by avoiding or paraphrasing what are seen as natural scientific terms like cause and effect. Just as an example, a journal issue that arrived on the day I was writing this chapter contained nine articles. Two were just nonsensical pieces with no new ideas, no evidence, and no sense of argument. All of the other seven contained some research and all used terms that are clearly causal if you think about what they imply in context. These terms included but were not restricted to 'influence', 'impact', 'moderate' (the verb), 'role', 'determinant', 'foster', 'maintain', 'assist', 'detract', 'improve', 'response', 'led to', and 'produced'. Statements included 'access to employment opportunities increasingly depend on...', '...partly a result of their own behaviour', and '...offers tangible employment benefits'. Again these are all clearly causal descriptions. Two articles also explicitly used the word 'effect'. Yet none of the articles had a research design that made any attempt to identify the elements of a causal model. Once you realise the enormity of what is going on here, it is shocking.

☰ Suggested reading

Morrison, K. (2009) *Causation in Educational Research*. London: Routledge.

3

Putting it All Together

SIX

Identifying the sample or cases

SUMMARY

- The 'cases' are the individuals, organisations or objects selected to take part in the research.
- The cases can be a 'population', in the sense that the study involves all eligible relevant cases.
- Or the cases can be a 'sample', selected from the population.
- If the sample is selected randomly from the population there are widespread techniques that are claimed to estimate the quality of the sample as a picture of the population, in terms of any numeric data collected.
- Where the sample is not selected randomly, where the data collected is not numeric, or where the claim about estimation is not accepted, then judgement about generalisation is required instead.
- The biggest threat to the rigour of a study at this stage is not whether a population or sample is used, or how cases are selected, but a low response rate and missing cases.
- In general, the larger the number of cases and the more complete the response rate is, the more convincing the study will be. In some designs there may be ethical reasons for limiting the number of cases.
- A power analysis can be a useful way of assessing the minimum required size for a study sample.
- However, power analyses are circular, and very sensitive to some rather arbitrary initial assumptions.
- All research reports should include a minimum set of information about the cases, such as the population, how many cases were selected, how many did not take part, and how many were later excluded for any other reason.

6.1 ▐▌ Introduction

The first common element of a research design is the set of cases involved in any study. As with all parts of research design, this set of cases has to be convincing to a sceptical audience. To be convincing, the number and range of cases has to be large enough and of sufficient quality to do the job required of it. The chapter starts by describing some useful terms.

Populations and cases

Technically, the population of interest to any research question consists of all of the cases that could be involved in that study. The term 'population' once had a slightly different general meaning, referring only to people, reflecting the derivation of the word. This meaning has been extended in social science to refer to the units of interest to the research. These units could be people, but they could also be groups of people in families, schools, businesses, or regions. Or the units might not consist of people at all. They might be bonds, cars, farmers' fields, texts, or indeed almost anything else. In this book, the units of interest in any research are called cases. Then the set of all cases that could be used in any research is referred to as the population. For example, a study of volunteer social workers in one city (Chapter One), which compared the volunteers to their colleagues, would have social workers as cases/units. The population would be all social workers in that city. There will also be a wider 'population' of social workers in other areas, and it is possible to consider the one-city population as a case or unit of that wider population, especially if these other areas could have been used in the research. Such 'nested' or hierarchical cases are considered later in this chapter.

Put another way, the population for any research is the largest group of units that the cases actually used in the research could be said to represent. The process of judging the research cases, to see how representative they are of the wider population, is called generalisation. Generalisation can take place in many different ways, several of which are discussed in more detail in this chapter. Generalisation can be by argument of similarity, by idiosyncratic transfer, or by statistical probability estimation. As readers may now guess, what all methods of generalisation have in common is that they must be convincing to a sceptical audience. From this, it is easy to see that the simplest way to convince a sceptical audience that the cases in the research genuinely represent the entire population of interest is to use that entire population as cases. So, if it is possible on resource, practical and ethical grounds to conduct the research using all possible cases of interest, this is the safest scientific way forward. In effect, this approach makes generalisation unnecessary. Using a whole population as cases is sometimes termed a 'census', like the 10-yearly census of population in the UK. But for social science and this book, a census, like a population, can refer to units other than people, and to areas or organisations other than nations.

In reality, there will always be cases missing even from a census design. In a census of population, some individuals may be abroad, seriously ill, homeless, unwilling to respond, or have difficulties with literacy. In a census of small businesses in one region, some businesses may be too new to be on the register used, some may be closing and have priorities other than assisting the research, and some may have once been larger and so are missed because they have only very recently become small businesses. Any non-response of this kind is a potential problem for research, but it is not unique to a census approach. Such cases would not have responded whether they were approached as part of a population study or a smaller sample. Their ability or unwillingness to respond is unaffected by how many other cases are involved. Wherever possible, it is preferable to use a complete set of relevant cases rather than to introduce the additional bias and error involved in selecting a sample from the population.

Of course, it is possible that working with a smaller number of cases will allow researchers to put more effort into gaining access to potential non-responders. This is one reason why research is sometimes based not on populations but on samples or simply some cases. Other reasons for using a sample include lack of time and resource to cover the population, or an ethical concern that the study may harm participants and so the approach is to minimise the scale of possible harm.

Samples and cases

The reason for not using the population, and focusing research efforts on a sub-set of cases or 'sample', must be clear in order for a research design to be convincing to a sceptical audience. This probably means that the reason must be made explicit in research reports more often than it currently is. In health science, for example, a study may be the first test of a new medicine on human subjects. Here, the test is for effectiveness but also for possible side effects. In this situation, it would be best to conduct the test using the smallest number of cases that could give a convincing demonstration of the use and safety of the medicine. The notion of power calculations to determine an optimal sample size is discussed later in the chapter. There will be many analogous situations in social science. New rules for banking, new qualifications for school-leavers, and new procedures for benefits payments should all be tested before being applied more widely. The test should be for effectiveness, relative cost, and for any unintended consequences. As with testing medicine, ethical considerations would suggest that the test should be rigorous, but conducted using the smallest possible number of cases needed to be convincing. The fact that such changes are usually made by governments and authorities without rigorous testing and without consideration of unintended consequences is part of the reason I claimed in Chapter One that many people do not care enough about social science research. It is because, unlike with medicine, the damaging consequences are diffuse and hard to grasp. People do not generally die suddenly as a visible consequence of sloppy social science research or public policy decisions. Hence, perhaps, what we have in the literature is too much sloppy social science.

Another reason for using samples is to save time for the researcher, who may want to spend a greater proportion of resource working with each case. Such research sacrifices breadth for depth (referred to in this book as in-depth work). Some commentators mistakenly refer to this kind of work as 'qualitative', but as I have explained many times elsewhere, this qualitative/quantitative classification is pointless (Gorard with Taylor 2004). There is certainly nothing about the scale or depth of a study that necessitates or precludes the collection of any specific kind of data. Scale is a design issue, while if the 'Q' words mean anything they are about methods of data collection and analysis (or what goes on within the 'O' element of the simple design notation introduced in Chapter One). A pilot survey might collect only numeric information but spend considerable time face-to-face with each case in order to reduce non-response, and ensure that the respondents understand the questions, and that the researcher understands any difficulties the respondents may have. On the other hand, a very large-scale study might interview all participants, given sufficient resource, because a full life history is required (e.g. Gorard and Rees 2002).

Sampling can also be a useful shortcut even when breadth is key, leading to results that can be almost as convincing as those for a full census of the population being studied but for a smaller cost. Most studies are subject to a law of diminishing returns, with each successive case adding less to our understanding, and doing little to change any emerging patterns.

It is not reasonable, and would probably be unethical, to conduct research with a sample that was too small to yield a convincing answer to the research questions. If time and resource does not allow a piece of research to be done properly, then it is better to do different research. If a sample size of at least 100 is necessary, then a sample of 25 is a waste of time for the sample, the researcher, and for anyone who reads the ensuing study. How do we decide on the number of cases needed to provide a convincing answer to a research question? Traditionally the way to answer this question has depended upon the type of sample used. This chapter discusses several kinds of sample separately, before suggesting that, actually, the way to answer this key question is often very similar regardless of the type of sample used.

6.2 ▮▮ Types of samples

Sampling can be divided into probability and non-probability procedures for selecting cases. The former includes random, systematic, stratified, and clustered sampling, and their combinations. The latter includes convenience, quota, opportunity and snowball samples, and unhealthy probability samples (with poor response rates, for example). See Gorard (2003) for more on all of these issues, and on how best to create a list of the population (or sampling-frame) from which to select any kind of sample.

Random and systematic sampling

When selecting a sample from a known population, for whatever reason, the single best approach is to select the cases randomly. Random sampling is free of the systematic bias that might stem from choices made by the researcher or others, and that is why it should be used whenever possible. Random sampling not only tends to provide a bias-free distribution of known and measurable characteristics (such as sex or income if the sample is of people), it does the same for unknown and even un-measurable characteristics (such as motivation or the later likelihood of developing a disease perhaps). The technique of random sampling is also very easy – perhaps the easiest method available. So it gives all of these key advantages to a study for very little cost.

As explained above, selecting a sample means starting with a known population. Cases can be chosen from the population by using any random number generator, weighted for the size of the population. All members of the population could be written on identical pieces of paper, or allocated a unique raffle ticket, and the required number of cases for the sample then drawn from a drum or hat. A printed or computer-generated table of random digits could be used. You would need to pick enough digits on each occasion to identify any case in the population. For example, use three digits in sequence from the table if there are up to 999 members of the population, four digits for up to 9,999 and so on. If any sequence of digits is beyond the range of the population it can be ignored. Imagine a population of 700 numbered members, and a random number sequence that starts:

0168733992432456245...

The first case selected would be 16 (016), the next three digits would be ignored as they are above 700 (873), and the second case would be 399. Where to start in the random number table can be determined by any other random or non-systematic event. It is a bit like dealing a deck of cards. If the deck is in order of suits, then giving every fourth card to a player at the table will give them a biased and structured hand of cards. If the deck is thoroughly shuffled, exactly the same process will give them a random, or near random, hand. This systematic approach mimics a good random sample. Even better, there is software that can select the sample for you. And even better than that is to get an independent party to select the sample for you using such software, so that you cannot unintentionally subvert the process.

A small problem can arise where you do not want the same case to appear more than once in the sample, because this would be a possible outcome of true random sampling (just like rolling two sixes in a row with one die). A case is selected at random from the sampling frame of the population, and copied to the sampling list. When a second case is selected there is nothing to stop a true randomiser from picking the same case again. Generally the researcher prevents this by deleting selected cases from the sampling frame (equivalent to pulling raffle tickets from a hat) or rejecting any cases already selected. This solution, known as sampling 'without replacement', could be seen to bias the true random sample. However, if the sample is small compared to the population (i.e. the sampling fraction is low) then the probability of repeated selection is very low, and the issue of replacement makes little difference in practice.

Two further things are worth noting at this stage. An incomplete random sample very soon becomes merely a non-random sample. All of the probability calculations about random samples are based on mathematical formulae that assume a complete random sample. A complete sample would be one where all of the cases that were selected agreed to take part, gave full participation, and did not drop out. Strictly speaking a sample with even one dropout or refusal cannot be random. It contains an important source of bias. As you may imagine, full response is rare. I have never encountered it. Whether you decide to continue treating an incomplete but randomly selected sample as still random is a judgement. It is a judgement that you must spell out and justify, just like any part of your research design argument. A sample of 1,000 cases with one dropout could be treated as just about complete. A sample of 1,000 cases with 800 dropouts (response rate of 20%) cannot be treated as random. To do so would be tantamount to research fraud. And yet I routinely encounter samples with low response rates treated as random (and that is only when the report bothers to state the response rate). This is another way in which social science is currently very weak. Non-response and how to deal with it is covered later in this chapter.

Finally, random sampling is conducted to minimise bias. It also has the advantage that it allows us to estimate the likelihood of things occurring in the sample by chance (like calculating the likelihood of getting a hand of all hearts from a properly shuffled pack of cards). We do not sample randomly because we can then estimate sampling variation likelihoods. We need to calculate the likelihoods because we have used random sampling. And once we have calculated such likelihoods we are left with the same analytical issues as when dealing with non-random samples – such as whether a pattern, difference or trend in our measurements is of substantive relevance (Chapter Twelve).

Stratified sampling

In a random sample the distribution of the characteristics of cases will be left to chance. In selecting 1,000 people from a general population, all could be male or all could be aged 13. This is very unlikely, and is more unlikely where the sample size is large. One can imagine rolling four sixes in succession with a die, but not

1,000. Where there is special concern over the small size of the sample, or the low frequency of one or more population characteristics, an alternative approach is to use stratification. Here, cases are selected in proportion to one or more characteristics in the population. For example, if sex is considered relevant to the study and the population is 58% female, then the sample is constrained so that it must be 58% female. In effect, the researcher creates two populations, one of men from whom 42% of the eventual cases are selected, and one of women from whom 58% of cases are selected. Selection within these sub-populations can and should still be random. The number and type of characteristics used in this way (as strata) are chosen by the researcher on theoretical grounds of relevance to the study. The researcher must use expert knowledge to decide which characteristics of the population could be relevant for the study findings, and then work out the pattern of distribution of these characteristics. This is not always an easy task, as the characteristics need to be considered in interaction, and the researcher may need to carry out a census anyway to uncover the nature of the population. So this approach to sampling is considerably harder than simple random selection. The researcher still needs a good reason not to use random sampling.

The stratified approach can lead to a high quality sample by reducing the risk of a 'freaky' result, at least in terms of the strata characteristics. Its problems include the fact that it can require decisions about complex categories (race, occupation) or on sensitive issues (income, age). Also, if several background characteristics are used then the selection process becomes difficult as each variable 'interacts' with the other. If both sex and occupational class are used, then not only must the proportions for sex and class be correct, but so must the proportions for sex within each class (if 23% of the population are female and professional, this must be reflected in the sample). If you also, quite reasonably, considered ethnicity, socio-economic status, or qualifications as important factors, then the calculations quickly become mind-boggling. You would need to know the proportion of the population who were white, male, had a professional background, with a first degree, and then you would need to reflect this in your sample. And you would need a large sample in order not to have increasingly sparse strata, which rather defeats the purpose anyway. Despite its lack of popularity judging from its rarity in the literature, random sampling is actually a lot easier than stratified sampling. And if the random sample is large anyway, stratified sampling is not needed.

Clustered samples

A practical issue with simple random sampling is that it tends to produce a sample from across the population. These cases may be country-wide or in a large number of organisational units (such as a few cases in every town). This can add to the cost of fieldwork. Clustered sampling is therefore often preferred, placing pragmatic resource considerations above purely scientific ones, although there are studies in which there is no choice. Perhaps a treatment does not allow individuals to be dealt with separately. An example could be an investigation of the impact of improved drinking water on individuals, which can only be feasibly applied to an area (which shares a well or a pipe). Using a clustered sample implies not so much a difference in selection procedures as a difference in defining population units. The cases we are interested in often occur in natural clusters such as institutions, organisations or areas. So we can redefine our population of interest to be the clusters (institutions) themselves, and then select our sample from them using one of the above procedures. The institutions become the cases, rather than the individuals within them. This has several practical advantages. It is generally easier to obtain a list of clusters (such as employers, schools, voluntary organisations, or hospitals) than it is to get a complete list of the people in them. If we use many of the individuals from each cluster in our selected sample, we can obtain results from many individuals with little time and travel, since they will be concentrated in fewer places.

Clustered random sampling is a valuable approach in many areas of social science, but the term is used in a variety of ways that can be confusing, with differing implications for the subsequent analysis. Imagine we wanted to measure the heights of the people at a conference, very accurately. Our population could be people at the conference, and our sample might be 100 of the conference delegates selected at random. We might check these delegates' heights with several instruments and at several different times of day, and then average the results for each person. In this example, our measurements would be repeated for each individual in order to maximise accuracy. And our outcomes would be the averaged heights for each person. So is our sample really the people, or is it the separate measurements of heights? Imagine each of 100 people had their height measured four times. Is our sample of 100 or of 400? Traditionally, this would be treated as a sample of 100 with four repeated measures for each. This is certainly how I would treat it. The sample is the level at which the randomness occurs, in the selection of the people. There is no probabilistic uncertainty in terms of how many or what types of measurements were taken for each person. There may be measurement errors, and missing data, but these are not random in nature. Thus, any probabilistic calculations of the type used in sampling theory and its statistical derivatives will be conducted with N=100. The repetition of measurements within the 100 cases is to increase the accuracy of the estimate for each case. It does not increase the sample size.

Does this situation change if there is probabilistic uncertainty about the measurements within each case, as well as in the selection of cases? Imagine instead a study of patient satisfaction in hospitals. The researcher selects a random sample of 10 hospitals, and then (and only then) a random sample of 100 patients within each of those 10 hospitals. What is the sample size here? Is it 10 hospitals or 1,000 patients? Both answers are possible. If the concern was primarily to compare variation in patient satisfaction between hospitals, then I would say that N=10, and that the repeated measures of individual patient satisfaction within each hospital are there to create a better estimate for each hospital. Put another way, the situation is similar to the repeated measurement of heights, above. On the other hand, if the purpose was to estimate patient satisfaction in hospitals in general, and the first step of selecting hospitals was for convenience (otherwise the sample could inconveniently consist of a few patients in all hospitals in the country), then N=1,000. On the first interpretation, there is a random sample of 10. On the second, there is a clustered random sample of 1,000. This is somewhat confusing.

A clustered random sample differs from, and is substantially inferior to, a real random sample of the same size because of the stages in sampling. In the height example, there was only one stage of sampling to select the people, who were then all measured repeatedly. So this is a true random sample of 100 people. In the same way in the hospital example, if all patients were involved in each selected hospital there would have been only one stage of sampling to obtain the 10 cases. But the more complex clustered random sample has a random sample of hospitals and then a random sample of patients within each. There are two stages of sampling. Although it has taken some time to get to this point I hope you can see the difference. To decide whether a sample is complex, consider how many stages of sample selection are involved. If there are none, you are dealing with a population study. If there is one stage of selection, the cases selected are the sample, and this is true however many measurements are made within each case. If cases are selected randomly from within clusters of cases (schools, hospitals, towns, companies etc.) which are themselves selected randomly, then you could have a clustered random sample. It is still perfectly proper to treat such a complex sample as a simple random sample of cases at the cluster level, and envisage the rest as repeated measurements (Cochrane 2012). In fact, this approach has two key advantages. It makes the subsequent analysis easier to conduct while at the same time making it more robust (less likely to be deceived by random sampling variation) than treating it as a clustered random sample.

It is important that the odds of selecting any cluster are in proportion to the number of individuals it represents (e.g. hospitals with more patients should be more likely to be picked). This does add a complication to the sampling process. However, the main problem with this clustered approach is the potential bias introduced if the cases in the cluster are similar to each other. People in the same house may tend to be more similar to each other than to those in other houses, and the same thing applies to a lesser extent to the hamlets where the houses are (people in each post-code area may tend to be similar), and to the regions where they live (and so on). This suggests that, if we have to use this approach, we should try to sample more clusters, and use appropriately fewer cases in each cluster (see Chapter Seven).

Non-probability samples

In terms of sampling quality, there is a quality hierarchy here. A random sample is the most convincing and rigorous. Systematic sampling is a way of mimicking random selection, and stratified random sampling is a variant used especially when the sample size is relatively small. Cluster random sampling is used when resource does not permit a genuine random sample, or when a treatment does not allow individuals to be dealt with separately. If none of these sampling types is possible, then some kind of non-probability sample can be used. Sometimes there is no possible alternative. Note that use of a non-probability sample must always be explained and justified in the research 'argument' that your report represents. If such a sample is used by others without justification, be suspicious.

An example of reasonable use of a non-probability sample is where a snowball technique is necessary. In some studies – of drug-use, truancy, or under-age sex for example – we are unable to produce a sampling frame even where the population of interest may be imagined as quite large. Indeed one of our key research objectives may be to estimate the size of an unknown population. In such a project we might quite properly approach a convenience sample to get us started, and once we have gained their trust ask each individual to suggest other informants for successive stages. In this way, we hope that our sample will 'snowball'. Difficult-to-reach populations can make probability sampling impossible. We simply accept this, and do the best we can with what is available.

Non-probability samples can also be used when the population of interest is very small and we are approaching cases as expert informants. We may want to ask government cabinet members about the background to a new policy, or directors of large banks how they decide on investment priorities. In some studies the number of experts is so limited that we must use whoever is available to us, since there are not enough to select cases at random from a list. Non-probability samples could also be used for pilot studies, where the intention is to trial a research design rather than collect usable data. Even here, however, a good pilot study will test out the actual sampling method to be used, along with the other components of the design of the main study.

The most common, and overused, form of non-probability sampling is the convenience or opportunity sample, composed of those cases chosen only because they are easily available. A researcher standing in a railway station, or shopping centre, or outside a student union, and stopping people in an *ad hoc* manner would create a convenience sample, clearly not a random one. This approach is often, erroneously, justified by the comment that a range of people use such places, so the sample will be mixed in composition. But large numbers of people rarely travel by rail, shop in city centres or use a student bar. These people would tend to be excluded from such a sample. Those in paid employment may be less likely to be in shopping centres during the day, while older people may be less likely to go out at night. The researcher may also make (perhaps unconscious) selections, by avoiding those who appear drunk or angry, or even scruffy. Even with a quota system, convenience sampling introduces a very real danger of biasing the sample, and it does so unnecessarily in far too many studies. It should be the sampling strategy of last resort.

6.3 ‖ Sample size

This is the point at which we can return to the question posed near the start of this chapter – how large does a sample have to be? The first answer has already been given. If possible it is best not to have a sample at all, but to use or involve the entire population of interest. If you want to talk to current Prime Minister's of the UK then the population has one case. You have no choice. If you want to analyse the 16-year-old school examination results of all pupils in England for one year, then the population will be around 700,000. But since the data already exists it is as easy to analyse the existing results for all pupils as for a sample. There is no excuse to use a sample. The number of cases required would be 700,000, or as many for whom there was appropriate data. If population data is not possible for any reason, but you still want to draw conclusions about the population, then the second answer would be that the sample should be as large as is feasible. For research purposes, the larger it is the better.

Small samples can lead to missing out on potentially valuable results. If you are looking for a pattern among the data you have collected from a well-designed study, then your success or failure is chiefly determined by three things. These include the 'footprint' or effect size of the phenomenon you are studying. This effect size is often very small in social science – imagine the likely impact of a national budget policy on household happiness perhaps – and its scale is not under your control. How easy it is to spot a pattern also depends on its variability. If the change in happiness is small but is the same for all households it is easier to detect than if it varies considerably between households. This is also not under your control. Finally, how easy it is to separate pattern from noise depends on the size of your sample. This is the only element of success/failure directly under your control. So make the sample as large as feasible.

Since random samples can provide a good picture of a population, random samples can be smaller than other types, such as cluster random samples, and yet be just as convincing. Oddly, however, the literature shows that practice tends to be the inverse of this. Convenience samples tend to be smaller than random ones, despite their obvious dangers of bias. Sampling is not tied to any design, or any method of data collection. A limitation on sample size may come from a lack of resource to include more cases. Another limitation already discussed may be that the study involves a small element of risk, and so we would want to expose as few cases as possible to this risk. So the third answer would be that we need just enough cases in the sample to get the job done. This then entails a random sample in preference to a cluster random sample that will require more cases, which is itself preferable to a non-probability sample which requires more cases again.

Traditionally, finding a sample of just the right size (and no more) has been done via a 'power' analysis. Power is the technical term for the ability to discern a finding if it is there in the data. Power is enhanced by a larger sample, larger effect size, small effect variation between cases, and by using the most powerful statistical approach available. Each of these can be converted into an equivalent of a change in another, and any one can be estimated if all others are known. Given the effect size sought, its variability, and the proposed probability of detecting the effect via a given statistical procedure, it is possible to calculate the required effect size (or have proprietary software do it for you). For example, around 200 cases would be needed to have an 80% chance of finding a significant difference at the 5% level between the mean scores in two sub-groups, if the effect size was 40% of the scores' standard deviation. The calculation of an effect size is explained in Chapter Twelve.

To calculate the sample size needed to have a certain discriminatory power, we need to decide on the other parameters first. We need a significance level (or alpha), and this is often 0.05 or 5%. We need to know the means and standard deviation of the two groups we are going to compare (or the effect size). If we then select a desired power level (beta), often 80%, we can calculate the minimum required sample size to detect that effect size 80% of the time at 5% significance. Hemming et al. (2011) provides the formulae to plug these estimated parameters into in order to derive a sample size for several slightly different situations (independent or repeated samples, for example). Alternatively, a number of programs and websites will conduct the calculation for you. Even better, since so many of the parameters are arbitrary or estimated, a heuristic will do perfectly well. Lehr's basic formula for sample size, assuming a significance level of 5% and power of 80%, is 16 divided by the square of the effect size (Campbell et al. 1995). So to discover an effect size of 50% successfully, 80% of the time, using 5% significance, the sample must be at least 64 cases (16/.25). This figure is for each arm in a comparison. So if there are two groups, we will need 128 cases in total. To compare three groups, we will need 192 cases, and so on. This heuristic calculation agrees well with the full algorithmic method in almost all circumstances. Campbell et al. (1995) also provide Lehr's formula for categorical data. Chapter Seven describes the adjustments that need to be made to the sample size when using clustered random samples.

However, power analysis has several problems. It does not really give you the answer as precisely as you may imagine. All of the factors are interconnected, so that changing any one will quite radically alter the computed sample size. And all of the figures used are themselves estimates or simply arbitrary thresholds. If we have not done the research yet, we cannot know the effect size precisely. We can estimate it, but if we estimated it as only 35% of a standard deviation rather than 40% then the required sample would jump considerably higher. Who can say beforehand whether 35% or 40% is the better estimate? In social science, such substantial effect sizes are rare anyway. Similarly, if we were prepared to accept only a 75% chance of finding the correct answer, rather than 80%, then the required sample size would go down. If we used a significance level of 1% for the findings, then the sample size would go up again.

For example, if we adjust the example above very slightly, so that we wanted a 90% chance of finding a significant difference at the 1% level between the mean scores in two sub-groups, if the effect size was 20% of the scores' standard deviation, then the sample size becomes around 1,500. Adjusting a few arbitrary and estimated values to a new set of equally plausible values means the computed sample size goes from 200 to 1,500. The whole procedure is circular and very sensitive to slight revisions of estimates. The effect size may be 40%, or it may be 20%. It would be a shame to go to all of the trouble of conducting a study and miss a 20% effect size. A study with more than one measure of interest will also have different 'power' results for each effect. Therefore, I repeat, your sample should generally be as large as possible. Another problem with this power approach is that it uses the idea of statistical 'significance' as introduced in Chapter Four. This is a confusing and rather abused concept, as explained further in Chapter Twelve. Finally, the apparently precise calculations for power take no notice at all of the more important issues of non-response in the sample, and measurement error in the scores. Nevertheless, there is a clear double-standard in operation here. RCTs and similar designs usually attempt these difficult calculations about the minimum sample size required to detect a pattern or effect. But the same considerations also apply to all work using any design and all methods. Yet most other work makes no attempt to calculate the power necessary. A lot of small-scale work, especially that labelled 'qualitative' by its authors, would have very little chance of finding anything convincing with the cell sizes often encountered. Any general claims it makes, in isolation and beyond the data actually presented, should therefore be treated as unwarranted.

6.4 ⊪ Non-response

All statistical procedures are idealised to a great extent, and all of the calculations associated with sample size and generalisation to a population are predicated on complete response. It is assumed that every case selected or asked to take part in a study will do so, but this just does not happen in practice. Non-response can be at the outset when it proves impossible to contact a case selected for the sample, or after contact when a case refuses to take part, or even after the study has begun and a case drops out. All of these kinds of missing cases, and any missing data from cases that do take part, can have a substantial impact on the study findings (Gorard 2008b). Yet, repeatedly in reviews of published research, it has been found that authors do not publish even basic information about their response rates (Kano et al. 2008).

There are several traditional ways of trying to deal with non-response, but all struggle to overcome the simple fact that the required data are missing. All missing data are liable to bias the study findings, and we cannot know in which direction and by how much. We cannot overcome these problems by using traditional statistical techniques like the standard error or confidence intervals, since their calculation is predicated in full response, and the only variation they can assess is due to random sampling not bias. Non-response is *not* randomly distributed. There are proven systematic differences between people who tend to take part in research and those who refuse – in terms of leisure, attitudes, education, income, social class, age and so on. All cases in any study are effectively volunteers and these willing participants could be very different from those who are not.

You could try replacing non-respondents with others like them, to maintain a desired sample size. But this will not reduce the bias, and it will invalidate any power calculations you have conducted. You could try to adjust for non-response in any stratum through weighting, by artificially inflating the existing scores of under-represented groups. But in all attempts like this, including imputing results, you are using what you do have to try and compensate for data you do not have. However neat the results might look, the dangers of being misled probably outweigh any gains. Here is an extreme example to make the point. Imagine a large survey of adults with an overall response rate of 99% but in which the response rate from the Traveller community was only 1%. Would it be reasonable to multiply the results obtained from a few Travellers by 99 to estimate what the majority of missing Travellers would have said, weighted at the same scale as the rest of the respondents? This would be very misleading if any of the 99% of Travellers who did not respond were different in some ways from the 1% who did.

Overall, I prefer instead a simple sensitivity analysis. You could calculate how many of the missing cases would have had to respond differently to the results you obtained, in order to change the substantive findings of the research. This is a tough but fair test that soon makes clear how inadequate many published samples are (assuming they report the response rate). Here is an illustration. Imagine we ask 100 business leaders in retail, and 100 in leisure industries, how optimistic they feel about the coming year. All 100 leaders respond in the retail sector, but only 80 leaders respond in the leisure sector (for an overall 90% response rate). In the retail sector, 50 leaders are optimistic and 50 are not (50% optimism). In the leisure sector, 45 leaders are optimistic and 35 are not (56% optimism). We want to conclude that there is therefore slightly more optimism in the leisure sector, but before reporting we conduct a sensitivity analysis. How differently would the non-responders have to have answered for our conclusion to be false? If the 20 non-responders were in the same proportions as the actual study, then 11 (56%) would have reported optimism and 9 not. It would only take 6 of these 20 people to respond differently in order to reverse the study findings completely (50:50 optimism in the leisure industry as well, since 35+9+6=50). So, despite a high 90% response rate, the difference observed is not very secure, and nothing should be made of it. Thinking like this is good practice. One thing you should definitely do with non-response is to record it accurately, and report it clearly. Then at least your readers can conduct this kind of sensitivity analysis, even if you are unwilling to.

Non-response affects all samples of all types, regardless of the methods of data collection or analysis. It is always an important brake on making convincing research claims. As non-response increases, the best quality random samples, even with replacement and weighting/imputing, tend towards bias and so become non-probability samples in most studies. This means that in practice most samples are really non-probability samples – because it is very hard to get and keep full response. And this means that most samples should really be treated as mini-populations in themselves, and any generalisation from them should be conducted with much greater care than at present.

6.5 ‖ Conclusion

Arising largely from medical experimental approaches, the group on Consolidated Standards of Reporting Trials (or CONSORT, see http://www.consort-statement.org/) has suggested a minimum set of information that should be made publicly available when reporting the results of experiments. Probably the best-known and influential part of this is their proposed flow diagram concerning what happens to all of the cases considered for, or involved in, any trial. I feel that an adaptation of this practice should be used in all social science reporting. We may have made some progress in areas of social science like education which was accused of routinely omitting basic details like the number of cases, even from high-profile peer-reviewed research reports (Tooley with Darby 1998). But it is still true that most reports I read or review omit to declare the response rate and how missing data or cases were handled in the analysis. Many studies present different numbers of cases in different sections without explanation or audit trail.

For me, this is one of the basic indicators of whether the researcher actually cares about the research they are doing, and the impact it might have. My proposal would be that a research report should, as a minimum requirement, make the following available:

- how many cases were assessed for eligibility;
- how many of those assessed did not participate, and for what reasons (not meeting criteria, refused etc.);
- how many then agreed to participate;
- how many were allocated to each group (if relevant);
- how many were lost or dropped out after agreeing to participate (and after allocation to a group, if relevant);
- how many were analysed, and why any further cases were excluded from the analysis.

This means that there is no single 'N' – the number of cases in any piece of research. There are the numbers sought, asked, signed up, involved at the outset, completed, and those used for the final analysis. Of course, these may all be the same N if the response rate is 100%, there is no attrition of cases, and so on, but this is very unlikely. Missing cases and data from any stage of research are important, and can fundamentally alter how we interpret the evidence from the cases we do have

(Gorard 2010b). Handling missing cases in a practical, safe and rigorous manner is discussed in subsequent chapters.

Exercises about cases

1 A researcher goes into a youth club and arranges three focus group discussions with some of the young people present. The cases, or sample, are the young people in the focus groups.

  a What is the population for this study?
  b How might the researcher assess whether the sample is genuinely representative of the population?
  c If one of the three focus groups was not with young people but with some of the staff and volunteer workers at the youth club, has the population for this study changed?
  d What difference would it make to your answers (a to c) if the researcher used a questionnaire instead of focus groups?

2 A study of voting behaviour in a national election is based on researchers trying to complete a quick survey instrument with every tenth person who turns out to vote in ten local polling stations. Around 80% of those asked did agree to complete the survey. Having finished the data collection, the researcher wishes to draw conclusions about national voting behaviour.

  a What is the sample and what is the population in this study?
  b This attempted generalisation from sample to national picture actually involves two rather different kinds of generalisation. What are they?
  c In the example described what are the most obvious limitations to each level of the generalisation from sample to national picture?

3 Researchers want a good sample of school students in a region for face-to-face data collection, but they want to limit time and travel as far as possible. So, they decide on a multi-stage sample. First they select a random sample of the schools in the region, and then they use all of the students in their fifth year at each school.

  a What is the population and what are the cases here?
  b Is this a clustered random sample?

Notes on exercises about cases

1 a The population consists of all young people attending the youth club (i.e. everyone who had a chance to be in the study).
  b In order to assess whether the sample is representative of the population, the researcher would need to know some of the relevant characteristics of the population and the sample. They can then try to convince their audience that the sample and population are very similar in all known characteristics (but only if they are, of course). The youth club may have attendance and other records, and the sample can

also be asked to complete a brief anonymous sheet about themselves. Relevant characteristics that can be easily assessed might be sex, age group, ethnicity, and the number of times attended. However, there may well be unknown characteristics on which the sample and population differ. The cases in the sample may have had more time available, be more opinionated, less shy, or more enthusiastic than the others in the population. This is why random selection of a sample is preferred, because it randomises the unknown as well as the known characteristics of the sample.

c Yes. Since the population consists of everyone who had a chance to be in the study, it must change as soon as staff and volunteer workers at the youth club are involved in the study. The population now might be all young people and all staff who were present in the youth club.

d It should make no difference at all. The sample and population, like all elements of a research design, are largely independent of the precise techniques used for gathering evidence.

2 a The population in this study is all voters who turned up to the ten local polling stations, and the achieved sample is 80% of every tenth voter who actually took part in the survey.

b The researcher is trying to generalise from the sample to the population, as standard, and is then trying to generalise from the population of ten polling stations to all polling stations in the country. The individuals are a sample of the ten polling stations which are, in turn, a kind of sample of a larger national population of voters.

c Although taking every tenth attendee is not ideal, and may be impractical at busy times, it should give a reasonably true picture of voters throughout the day. The bigger problem is the 20% of voters who refused to complete the survey. We have no reason to believe that this 20% is the same in all other respects to the 80% who took part. As ever, the non-respondents could be busier, less confident, or even slightly embarrassed by their voting behaviour. This is a serious limitation to the generalisability of the sample, and should be mentioned in any report of the research. It will reduce how convincing readers will find the results. The attempted generalisation from the ten polling stations to the national picture is even more problematic. The example does not state how the polling stations were selected but they are clearly not a fair representation of a whole country. The number of cases is small, and they are local to one area. These limitations will, inevitably, make the local picture less convincing than if the response rate was 100%, and make the national picture less convincing than if a somewhat larger number of polling stations had been chosen at random across the country. However, this is quite normal in real-life research. None of these limitations is fatal, as long as the researcher does not try to hide them, or to pretend that they can be overcome with statistical jiggery-pokery (Chapter Four).

3 a The cases are the schools, since it is these and only these that are being selected. The population is the set of all schools in the region (i.e. all of the cases that could have been selected).

b This is not a clustered random sample. It is a relatively simple random sample of schools. The only sampling variation that exists, and that could be assessed by sampling theory statistics, is at the school level. The research is then a census of each school's fifth year. To be a clustered random sample, the researchers would have had to pick students at random within each school chosen at random. The cluster sample actually used here is preferable, if resource allows, to the clustered random sample since it eliminates sampling variation at the within-school level.

⊑ Suggested reading

Chapter Four in Gorard, S. (2003) *Quantitative Methods in Social Science Research*. London: Continuum.

SEVEN

Preparing for comparative claims

SUMMARY

- An obvious but too often disregarded principle in social science is that a comparative claim must be based on an explicit comparator.
- A comparative claim is always more convincing when it is stated in advance.
- Dredging for results by creating sub-groups after data collection could be appropriate in exploratory studies, but must not be mistaken for anything more than this.
- Naturally occurring groups of cases are useful for making descriptive comparative claims using a cross-sectional design. However, any other kinds of claims are hard to untangle.
- Close matching of groups can make analysis of comparative results easier.
- Where feasible, randomising cases to sub-groups is safest because it caters for differences in terms of known variables that could be matched as well as unknown variables that can never be matched.
- Blocking and minimisation can be used in conjunction with randomisation to try and reduce fluke distributions of cases.
- Cluster randomising to groups is a convenient alternative, but not one to be undertaken lightly because it introduces complications and further possible bias.

7.1 ‖ Introduction

Chapter Six discussed making design decisions about the nature and number of cases involved in any study. It argued that the main concern must be how convincing the set of cases is, as a representation of the population of interest to the research. This chapter considers how the cases within a study can be sub-divided into two or more groups for comparison. This allocation of cases to sub-groups is the second element of a research design. There are many reasons why a researcher might want to divide their cases into sub-groups. A sub-group may be simply to provide more detailed description, or it may act as a control, or form the basis for discovering a difference. The chapter considers naturally occurring groups, those defined by the researcher, matching pairs of cases across groups, and randomisation. As with all aspects of research, including design, the researcher should be looking for a way of generating sub-groups of cases that will provide the most convincing eventual research claims.

7.2 ▏▎ Why have comparator groups?

It may seem strange to ask why we want to build comparator groups into our research design, but my experience suggests that plenty of studies have made, and are still making, comparative claims without appropriate comparators. I have noted before how common this strange phenomenon is (Gorard and Fitz 2006). In the field of school choice, for example, Willms and Echols (1992) used data from one year to show that parents not using designated local schools in Scotland were, in general, better educated and of more elevated social class than those who did. What Willms and Echols could not show with data from only one year was any increase in such social segregation between schools. They did not have a comparator from another year. Yet, in their conclusion and their summary, the authors say 'The results suggest that the choice process is increasing between-school segregation' (p. 339). This is a good paper and an innovative analysis, yet the authors are over-claiming. Even worse, their paper has been repeatedly cited by others as direct evidence that segregation had increased. The authors could have legitimately said something like:

> 'We predict on the basis of what we found that segregation is or will be increasing. The next step would be to monitor the situation with data from several years'.

On the same topic, Fiske and Ladd (2000) reported that 'the most obvious negative consequence of the Tomorrow's Schools reforms is that enrolment in New Zealand ... became increasingly stratified'. All of their key tables (for instance, table 7.2) presented data for the years 1991, 1996 and 1997, and showed a slight increase in segregation from 1991 to 1997. But 1991 was the first year after the new policy, whereas 1990 was the last year before the choice reforms. As Fiske and Ladd admit in a footnote on page 194, 'the indexes fell substantially between 1990 and 1991'. By 1997, segregation in New Zealand was still substantially lower than in 1990. Therefore, the lowest figures for social stratification of schools in New Zealand appeared after the introduction of choice reforms, and the highest recorded level of stratification is, by some way, in the only year for which they had data before the reforms. Bizarrely, Fiske and Ladd had an appropriate comparator for their claim but neglected to use it and so published the wrong conclusions. This whole field is full of explicit comparative claims without an appropriate comparator, and it is strange that no one else seems to have noticed. These publications have been repeatedly cited by others, including some of the most high-profile researchers, as though their comparative claims were valid.

In my experience, this problem of unwarranted comparative claims is not unique to the field of school choice. I was recently co-author of a report in which another author offered the following complete statements:

> 'The poorest children are eight months "behind" by 5 years of age';
>
> 'Poorer children who performed badly at age 7 are less likely to improve their ranking';
>
> 'Persistent absentees are nearly three times more likely to be in the poorest 20% of families';
>
> 'Disadvantaged pupils also have three times the likelihood of receiving either a fixed term or permanent exclusion during their time at school'.

The other authors, all successful high-profile people, were surprised that I objected to these claims. I hope you can see why these statements are incomplete. In the first example, what are the poorest children eight months behind? The answer could transform our understanding of what that claim means. They could be behind some expected level, behind an average score, behind everyone else (not the poorest), or only behind the richest. Each interpretation would mean something very different. An additional problem is that the claims mix apparent precision with considerable vagueness. 'Behind' in terms of what measure? Who and how many are the 'poorest'? This could be six children, 5%, 10%, or 20% and so on. The answers to these questions would also alter our understanding of this claim. In the second claim, 'less likely' than what? In the third, 'more likely' than who? And, is 'more likely' the same as 'as likely'? And in the fourth, 'three times the likelihood' of what or who? Social science is not journalism; nor is it a political manifesto. Social science research is presumably funded to give us good answers to important questions. Claiming that poorer children are 2.75 times as likely to be excluded from school is nonsense, because the comparator is unknown. Knowing that children from families living on incomes below the official poverty line in their country are nearly three times as likely as all other children to be excluded from school is a proper social scientific claim, because it has a comparator.

This problem is also not unique to my field of education, of course. It is prevalent throughout the social science literature. Many researchers seem to ignore design in their research – perhaps it is deemed too 'scientific' for their free-thinking approach! But later they have a difficulty in making any useful or interesting claims on the basis of what they find. So they make disguised or implied comparisons. A study that involves only homeless people might claim that something is a special problem for the homeless. But how could the researchers know this, if the study did not also include a group who were not homeless and for whom that 'something' was found to be less of a problem?

Such widespread nonsense stems from lack of consideration of design, as discussed in Chapter One. When pressed for a design, there is then over-reliance by weak researchers on the vague concept of a case study. A case study is a study of one case, as defined in Chapter Six. Once a study has several cases it has usually become comparative, cross-sectional or something similar. If the case is considered over extended time, the study becomes a longitudinal design or similar (Chapter Eight). If the case involves evaluation or manipulation of variables, it becomes an experimental design or similar (Chapter Nine), or perhaps action research or similar (Chapter Ten). In a sense then, a case study is just the absence of these design elements. It is the simplest possible use of design notation (other than a blank page!). It is:

N   O

Yet Yin (2009), considered an expert on case studies, claims that case studies are especially good at addressing explanatory research questions like 'how?' and 'why?'. I can see no justification for this at all. Why would *not* having a comparison group, any before-and-after data and an intervention lead to this extraordinary claim? All such claims do is let poor researchers off the hook of having to consider decent designs for their questions. A case study is simply about collecting data for a description of one case. This is so, however detailed the data that is collected. The problem here arises partly because of the widespread confusion between methods of data collection and research design, and partly because researchers want to find a coherent-sounding reason for being 'qualitative' (i.e. rejecting the use of numbers).

I repeat, in selecting one case you might want it to be a company, and to look carefully at their accounts, or to interview the chief executive. You might want it to be a village in a developing country, and to live there for a week doing in-depth observations, or you might simply want to count the number of daily trips for water. The kind of data you collect is independent of the case selection itself. If you look at individuals within 'cases', such as employees of the firm, or houses in the village, and you wish to draw conclusions about these individuals, then these are now your cases, not the company or the village. And if you look at all or several individuals then you are no longer conducting a single-case study. You might be trying to represent variation within the larger unit (company or village) or you might be working with all individuals as a census. If you wish to make warranted claims about similarity, uniqueness, difference, change, cause, or anything else of real social scientific interest, then you will need more than a case study. You will almost certainly need a comparator. An implied comparison, like saying something is especially good, is a real comparison and needs an explicit comparator in the research design. Care is needed to be precise and meaningful in making comparative claims.

7.3 ‖ Initial design or dredging?

A rather obvious point, but one that is too frequently missed both in practice and in methods resources, is that a planned comparison between groups of cases or measurements is intrinsically more convincing than one based on dividing the cases into groups after data collection. There is a considerable difference between:

N   O

N   O

and

O   [N]

O   [N]

In the first design, the cases are divided into two non-random groups, and then data are collected from both, and compared to see if there is any difference. In the second, data are collected from all cases, and then the cases are divided into groups, perhaps on the basis of differences in the data. Although they are not traditionally portrayed as such, these are quite fundamentally different designs. And the same crucial difference of timing would matter whether the cases were divided in some other way, and if there were more than two sub-groups. Why is this?

There are a number of reasons why this difference matters, but perhaps the two most obvious are the importance of prediction and the dangers of being misled by 'dredging'. Imagine, for the sake of illustration, a 'magician' entertainer who asks two members of the audience to pick a card of their choice from a standard well-shuffled deck of playing cards. The magician asks the two of them to reveal their cards, and perhaps they are the ten of spades and the three of hearts. The magician then states that the first person (ten) picked a higher numbered card than the second person (three). How impressed would you be in the audience that the magician had successfully identified ten as being higher than three? Not very impressed, I suspect. Such a magician would probably not have a successful career. Imagine that they could do this again and again, always saying which of any two cards was the higher. This is still not impressive. On the other hand, imagine the same scenario but with the magician saying each time which card will be higher before the cards are revealed – perhaps even before the cards are picked. If the magician can do this once they might be lucky. If they can do this time after time, there is almost certainly something other than luck involved. The same action (stating which card is higher) is infinitely more interesting and convincing when done before the action to reveal it, than when done after. The same is true with data collection. Or at least it should be (Gorard 2011).

Take any reasonable size set of cases, and any measurement related to those cases. It is likely that subsequently dividing the set of cases into any two groups will lead to an average measurement that is not exactly the same in each group. The average height of the people on the left-hand side of a lecture room will not be exactly the same as the height of those on the right. The average expenditure of all registered companies whose name starts with a vowel will differ at least slightly from the expenditure of the companies starting with a consonant. In itself, this probably means nothing. If the direction of the difference, and perhaps an idea of its scale, was predicted before the measurement was taken and the difference was calculated, then this would probably be more convincing as a finding of substantive interest. Social scientists are not stage magicians. This prediction must be open and genuine. The sub-groups (side of the lecture room, names of companies etc.) must be specified at the outset of the research. The measurement to be used must be specified in advance. And at least the direction of the difference, and ideally its scale, must be predicted, whether on the basis of theory or prior research. Such a design would be very different from taking the measurement from all cases, and only then creating lots of possible sub-groups to see which had large differences in their average measurement. Such a prior design would also be very different from taking a whole series of measurements, and then looking to see which measurements showed the greatest difference between any two sub-groups. The shocking thing is that social scientists so frequently use both of these weaker approaches at the same time, and almost entirely without critical comment by their peers.

A typical example might be a researcher collecting data on the background, health, well-being, happiness, and aspirations of a large number of people. Having collected the data, the researcher then runs a complete analysis comparing each sub-group, as defined by background, in terms of all of the other variables for health, well-being and so on. The background data might include the age, sex, ethnicity, and parental occupation of each respondent. If there were seven categories for parental occupation, then each measure such as level of aspiration can be divided into seven average scores – one for each occupational group. Now the researcher can discover if one or more of these seven averages differs noticeably from any others. There almost certainly will be such a difference. If there is not a big difference, then there may be a bigger one in relation to ethnicity or age. Or maybe the biggest difference is within occupational class, but for health not aspiration. Using software the researcher can calculate and compare hundreds and even thousands of average scores across groups, with only four background variables and four measurements. This is called 'dredging'. Something will turn up. It always does. Like a stage magician, the researcher can then present the 'significant' result in isolation from the hundreds of calculations from which it emerged, and this makes the result appear more convincing and interesting than it should be. Be very wary of this when reading research reports.

Dredging is fine as a research approach, as long as it is reported as such, and the results are considered exploratory and indicative but nowhere near definitive. Dredging is a way of generating research questions or ideas for investigation. But that is all it is. If dredging, in the example above, found that the aspirations of one small ethnic group were noticeably higher than all other groups, this might be worth publicising and pursuing through further study. If, on the other hand, a researcher genuinely predicted, on the basis of theory, that this small ethnic group should have higher aspirations, and only then collected the data, and did only that one calculation, then the result is much more impressive. Note that is so, even though the actual measured and published results may be exactly the same in both approaches. That is the power and importance of prior research design. It rightly makes research claims more convincing. Limitations of design usually cannot be overcome *post hoc*, leading instead to data dredging with considerable danger of misleading results (Coe 2010). If we ignore design, as many 'researchers' do, we will be misled by sleight of hand. My guess is that most readers will already have encountered this situation, but will not necessarily recognise it for what it is. As a rule of thumb, decide on the sub-groups before conducting the research and keep these groups clearly labelled as such in the subsequent analysis. And also remember to note the difference in the work of others between groups planned in design and those created by dredging. If the research report does not make this difference clear, ask yourself why this is so.

7.4 ||| Unmatched sub-groups

Unmatched sub-groups of cases might be used in a design for at least two very different purposes. The groups might be deliberately heterogeneous, formed to make an explicit comparison between two contrasting sets. An example could be a consideration of the earnings of professional employees compared to unskilled employees. In this case, the groups are properly unmatched and could not be any other way. Quality issues include the completeness of coverage, and the validity of the classification into professional/unskilled employment, plus the usual measurement issues about revealed earnings. The result could really only be descriptively comparative. It would tell us nothing, in itself, about what caused any difference observed.

The simplest design with two pre-existing comparator groups, formed in a non-random (N) way such as natural clustering, might be:

N   O

N   O

This comparative or cross-sectional approach is excellent for descriptive work intending to establish a difference or similarity between two groups. Often, the sub-groups used by researchers are quite properly based on pre-existing classifications. Another example could be establishing the relative satisfaction of patients in private and publicly-funded hospitals. In the previous example about aspirations and health, the sub-groups were created by age of respondent and categories such as ethnicity, sex and occupation. If the researcher used standard classifications, and planned the analysis from the outset, then each of the sub-groups were pre-existing and pre-defined. The design is then quite complex to portray in notation, since there are so many sub-groups and their defining characteristics are not hierarchical (sex is not a sub-category of ethnicity, or *vice versa*). One thing to watch out for with complex designs involving large numbers of categorical variables is that the active sample size shrinks dramatically. All of the points made in Chapter Six about the need for a substantial sample overall, also apply to each cell in any table of comparisons. If your estimate is that 100 cases are needed as a minimum to represent any population, then something of the same order of magnitude is also needed for each sub-group if you divide your sample in any way. Thus, a comparison of two groups of hospitals might need around 200 cases in total. The aspiration example might require thousands of cases, otherwise there will be sparsely populated or empty cells for some of the necessary comparisons. This issue is often overlooked.

Establishing a causal pattern or explanatory theory using an unmatched comparative design like the ones discussed so far is almost impossible. Children attending a private fee-paying school, for example, might tend to attain at a higher level at age 14 than those attending state-maintained schools, but we cannot attribute this difference to the school attended. Because the children are not randomised to the type of school we cannot be confident that the two groups were similar at the outset. In fact, most commentators would accept that the population of the two types of schools were already very different in ways that could easily influence their later attainment. Children attending private schools may have more parental attention in the early years, more books at home and so on. The design cannot cater for these pre-existing differences. It is the design itself that is deficient for causal purposes. This means that the same design cannot be used for a causal claim with anything else substituted for schools and attainment, even if it sounds more plausible at first sight.

Where research is attempting to isolate the impact of an intervention (Chapter Nine), the standard approach is to have two or more groups and to vary the timing, strength or appearance of the intervention between them. In this kind of design, one sub-group (or more) is acting as a comparator for the intervention group. In a natural experiment, these groups will often be unmatched. It is possible to learn something about the success of a new policy in one country by contrasting it with what happens in another similar country, or about a new law or practice or funding regime if it takes place at a regional or local authority or even at institutional level. Such comparisons are not ideal in scientific terms, but they are easy to set up and ethical to work with, and much better than not having an explicit comparator at all. Their chief problem comes at the analysis stage, in trying to decide whether any differences in the observed outcomes between two groups are due to the intervention or can be explained by the other myriad initial differences between the countries (or regions etc.). One way of reducing the difficulties for analysis in situations like this is to match the comparator groups more closely.

7.5 ‖ Matched comparisons

A simple matched comparison design could be portrayed like this:

M   O

M   O

'M' is used to distinguish it from the natural comparative design above. The idea behind matching cases across the two (or more) sub-groups is that it provides a fairer comparison than with unmatched groups. Some commentators even envisage that it leads to results as robust as randomisation, but this is dubious. Continuing the earlier example, children in private schools could be matched with others whose parents have the income to use private schools but choose not to. But this assumes, with little justification, that children from families who choose to spend on education in this way are otherwise the same as children from those who do not. The same problem emerges however many variables are used to try and make the match. If children are matched on prior attainment this may ignore the fact that one group had already been more heavily coached, or was more motivated or had greater access to computers or highly-educated relatives. One can never be confident that the subsequent difference in attainment is not a consequence of omitted data in the matching process.

Matching can be as simple as the approach used in stratified sampling, with cases randomised to groups within a pre-determined stratum like sex (Chapter Six). Each sex could have its own lists of cases, which would be allocated to sub-groups separately. In this way each group would have the same number of women, or of whatever variable was used for the stratum. As with stratified sampling, matches can be made on more than one variable at the same time, such as sex within social class. This could ensure that each group had the same number of working-class women. Presumably, the more variables involved in matching the better the results could be. But as with stratified sampling, the problem is that this can quickly get very messy and complex, with too many categories and not enough cases.

A number of compromises have been suggested to overcome this problem, mostly with considerable similarity to each other. In essence, the idea is to conduct a multivariate analysis beforehand with all of the variables to be used for matching, and so reduce them to the most important, or those that are latent (underlying several others). An appropriate technique might be principal component analysis, which can yield a score for each case on one or more aggregated variables. Matching can then go ahead using these scores instead of the much larger number of known variables. The two cases with the closest matching scores are then constrained to be in separate groups.

Propensity scoring

Rosenbaum and Rubin (1983) proposed propensity score matching as a solution both to having too many variables to cope with when taking matching seriously, and to the fact that there will be inter-correlations and interactions between these variables. In outline, propensity scoring works as follows. We have a group of cases, perhaps a naturally occurring or clinical group, which will be given an intervention. The cases could be everyone in a particular city where a new policy is being piloted, or volunteers for a social work training course. We also need another set of cases, not receiving the intervention, with no overlap with the treatment group. This second set could be those living anywhere that the policy was not being tried, or they could be volunteers not selected for the training course. In the absence of randomisation, this set is unlikely to be similar to the intervention group. No two cities are otherwise alike, for example. It is the same problem as with any set of unmatched cases (above).

In order to see whether the intervention is effective, we need to create a group from the second set that is comparable in all respects to the intervention group, other than the intervention (Gorard and Cook 2007). The assumption of propensity score matching is that the difference between cases in the treatment group and the rest can be explained purely in terms of observable characteristics. This is a very strong, and probably unrealistic, assumption. It necessitates a lot of high quality information about the cases in both groups. Theory and prior syntheses of research (Chapter Three) can be used to help decide on the relevant variables needed. If some key variables are indicated but not available then propensity scoring should not proceed. There is a temptation to use all available variables, but this necessitates a correspondingly large number of cases (for the usual statistical reasons, see Gorard 2003). So, if the number of cases is small, perhaps less than 10 times the number of variables, again propensity scoring should not be attempted.

The original intervention group, such as the cases in one city in the example above, will have an outcome measure, which can be used to decide whether the intervention was successful or not. This outcome measure might be the proportion of successful activities led by a social worker in the year following their participation in additional training. Once we know the outcomes for each participant, and for all cases in the second set who did not participate in training, and the scores for the relevant variables for participants and non-participants, we can work out which variables could be related to the outcome and also to whether an individual was a participant. There are a number of ways of doing this. Logistic, logit or probit regression can be used, with participation in the intervention or not as a binary dependent variable, and with all other measures as predictors of participation (Bryson et al. 2002). The predictors could include the intended intervention outcome measure (percentage of successful activities both with and without training). The ensuing model will show, via the size of the coefficients, which background variables are particularly related to patterns of participation in the intervention. It will also provide a probability for the expected participation of each case. This is the propensity score.

The next step is to find the case in the second set with the closest propensity score match to each of the cases in the original treatment group. There are a number of ways of doing this, but using the nearest neighbouring score is probably the simplest. The final step is to calculate the average 'effect' of the original treatment (Dehejia et al. 2002). This is done by finding the average difference in outcomes (the number of successful activities for social workers, in the example above) between the treatment group and the group formed of the closest propensity score matches, as for a standard experimental design (Chapter Nine).

In some ways this sounds more complex than it is in practice, as long as you are familiar with logistic regression and similar modelling techniques. However, it is more complex than random assignment, and so should not be undertaken lightly. Random assignment to groups before treatment is so much more superior to any kind of matching that it should always be used if possible. It is also easier. Matching requires more variables to be known at the outset (to match with). It requires more cases as a minimum to reflect variation in those variables and their interactions, than random allocation does. Matching makes assumptions that random allocation does not need to, and which are immediately questionable – such as that the difference between participants and non-participants can be fully explained by known measurements. Omitted variables here lead to bias in the estimates of treatment effectiveness. Unmeasured, unknown and even unimagined variables can only be handled through randomisation. There are a large number of analytical decisions to be made in matching, any one of which could lead to different outcomes. For example, the nearest neighbour to one of the treatment cases could itself be nearer to a different treatment case. Which then should be used? What happens to cases with no near matches? Decisions like these can bias the selection, by leading to systematic exclusion of very high or very low probabilities that have no good match, and so reducing the number of cases further. It is actually very instructive to try propensity scoring with a convenient dataset even if you are not intending to use it, because it reveals in this way the systematic selection bias that occurs in standard statistical modelling approaches to looking for causation. Matching could even make these biases worse.

Given all of the above, it should be no surprise to learn that where it has been possible to compare the results of propensity score matching, and similar statistical modelling approaches, with the results of randomised treatments, there is often a considerable difference (Ty Wilde and Hollister 2002). This then means that different conclusions can be drawn from the same dataset where there is a true control group and where one has been created artificially by matching, which means that money could be wasted and futures harmed wherever matching is used in preference to randomisation. When we want homogeneous groups, matching may be better than not matching, but perhaps not by that much (further examples in Chapter Ten).

7.6 |ı| Randomised comparisons

One way of improving a comparative design is to randomise cases to the two (or more) groups:

R   O

R   O

As long as the number of cases is high and each had an equal chance of being in either group then this design provides protection against biasing differences between the groups. In this design, the matching of cases does not matter. The known variables that cases could have been matched on are treated in the same way as the variables that might be omitted or unknown in the matching process. And in practice, the ensuing balance between two large random groups, in terms of the known variables that could have been matched, gives some confidence that unknown but important background variables will also be unbiased between the two groups. It is a somewhat provocative description of random allocation that it is the 'gold standard' in research, but given what has been said above it is possible to see why commentators use it. They are trying to convey that randomisation is to be preferred whenever it is an option. The actual technique used to assign cases by selecting random numbers or elements can be the same as when selecting a random sample (Chapter Six). There is a range of alternative methods that will produce a random or near random assignment to groups. These include alternating cases between groups as they appear in sequence (or in threes if there are three groups, and so on). Of course, like all methods, such alternation requires that no interference or unwanted manipulation of order takes place, and that the initial order of appearance is meaningless. Assuming these, then alternation or something like it is an entirely suitable way of allocating cases.

One of my main concerns about the use of the phase 'gold standard' is that it suggests that, as long as we use random allocation to groups, everything is fine. Of course, this is not so. A simple comparative design such as that above, even with randomisation, has no further time element and so still cannot be used to identify causation securely. In the example of comparing state and private school outcomes, once the pupils are aged 14, it is too late to randomise the children to schools that they have attended since age 11. A more complex design than a comparative one is needed. Dropout, subversion of the allocation process, contamination and a host of other threats to the validity of a research design apply to randomised designs as much as any other (Chapter Eleven). One of the most common threats is post-randomisation bias. If dropout from two or more groups is uneven once the cases discover which group they are in, this causes bias. Perhaps people are disappointed to be in the control group. Even if there is no such dropout, discovering that one is or is not in a specific group can lead to de-motivation, which would then bias the estimate of the resulting effect size. However, it is important to note that such problems occur in all designs, and in any kind of sample. They are not specific to random allocation. The bias in a convenience sample with naturally occurring sub-groups will be far worse.

Minimisation

As with random sampling, it is possible and sometimes desirable to use theoretically or empirically important strata to sub-divide the cases before allocation to groups. This reduces the likelihood of a fluke random distribution, and for this reason tends to be used with smaller samples where volatility will be higher. A separate list is made of cases with different values on one or more stratifying variables, such as sex, and each list is then randomised to groups separately. This leads to balance in the number of cases with a specific characteristic (such as being female) in each sub-group. But this approach quickly becomes very complex and almost impossible to do as soon as several stratifying variables are used at once.

One somewhat superior approach is to use 'minimisation' (Pocock and Simon 1975). This involves computing a large number of potential ways of creating the sub-groups. In each solution, the total imbalance between the two or more groups is calculated as the sum of the imbalances for each stratifying variable for each individual case. Then a grouping is chosen for the design which minimises the overall imbalance of the comparator groups. Either the grouping with the smallest imbalance is selected, or the grouping can be selected randomly from among a number of groups with relatively small imbalances. As ever, if possible, plain random sampling is better. Minimisation is more complex, could inadvertently introduce bias in unseen variables, and so is perhaps best used only when the number of cases is very small (Altman and Bland 2005).

Cluster randomisation

Some interventions have to be conducted with groups of cases. For example, providing a new well for drinking water in a developing village would provide better water for everyone within reach. It is not possible, and not desirable, to limit access to the water. This means that a study of the impact of better drinking water cannot randomise or match individual people as cases to treatment or no treatment. Only entire villages can be considered. In the same way, cleaning a hospital ward to a higher standard to protect patients from cross-infection could, if it has any effect, have an effect on all patients therein. Similarly, in social science there are occasions when it is preferable to treat groups of individuals as inviolable clusters. An obvious example would be teaching units in schools. It is possible to allocate pupils randomly to teaching interventions, but schools are much more likely to agree to take part if their existing teaching structure is respected. An additional advantage of allocating clusters of cases to sub-groups, rather than individually, is that it can help to control 'contamination' in an intervention study. Contamination is an analogy derived from health studies, where a treatment or intervention is leaked from the intervention group to the control or comparison group. Dilution of effect might be a better description. In a teaching example, if new learning materials were given to random individuals in and across schools, they might copy them or share them with friends or relatives in other treatment groups. Since those others could be in the control group, this sharing will reduce the apparent effect of the new materials. This may seem unlikely, but it can happen. Using clusters, like entire classes or entire schools allocated to treatment or control, makes this contamination even less likely.

There has to be a good reason for using clusters. As with all aspects of design, the use of a cluster approach should be reported, and the reasons for using it clearly set out. One problem that is worse with clusters than with individual random allocation is that if one individual refuses to take part after allocation (the parent of a child in one class refuses permission perhaps), then often the entire cluster has to be dropped. This causes greater bias than if an individual drops out (Puffer et al. 2005). There are a number of steps that can be taken in design to minimise this bias. Participants should be signed up for participation in the study individually. Only then should the viable clusters be allocated randomly. This does not entirely prevent cluster dropout but it helps limit post-allocation demoralisation.

Where clusters are used, they generally and automatically become the units for analysis (Chapter Six). If entire classes in schools are randomised to sub-groups, then the only probabilistic uncertainty is at the class level. This is the level at which the analysis should be, 'thereby keeping the unit of analysis the same as the unit of randomisation' (Cochrane 2012). To do anything else makes the analysis more complicated for no analytical gain. The only uncertainty in this situation that is relevant to statistical sampling theory lies in the cluster allocation.

It becomes somewhat different if randomisation is used within the cluster as well. Perhaps schools are the clusters, randomly allocated to treatment or other sub-groups, and teaching classes are then selected randomly within schools. This would be a cluster-randomised design, and there would be probabilistic uncertainty in the selection of schools and of classes within schools. This process of nested probability sampling could be extended to three or more levels. Perhaps regions are randomly selected before schools and then classes. Perhaps pupils or lessons are also then randomly selected within classes. This has implications for the size of the sample, and for the understanding of effect sizes.

It is possible that cases within clusters are more similar to each other in some respects than they would be to cases in the population more generally. If so, this can lead to what is called a 'design' effect that is claimed to artificially reduce the standard error of a sample, leading to the possibility of a misleading result from statistical analysis. Of course, this only applies if your analysis is based on the use of standard errors (Chapter Twelve). And even if your analysis is of this kind, such as significance testing, you can easily counter the problem in a variety of ways – most simply by lowering your threshold for significance.

The recommended way to estimate the impact of any design effect, for sample and power purposes, is to start with an estimate of the extent to which the scores of cases within any cluster will be correlated with each other, over and above what would be expected for the wider population. Of course, in practice we will not know this figure, so the process starts from what is effectively a guess or hypothetical assumption. Then to retain the same power as a sample of individuals, a cluster design needs to multiply that sample size by the design effect. The design effect is usually portrayed as 1+(m–1).rho, where rho is the intra-cluster correlation, and m is the average number of cases in the clusters (Campbell et al. 2004). So in a study with an intra-cluster correlation (assumed) of 0.1 or 10%, and clusters of around 20 cases each, the design effect would be 1+19/10 or 2.9. A study with these characteristics would therefore need a sample nearly three times as large as an equivalent study using individual randomisation. It is easy to see why simple randomisation might be preferred.

A few myths have grown up about such clustering. These include the idea that *all* important social science groupings are hierarchical in nature, and that special and complex analytical arrangements such as hierarchical linear modelling are always necessary when dealing with clusters (Hutchison 2009). Both claims are clearly wrong but are repeated as analytical facts by some commentators. Perhaps the most commonly used social science explanatory or grouping variables are the sex, social class, and ethnic origin of people. It is obvious that these are not hierarchical in the same way as schools within regions. These key social variables intersect and interact with each other. None nests neatly within another. The claim that special analytical arrangements are needed when dealing with hierarchical clusters alone is based on the idea that cases within clusters are not independent, because they may be more like each other in some important respects than cases in other clusters. This may well be so, but conversely may not be so. For example, a mixed-ability class in school represents a kind of attempt at stratified or minimised grouping. Some of the most similar cases, such as the most able or talented, are constrained by mixed-ability to be in different clusters. It is also clear that the same claim of similarity is much more likely to be true of cases within the categories of variables like sex, class and ethnicity. Does this then mean that the women in a sample must be treated as non-independent cases, whose similarity leads us to underestimate the standard error? If not, then the argument cannot be made uniquely for nesting clusters. If so, then the special analytical arrangements for clusters need also to cover sex, class, ethnicity, talent and hundreds of other possible inter-correlating variables as well. But the methods proposed, such as hierarchical linear modelling, only work with nesting hierarchical variables, which is perhaps why their advocates seem to suggest that all key variables must nest. This is to put the cart before the horse!

It is far easier than these advocates of complex methods suggest to conduct an analysis that respects all variables, and permits results presented at any level at which data has been collected. As the BMA, Cochrane and other authorities suggest, the analysis can be conducted with the clusters as cases. This avoids any difficulties and is a tough test of effect sizes. If there is no probabilistic sampling variation at any level in an analysis, then no complex approach is needed or appropriate, because a census of population represents a population, even if it is only part of a larger study. If there is sampling variation at more than one level, the data can even be analysed just at the lowest level (pupils or lessons in the example used). Anyone wishing to safeguard against being misled on account of the non-independence of cases within clusters can then increase the sample size, lower the significance level (if they use such a thing), or use a number of other simple adjustments or alternatives (Bland 2003; Gorard 2007). Decent research design is robust, and should generate results as needed to answer the research question. If the research questions concern what is happening at different levels in a process, then the design must relate to each level. In general, therefore, the need to use complex modelling and dredging of datasets after the event is an indication of poor quality design.

⚌ Exercises on comparator groups

1 Two professors are arguing about their new research project. It is a psychology experiment about human perception, taking place in a laboratory setting. The first professor wants to allocate the research participants to two groups randomly, and their reason is that they want to conduct some statistical tests, which means they must use randomisation. The second professor disagrees. They want to match the large number of research participants by sex, age, ethnicity and social class to find the closest pairs, and then put one of each pair in each research group. This, they claim, will lead to less biased variation between the two groups, of the kind that might affect the results. Which professor is correct?

2 A colleague of yours is studying the occupational income of recent graduates to see if there is a value in monetary terms in attending university. Naturally, they also have a

comparator group of people who did not attend university. Their finding is that people with degrees earn slightly more than people who did not attend university. This is not surprising. Your colleague is also interested in the graduate 'premium' for men and women separately. They find that, despite the overall finding, men who did not attend university actually earn slightly more than those who have degrees. The colleague also calculates that women without degrees earn more than women with degrees. This must surely be wrong. How could it be possible for men and women combined to earn more as graduates than non-graduates, but for men to earn more as non-graduates *and* women to earn more as non-graduates?

3 Find an empirical research article in your own area of interest that makes a comparative claim.

   a Does it have an explicit comparator?
   b Does it explain how many other comparisons were made as part of this study?
   c If a lot of other comparisons were made but not reported, would this influence your judgement about the significance of the comparison reports?
   d Were the other comparisons specified before the study was conducted? Was the result of the comparison predicted before the study was conducted? What difference would this make to your judgement of the findings?

⇌ Notes on exercises on comparator groups

1 Strictly speaking, neither professor is correct. We do not randomise cases to groups in order to use statistical tests. That would be like saying we use crockery when eating so that we can do the washing up! We can conduct the tests in order to estimate the random sampling variation *if* we have randomised cases to groups. However, for a large group, randomisation is almost always the best method of allocation, if we wish to minimise unwanted bias between the groups. It is true that matching cases between groups on the basis of known characteristics like sex and age will lead to well-balanced groups for these variables – but for these variables only. If the experiment is about perception, then there is a whole range of possible characteristics that might influence the results. The groups might differ in health, visual capacity, intelligence, or motivation, for example. A researcher cannot balance all possible differences between cases in a finite sample, and, in most studies anyway, a researcher does not know what the key variables will turn out to be. So, randomisation – which gives each person an equal chance of being in each group, regardless of known characteristics like age and regardless of unknown ones like motivation – is better than matching.

2 Strangely, this is possible. It could be an example of what has been called Simpson's paradox, after the work of Simpson (1951) but which is probably much older. Look at Table 7.1. It shows the situation your colleague described. In the local currency, men earn 65,000 after a degree but 75,000 without a degree. Similarly, women earn more without a degree than with. How can this lead to the overall finding that people earn more with a degree (60,000 on average) than without (50,000)? It is sensitive to the number of cases in each cell. Assume that the study had 100 cases with degrees and 100 without, and 100 cases were men and 100 women. But let us say that men are more likely to have degrees. So imagine that 80 men but only 20 women had degrees. This means that the average income for those with degrees is 80 times 65k plus 20 times 40k all divided by 100. This is 60k. The average income for those without degrees is 20 times 75k plus 80 times 44k all divided by 100. This is 50k. So, it can be true that the pattern for the overall sample is the opposite of the pattern for *all* sub-groups. There is no reason to doubt your colleague's findings.

Table 7.1 Average income of graduates and non-graduates, for males and females

	Degree	*No degree*
Men income	65,000	75,000
Women income	40,000	44,000
Average income	60,000	50,000

Source: imaginary data

Note: there are 100 cases in each column, 80 men have a degree, and 80 women do not have a degree

This 'paradox' can have implications for meta-analysis which might sum several studies, each of which finds one thing and produces a synthesised result that shows the opposite! Changing the level of aggregation of data and forming sub-groups are important steps in research, but both can have unpredictable consequences. Research design requires care, and then more care.

3 a If you have been doing the exercises in each chapter as you go along, you should be getting quite good at this kind of audit by now. You may also be getting less surprised at how poor much published research is and how easy it is to find simple flaws like implied comparative claims without a comparator.

b The number of comparisons is important, because it provides the 'denominator' for how convincing any claim is.

c In traditional statistical analysis it is assumed that calculations are based on making only one comparison. For example, a claim that a finding is 'significant' at the 5% level should be understood to mean that if the finding were not true then there was a less than 5% chance of collecting data suggesting the finding to be true, by random sampling variation alone. The 5% (or 1 in 20) calculation assumes that only one test for significance is made. If more than one comparison is made, the 5% is misleading. If tens or sometimes thousands of comparisons were made then the 5% means nothing. Rolling a double with two dice has a chance of 1 in 6. Rolling at least one double in 100 throws is to be expected. The number of throws is crucial information, yet this is usually omitted in research reports. Such an omission makes me very suspicious, especially of the use of significance in large complex statistical models. Note that exactly the same problem arises even if probabilities are not calculated and no statistics are involved. Quite how remarkable a pattern in your interview data is depends partly on how many patterns you sought, and whether you predicted the pattern before collecting the data. I seldom see any reports that make this explicit, which is shocking once you realise how important this factor is in being convinced by any findings.

d Quite clearly, if the comparisons were built into the research design from the start then they ought to be more convincing to the reader, like predicting the result of the card trick at the start of the chapter. I wonder, though, whether the readers and critical consumers of social science remember to make this distinction when reading research.

⊒ Suggested reading

Chapter Nine in Shadish, W., Cook, T. and Campbell, D. (2002) *Experimental and Quasi-Experimental Designs for Generalized Causal Inference*. Belmont: Wadsworth.

EIGHT

Matters of timing and sequence

SUMMARY

- Trend, or repeated cross-sectional, designs are useful for describing historical changes over time.
- They are of limited use in explanatory research, and there is a danger of confusing changes over historical periods with changes in the life of an individual.
- Longitudinal, or panel or cohort, designs are useful for tracking changes over the life-course of individuals.
- They can be excellent at uncovering possible risk factors for subsequent events.
- The two approaches can even be combined, as with the UK Labour Force Survey. This example shows that there are many more designs based on the flexible elements in this book than are found in traditional research resources.
- However, both kinds of studies suffer defects in terms of providing convincing causal accounts. The problems include regression to the mean, attrition, early design errors, unpredicted events, and changes in society.
- Neither design is very good for predicting subsequent events.
- The chapter ends by considering the role of place in design, and also whether retrospection can overcome some of the deficiencies and costs of longitudinal work.

8.1 ‖ Introduction

A third key element of research design, after the selection of cases and their allocation to groups, is time. The comparative designs in Chapter Seven were all cross-sectional, meaning that they took place in one time period with data collected as a 'snapshot'. Of course, a cross-sectional design does not imply that all data is collected at exactly the same time. Fieldwork is a real-life process and even a large team will not be able to gather all of the evidence simultaneously. But having to space out your interviews with different people over a month-long period in order to fit them in and accommodate the participants is very different from designing a study that interviews people once at the start and again a year later. The sequence in which events take place is particularly important when the research is evaluating a causal model – the cause must come before the effect (Chapter Five). However, as Chapter Two showed, when outlining a full cycle of research activity, the order in which events and processes take place is an important factor in all studies, whether causal or not. This chapter looks at the concepts of repeated cross-sectional, longitudinal and related study designs.

When discussing the comparative designs in Chapter Seven, I introduced the problem of trying to assess whether the difference in examination results attained by pupils at state and private schools was due to the activities of the schools, or to some pre-existing difference between the pupils who attend such schools. A cross-sectional design can really only establish whether there is an average difference in school outcomes between the two sets of schools. It cannot help decide on when that difference emerges. Even the supposed gold standard of randomised allocation cannot help because once the pupils are aged 14 it is too late to randomise the children to schools. A more complex design is needed that involves time as an element.

At the start of Chapter Seven, I pointed out how strange it is that so many researchers make comparative or implied comparative claims in their research reports without an appropriate comparator. It is at least as hard to get many researchers to see how important the time element is in any study, but especially for a study that eventually wishes to make warranted causal claims. In fact, several of the examples of missing comparators in Chapter Seven concerned purported changes over time (with data from only one time period). It is as problematic to claim changes over time with data related to only one time period as it is to imply differences between groups with data from only one group.

8.2 ‖ Repeated cross-sectional designs

As soon as time becomes an element of a design, it is vital to distinguish between tracking cases over time (see next section) and working with different cases at different times. The latter could be a repeated cross-sectional design, with the simplest arrangement perhaps expressed as:

N	O		(Group1)
N		O	(Group 2)
N			O	(Group 3 etc.)

This could represent the quarterly reports of unemployment for a region, with the 'O' being a measure of the numbers unemployed. Such a design is also called a trend survey, because it shows the trend over time for a measure or series of measures. An example from the UK (England) is the Annual Schools Census. This official document is completed by all school-age educational establishments to some extent, and by all state-funded schools completely. It is a census of the school-age population, and collects official data on the number of schools, pupils, teachers, teaching assistants, and a range of possible indicators of pupil disadvantage such as eligibility for free school meals and special educational needs. The data can also be linked to pupils' entry to, and results in, formal examinations. Among other things, this annual census can be used to portray the historical pattern of stratifying pupils with similar characteristics in the same school (Figure 8.1). This figure shows that pupils from poor families – those taking free school meals (fsm) – are clustered with others like them to a certain extent. Around one third (0.3 to 0.4 on the y axis in Figure 8.1) would have to exchange schools for there to be no clustering by poverty. The figure shows also that this level of clustering changes over time, and that the annual changes are the same in primary and secondary schools. I found the latter result surprising, since the process of selecting and allocating school places is very different between the two school sectors. This result might suggest the pattern is not related to the school intake process, but to something else. The result therefore suggested a number of follow-up questions. This is exactly how secondary data analysis works best.

As illustrated, a trend design is excellent for descriptive work and inspiring new research questions, but cannot by itself address causal questions, such as why are there changes over time in any trend? Another survey of the same basic design, also widely used in social science, is the United Nations Crime Trends Survey (CTS).

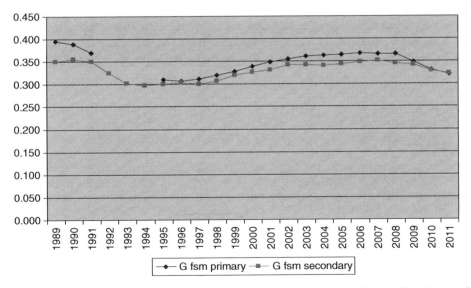

Figure 8.1 Gorard Segregation Index, for free school meal take-up (fsm), all maintained schools, England, 1989–2011

Data and methods in Gorard and Cheng (2011)

This is now annual, and based on incidents of being the victim of crime that have been reported to the legal authorities in each member country of the UN. As you can imagine, this means that the completeness of figures is quite variable between countries, some acts are crimes in one country and not another, and levels of reporting also vary considerably. This means that cross-sectional comparisons between countries are difficult. Even the UK Annual Schools Census has changed its format, completeness, and methods of coding variables many times, making comparisons over time difficult as well. Nevertheless, as long as they are presented with suitable cautions, figures from a repeated cross-sectional design can be informative. But the addition of a time element does not automatically add to the rigour of the conclusions that can be drawn. In fact, concurrent changes over time and between the ways cases are contacted can make it more problematic.

To illustrate this, imagine that a national government is concerned to improve rates of adult learning. It introduces a number of measures to encourage adults to participate in formal education or training, and it publishes a target for progress. An initial target is to increase the proportion of all adults aged 18 to 70 who have a qualification, equivalent to that expected of a school-leaver, from 42% of the population to 65% after five years. In the year that the new measures are introduced, 42% of 18–70-year-olds have this level of formal qualification, and this figure increases by about three percentage points in each successive year. This is trumpeted as a clear success for the government policy, but it might not be. It is likely that the older people in this country generally have lower levels of formal qualifications than younger ones. If so, then the percentage of the 18–70-year-old population with the qualification will go up each year, even if no adults aged 18 or over take any qualifications. What this government has done is to confuse changes in successive cross-sectional figures with changes over the life-time of an individual. They have confused what I have previously referred to as the two 'dimensions' of time (Gorard et al. 2002).

8.3 ||| Longitudinal designs

A longitudinal design is what is needed to look at changes over the lifetime, or at least part of the lifetime, of an individual. It is repeated measures (or observations), not repeated cross-sections. A design can be considered longitudinal if it involves observation or data collection from the same cases at two or more clearly separate points in time. The most important difference from a repeated cross-sectional design is that the cases are the same on each occasion. In its simplest form, it would be:

N   O   O

This can be adapted to many episodes of data collection, such as:

N   O   O   O   ......

The number of episodes does not fundamentally alter the nature of this design, its advantages and its many limitations. It is a good way of describing the sequence of events. It is even better for the clues it can provide to generating alternative explanations for eventual outcomes. For example, we might have a comparative cross-sectional finding that the age at which people die is related to their income. Poorer people in a certain society tend to die younger than the wealthier do, based on using data on income at the time of their death. This might be an interesting, and shaming, descriptive research result but it immediately leads to the query whether it is poverty/income that is the cause of earlier death or not. In order to progress we would need some more of the life history of each person.

Such a design, when individuals are the cases, is also referred to as a panel or cohort study. The panel or cohort is the group of cases being followed over time. The panel can be a sample from a more general population, selected by any of the methods in Chapter Six, usually randomly or via random clusters. Or the cohort can be a population in its own right such as when all of the new-born infants in one week are followed up. In the UK, there are a number of such birth cohort studies. These include the National Child Development Study (NCDS) started in 1958, which now has respondents in their 50s, the British Cohort Study (BCS) started in 1970, and the Millennium Cohort Study (MCS) started in 2000. These are all attempts at a longitudinal census of neonates born in a short period, and they initially consisted of around 16,000 cases each. At the outset, it is the families who agree to take part and provide most of the responses, with the child becoming a primary respondent with age. A whole range of measures, issues and methods of data collection are involved, and a lot of descriptive research questions can be answered. For example, the cohort will include those who turn out to be unemployed, and those who are employed, and so it can provide a suitable comparison for identifying possible risk factors for unemployment. Researchers have used these ongoing studies to look at a range of risk factors for later achievements (e.g. Mensah and Kiernan 2010; Sullivan et al. 2011).

There are also ongoing studies based on samples of the wider population, using postal address files as a sampling frame to select households at random. Then the household can become the unit of participation, as with the British Household Panel Survey (BHPS) conducted since 1991. Or one individual can be selected from the household, making the sample a cluster-randomised one, sometimes with several levels of clustering (area, household, individual). An example would be the British Social Attitudes Survey (BSAS) based on adults aged 18 or over, selected within households, within postal districts. Another example is the UK Family Expenditure Survey (FES) which has a very similar sampling approach. Many of these complex samples are also weighted afterwards, perhaps to try and overcome problems of non-response bias, to calibrate to known population characteristics – post-stratification – or to overcome bias from having boosted the sample for some smaller home countries of the UK or for some hard-to-reach or scarce sub-groups. Complex samples then often involve complex, sometimes needlessly complex, treatment in analysis. This makes a simple birth cohort or a clear random sample much more appealing because both are so much easier to analyse. Nevertheless, these panel surveys and others like them in all areas of social science can provide a fascinating picture of growth and change, and can be set within the context of concurrent social, economic and political changes.

The range of variations in designs involving time is limited only by our imagination. It is perfectly proper, and quite common in clinical studies, to have two cohorts in the same study. One may have been subject to a treatment like a vaccination, while the other is a comparator. It is possible to compare two or more birth cohorts over time (e.g. Bynner and Joshi 2002). This would be a bit like a repeated cross-section design but the repeated cohort design would allow a comparison of the changes in risk factors between time periods. Some well-known studies build a combination of approaches into their standard design. For example, the UK Labour Force Survey (LFS) has been conducted since 1973, by the Office for National Statistics (a one-stop shop for so many resources for secondary analysis). A sample is constructed and interviewed every three months. Each sample has around 11,000 cases selected for the first time – a cross-section or 'wave'. Each wave is then interviewed on four successive occasions, which means that on each occasion, 11,000 cases are new, and 11,000 each are having their second, third, fourth or fifth interviews. The LFS is both longitudinal and a trend design. This allows a number of estimates to be made, such as projections of unemployment on a monthly basis, but it can also make analysis very complex. The point of this example, other than to remind you of these powerful sources of data for your own project, is to exemplify that once you have understood the elements of research design these can be combined in many different and often unorthodox ways.

8.4 ‖ Limitations of sequence alone

The designs discussed in this chapter have used time only but without a direct comparator or intervention. Apart from for descriptive and exploratory work, these designs have a number of problems. If the design merely associates data collected initially with data collected subsequently, then this is not intrinsically any more powerful than an association between two groups of data collected at the same time. As discussed in Chapter Seven, an association between school attainment and a pupil's attitude to school at age 14 cannot be used, in itself, to demonstrate that either is the cause of the other. In the same way, a link between prior and later attainment at school does not mean that the prior attainment 'caused' the later attainment. Nor could the same simple longitudinal design be used to justify a causal explanation with anything else. In my reviews of evidence, I have come across tens of thousands of studies using causal language for associations between data collected at the same time, and thousands more using causal language for simple associations between data collected at different times. Both are completely unjustified.

A simple longitudinal design is sometimes more convincing for causal purposes where a natural intervention (X) occurs between the two (or more) episodes of data collection:

N   O   [X]   O

However, this design still has many defects that can be fatal to the validity of any attempt to draw robust causal conclusions. For example, a change between the observations before and after the intervention (X) cannot be attributed to X until it is clear that the change would not have happened in the absence of all interventions, and that it would not have happened in the presence of any intervention that was attempted (a Hawthorne effect, as described in Chapter Eleven). There is a danger that enthusiastic and well-funded developers and researchers do produce an effect through an intervention, but it is not the specific intervention that is the cause. Almost any coherent approach with that level of resource commitment and freshness might have produced the same or a larger effect. What is needed is a fair comparison group. Children's literacy tends to improve with age, especially when young. It would not be reasonable to claim that an improvement in literacy between ages 5 and 6 was due to a specific approach to teaching unless the 'natural' improvement that also occurs for those children not subject to the intervention had been accounted for. Software manufacturers can rightly claim that after using their product for literacy education for some extended time, the average literacy of a group of children will improve. But they cannot also rightly claim that the product causes the improvement, else this is the common fallacy formally termed *post hoc ergo propter hoc*. Another well-worn example would be a purported cure for the common cold. Such a 'cure' cannot be warranted by a simple before-and-after design because colds disappear after a few days anyway with no treatment. This means that a claim for any cold treatment that causes 90% of colds to disappear within a few days is unjustified.

One common problem with before-and-after studies and with trend designs is regression to the mean. Where a score or measure is particularly high or low then a subsequent score is likely to be closer to average just because of the natural volatility of numbers. In the same way, the child of a very tall person is likely to be slightly smaller than the parent. This is normal. If a person takes an aptitude test and scores 100% and then takes a similar test, there is only one kind of change possible. If the score is different on the second test, it must be lower than in the first. Tversky and Kahneman (1974) briefly discuss the example of pilot training to illustrate the practical importance of this phenomenon. When pilots do a particularly poor landing they are reprimanded and then tend to land better the next time. When pilots do a particularly good landing they are praised and then tend to land

(margin handwritten note: good example of regression to the mean)

worse the next time. It would be tempting to conclude that praise is harmful and reprimand beneficial. But using the warrant principle (Chapter Four), if this were not true how else can we explain the pattern? It could just be that within normal variation a particularly bad landing will more often be followed by a better one next time, and *vice versa*. This would be regression to the mean. Attributing the change over time to the use of praise or criticism could be dangerously misleading. Jerrim and Vignoles (2011) present evidence of a similar phenomenon complicating their analysis of the social mobility of high ability children from poor homes.

There are many other problems and limitations in time-based work, most notably perhaps concomitant changes in society and an increased chance of participant dropout. Some of the birth cohort studies can identify risk factors, such as those for adult unemployment, but only for a past era that has long gone. For example, the UK NCDS started in 1958 and may now be used to suggest possible reasons why people aged 50+ become unemployed, but the reasons are grounded in events and the context of the past 50 years. There is no way of knowing that the risks will be the same nowadays or in the future. This is a problem because such studies are very costly to discover something that is largely of historical significance. Because they are costly they are used to cover a wide range of topics, giving them a lack of focus perhaps. At the outset, the designers try to imagine what the issues will be for the future, and so use suitable questions with the first wave. But there is no real way of doing this. How could the designers in 1958 know that the word 'mannequin' would almost entirely disappear from use, but that ICT and social networking would become terms in common use instead? What seemed like the key issues in 1958 might turn out not to have been key issues at all. Questions have to be re-phrased to suit a newer vernacular, and this limits comparability between responses to questions over time (even though this was part of the reason for doing such a study in the first place!). Unexpected issues arise for which the research foundation has not been laid (such as the role of the internet, or the impact of AIDS), and early design errors can never be undone. Being in a longitudinal study is a life-time commitment. This may influence both the kinds of people who stay with the study and their behaviour.

Just as importantly, the longer a study goes on and the longer the gaps between events, the greater the non-response is of those cases involved initially (dropout). Dropout is a huge problem for cohort and panel studies because it is not random. The earliest UK birth cohort studies have lost about 4,000 to 5,000 of the original 16,000 respondents. This is pretty good and represents considerable effort on the part of the researchers involved, but the dropout is still inevitable and huge. Some very influential studies have ignored such dropout and come to erroneous conclusions, about social mobility for example (Gorard 2008a).

One way in which longitudinal datasets ought to be useful is to contribute to an important debate in psychology about the relevance of things like motivation, intention and aspiration for later life events. On the one hand, a number of authors have used limited designs but with increasingly complex *post hoc* modelling to suggest that such psychological factors are the causes of later events, such as academic achievement or job success (Marsh 1990; Green et al. 2006). On the other hand, longitudinal designs have suggested that the link between prior psychological reports and later decisions is weak, and far weaker than many people imagine. For example, de Groot et al. (2011) found that real-life events intervened and prevented a solid link from intentions to actions. People might have to move house because of an unplanned end to a relationship, such as a divorce, or might not be able to move house as planned, because of an unplanned loss of income perhaps from being made redundant. Even in those situations where constructs such as attitudes and preferences correlate highly with something explicit (a later behaviour for example) there is a danger of tautology (Gorard et al. 2011).

In most studies, predictions from psychological events are not literally 'predictions' at all, because the research calculations are done after the occurrence of the events they are meant to be predicting. Unfortunately, the term 'prediction' is used in social research involving statistics in a somewhat different way than in science or the vernacular. Predicting the arrival of a comet or the winner of a race must be done beforehand in order to be a true prediction (Gorard 2011). Parcelling out the variation in a set of already established outcomes cannot be prediction in the sense needed to demonstrate this important step in a causal model (remember the stage magician in Chapter Seven?).

Further, it is not clear that even those studies claiming to be able to 'predict' retrospectively, as it were, are correct in their claims. One such study is by Croll (2009, p.400), who says of his use of data from prior years of the Youth Survey from the British Household Panel Survey, 'The results show that most children can express intentions with regard to future participation very early in their secondary school careers and that these intentions are good predictors of actual behaviour five years later', and that 'The results show the value of focusing on intentions for participation at a very early stage of children's school careers…'. But the evidence presented does not match these claims. For example, 52% of 11-year-olds said they wanted to stay on and eventually did so, while 7% of 11-year-olds said they did not want to stay on and eventually did not stay on. Overall then, only 59% of Year 7 pupils acted out their previously-reported intentions at age 16. Of the remainder, 22% at age 11 did not know whether they wanted to stay on or not when aged 16, and 19% did the opposite at age 16 to what they reported aspiring to at age 11. Put simply, a gambler betting who would stay on using only pupils' expressed intentions at age 11 would be right 59% of the time. But because so many pupils did stay on in fact (72%), this gambler would lose heavily to another gambler who simply bet that all and any pupils would stay on. The latter would be correct 72% of the time. Knowing the expressed intentions actually makes any prediction of the future less accurate than not knowing it, and this means that Croll (2009) is inadvertently quite wrong to say that intentions are good predictors of actual behaviour here. Something more than a sequence is needed, and that is the subject of Chapter Nine.

⇌ Exercises on timing

1   You read an article in a social science journal showing how a small early investment in overcoming personal poverty leads to significant impact on the chances of poverty in later life. The researchers have evaluated a programme to provide pocket money to children and young adults from the poorest 5% of families in one area. By age 16, the families of well over a third of these young people are no longer among the poorest 5% in that area. In fact, a few families are now among the richest 50%. This is an impressive result for what amounts to a very small investment, and in their paper the researchers call for their programme to be rolled out across the country.

 a   What is the key logical error being made by the researchers here?
 b   Using the warrant principle, if their conclusion was actually incorrect then how else can you explain their dramatic findings?

2   You have just read three studies on the same topic. They each investigated the extent to which individuals' job or career episodes have been getting shorter since 1950. The first study contacted a large number of school leavers in 1950, signed them up for a longitudinal cohort study, and then contacted them every decade until 2000. Among other things, the researchers noted any job changes or change in status from employed to unemployed. They found that after some initial volatility, people reported reasonably stable periods of employment but that these periods got progressively shorter over time. The second study contacted individuals who were aged 30–34 in 1960, 1970, 1980, 1990 and 2000 respectively. These researchers found that reported periods in the same employment remained about the same across the decades. The third study took place in 2001, and asked respondents aged 65+ to report their periods of employment back to 1950. This study found that periods of employment grew longer over time. So the three studies drew very different conclusions about an important issue for employability and career management.

 a   How is this possible? From what you know, suggest one way in which each design could be superior to the others, and one way in which each design could be inferior.
 b   Which study is correct?

3   We have nearly finished discussing the separate elements of research design in this book, and a lot has been said about time and the sequence of events. Time is certainly important. But then so is place or location. Consider why place is important in social science, and why it is not traditionally considered to be an element of research design along with time. Perhaps discuss this in a seminar group or similar.

⇌ Notes on exercises on timing

1   a   The key logical error in this claim is known as *post hoc ergo propter hoc*, literally meaning – after this so because of this. We have no idea what would have happened if the pocket money intervention had not taken place. More formally, we could say that the result has no 'counterfactual'. This would be a very unsafe result to use as the basis for rolling out the intervention more widely, assuming that this was the only evidence available and the only reason for doing so.

b   If the giving of pocket money was not effective, then plenty of other reasons are available to explain the lifting of so many families out of poverty. One is regression to the mean. The poorest 5% have less 'room' to become poorer over time, but plenty of room to become less poor. Those in the middle of the income distribution can become poorer (or richer). Thus, it is perfectly possible that this change would have happened over time anyway. Without a comparator group not receiving the pocket money, we do not know whether the intervention was effective or not. Chapter Seven established that a comparison alone was not enough. This chapter has shown that a change over time is not enough. The solution, of course, lies partly in using both, as illustrated in Chapter Nine.

2   a   I hope you can see that such a set of three studies is perfectly possible. Even studies with the same design find different things and come to opposing conclusions. This variability is part of the justification given for meta-analyses (Chapter Three). Here though there may be more than mere idiosyncrasy in play. Perhaps most obviously, the second study is answering a very different research question to the other two. Remember the two dimensions of time? The second is repeated cross-sectional, and looks at whether successive age cohorts have different lengths of spells of employment. It is largely about history. This history is also relevant to the first and third studies, but these are primarily about changes in employment patterns over the life-course of each individual. So, it is perfectly feasible for there to be genuinely little change over historical time – and 30–34-year-olds can expect about the same length job spell in any decade. And it is feasible for this to be coupled with either a decrease or increase in the length of these spells as they themselves get older. Put another way, it could be a biographical and not a historical pattern. A common problem with longitudinal designs like the first study is that cases tend to drop out over time. It could well be that the people with the most unstable lives were also the most likely to drop out of the study. This could be enough to bias the results, and give the appearance of longer employment spells over time. But this is not what was found. A common problem with a retrospective longitudinal design like the third study is that people are reliant on imperfect memories to a greater extent. Perhaps it is easier to recall longer periods of employment, and this was enough to bias the findings. We do not know. I hope you can think of other issues affecting the interpretation of both studies.

   b   I also hope that you did not propose a definitive answer to the question 'Which study is correct?' We do not know. Using ideas about the relative merits of the designs, we can offer an opinion, and a justification for that opinion. Given what I said above, maybe the prospective longitudinal study is the more trustworthy. But this does not mean that retrospective studies do not have an important role. Sometimes they are all we have. Perhaps we should look at the scale, non-response, measurement qualities and other issues before deciding. The level of dropout from the longitudinal study could be a determining factor in which study we prefer.

3   Place or location can be a key part of understanding how and why things happen. It could be the physical geography, with valleys making lateral communication between settlements difficult. It could be the population density, the nature of local investment and employment opportunities, or the availability of resources from water to oil. A coastal area has very different features to an inland plain, both structurally and probably in the kinds of people living or arriving there. Patterns of migration and in-migration are fascinating and crucial topics for social science. Place matters (Selwyn et al. 2006). I am not entirely sure why place is not itself an element in traditional design resources, and has no symbols in design notation. The meaning of place is partly

covered by sub-groups, I suppose. These groups could be cases in different regions, for example, such as a comparison of unemployment rates in the north and south. But perhaps also many designs are intended to be unspecific as to place. If a policy works it should work in all areas, seems to be the idea. But this idea is often wrong (Gorard et al. 2003). In some studies, the role of place is paramount and should be represented as such. Perhaps we need a third dimension in design notation, with time across the page, groups going down, and the places for these groups and timed events going 'into' the page.

⇌ Suggested reading

Chapter Six in Gomm, R. (2004) *Social Research Methodology: A Critical Introduction.* Basingstoke: Palgrave Macmillan.

NINE

Evaluating controlled interventions

SUMMARY

- An active research design involves an intervention or treatment, usually delivered to only some sub-groups. The sub-groups not receiving the intervention are used as the 'counterfactual'.
- In a true experiment the intervention itself is at least partly under the control of the researchers. Control is greatest in laboratory settings, most commonly used in psychology.
- Field trials and naturalistic experiments cede some control in exchange for greater realism and external validity. Natural experiments cede even more control, and are dealt with in Chapter Ten.
- A post-test only experiment with two groups allocated at random is a simple powerful design.
- Adding a pre-test allows researchers to compare gain scores between groups. This allows for slight variation in the initial scores between groups, but it introduces further complications (Chapter Eleven).
- Generally, experimental trials are powerful, relatively inexpensive, easy to conduct, and make subsequent analysis simpler. Despite some claims to the contrary they present few specific ethical concerns.
- Nevertheless, if they are done, then they are best done well. Planning an ideal study and then compromising on that ideal where necessary is a good way of promoting ambition and rigour in research.
- Consideration of stepped-wedge designs, crossover trials, and intention-to-treat analysis might improve evaluations in realistic settings.
- Even more importantly, an experimental design works best with clear outcome measures coupled with in-depth observation of fidelity to the treatment.
- A treatment can have a clear impact on those not in the treatment group, and this kind of unintended consequence is an important factor to consider in the results.

9.1 ▮▮ Introduction to active research designs

Just as research can involve comparisons or not, and can take place in a sequence of time or not, research can involve a specific intervention or not. An intervention is a deliberate change in circumstance that could influence an outcome of interest. A new law on gambling might be the intervention, and a reduction in the number of people with gambling addictions might be the outcome of interest. A new official form for collecting employment records might be the intervention, and a faster service time for clients might be the outcome of interest. A research design without such an intervention would be considered 'passive' rather than active. The birth cohort studies described in Chapter Eight are all passive, in that they involve following a large group through their lives and taking repeated measures, creating any counterfactuals (groups who did and did not experience an event) after the event. This is a good way of uncovering possible causes, but a weak way of assessing causal models. It is preferable when dealing with causal questions to create two homogeneous groups at the outset, vary the potential cause differently for the two groups and then measure the outcome of interest (Chapter Five). This would be an 'active' design or experiment, and a 'controlled' trial, or a randomised controlled trial where the groups are randomised to treatments at the outset. The 'control' or comparator group is the counterfactual, and it is this that defines the effect for the treatment group, by allowing us to estimate what would have happened to them otherwise (Shadish et al. 2002). If we could somehow give each case the treatment and not the treatment as well then each case could provide its own counterfactual. But this is seldom possible in social science. Similarly, if all cases responded to the treatment in the same way then we would not need so many cases, of course. But again this is rare in social science.

The study could take place in a laboratory to achieve the greatest control of the environment, and strong internal validity (Chapter Eleven), or alternatively in a field setting to provide more realism. A field experiment or trial might involve giving a group of accountants extra help in identifying tax evasion, or setting a group of students more homework. Either of these would be a naturalistic field experiment, similar to a laboratory set-up since the experimenter intervenes with a treatment but in a real setting (Bernard 2000). Or you may want to evaluate, in the most rigorous way, an intervention that is happening anyway – the effect of increasing population density on the transport system, or the effect of ageing on short-term memory perhaps. Here the intervention would be uncontrolled, and designs appropriate for these non-manipulated interventions or natural experiments are dealt with more fully in Chapter Ten. Finally, trials can be used primarily for testing and developing causal theories, as has been common for some time in psychology (Festinger and Carlsmith 1959), or to evaluate the effectiveness of interventions. Note that some methods resources, and some examples here, refer to the counterfactual as a group for whom the intervention is withheld. But the comparison does not have to be between an intervention being totally present or absent. The intervention can also be varied in strength between the groups to see what effect this has on the designated outcomes. Despite these differences of purpose and setting, the underlying design for all of these evaluations of controlled interventions is very similar.

9.2 ₪ Two common experimental designs

To create an experimental or quasi-experimental design, an intervention can simply be added to any of the designs discussed in the book so far. In fact, several of the examples have involved interventions. The basic cross-sectional design looks like this:

N   O

N   O

where two naturally occurring groups (N) are compared in terms of an observation or measure (O). If these were heterogeneous, or non-equivalent, groups, like recent in-migrants compared to locally born people in a region, then a natural intervention (X) like an economic recession could affect both:

N   [X]   O

N   [X]   O

This design might provide some idea of whether the recession was differentially problematic for in-migrants, for example. But it would be an extension of the before-and-after design in Chapter Eight with all of the same limitations and problems, like regression towards the mean. This would be true even if the design was a true comparative before-and-after, like:

N   O   [X]   O

N   O   [X]   O

What the design really needs is a counterfactual group, for whom the recession did not take place, or where the recession was either weaker or stronger. This could be:

N   O   [X]   O

N   O   [X]   O

N   O   O

However, while more complex and expensive to run, this design does not really solve the problem because the groups are still unmatched. The third group might have differed in some way anyway, or been subject to some other influence, and this could explain any difference in outcome. Perhaps we need to look at in-migrants and others, both in the recession area and elsewhere. This is now four groups. But even so, there may be differences between the areas other than the recession. Also the type, relevance and meaning of being an in-migrant may vary between the areas. The intrinsic problem here is that the intervention is uncontrolled. Uncontrolled interventions like this are often among the most important to understand for social scientists, and so the issue of how to evaluate them is a focus for Chapter Ten.

Another way of envisaging the basic cross-sectional design is where the groups are intended to be homogeneous (random, matched or using a cut-off), such as:

R   O

R   O

A controlled intervention could be added to this basic design to give:

R   X   O

R   O

This is the format of the classic post-test only experiment, in which two similar randomised groups are tested or measured for an outcome after only one group has received the intervention. As illustrated in this chapter, there are many variations on this standard and powerful basic design.

Coming at it another way, the basic longitudinal design looks like this:

R   O   O

where two or more episodes of data collection take place over a considerable elapsed time period for one group (here for a random sample). This is a descriptive or exploratory approach, and it is passive. As with the basic comparative design, it can be strengthened by the addition of a manipulated intervention if the research is causal in nature, to give:

R   O   X   O

This is, again, a before-and-after design with all of the limitations and problems that ensue. We could never know whether a difference between the first and second observations was caused by the intervention, or whether it was caused by something else, or would have happened anyway. Again, we need a counterfactual to help test this. So we add an appropriate comparator group not subject to the intervention, to create:

R   O   X   O

R   O   O

This is the format of the classic pre- and post-test experiment, in which two similar randomised groups are tested for an outcome both before and after only one group has received the intervention. Here the outcome of interest would be the difference in the change between the pre- and post-tests scores for each group. This chapter considers such powerful designs that combine *all* of the elements of design in one study (allocation, comparison, sequence and intervention).

A simple example

Experimental designs do not have to be complicated, nor large-scale. A useful and informative study of an existing intervention could be conducted during a one-year full-time masters course, while a more elaborate study with a pre-pilot is easily possible for a part-time student or doctoral researcher. See, for example, the trial in one school by Smith and Gorard (2005). This is nothing like a definitive trial. It is a small piece of work done at the request of one school, but it illustrates how easy it is to 'piggy-back' an evaluation onto an intervention that is going to take place anyway (so eliminating many resource and ethical issues). It involves a 'process evaluation' which allows the researchers to understand something about how the intervention was introduced (and which incidentally shows how experiments, like all designs, are independent of the increasingly ridiculous 'qualitative' and 'quantitative' terms). The study involved a school which was enthusiastic and eager to take part; in fact it was the school's idea and conducted at their request. This shows, in line with my experience, that trials are not that hard to organise, although just like any other form of research, they can only generally be conducted with the 'willing'.

The school was planning to implement a new method for providing feedback to their pupils. They planned to cease providing summative marks and grades for assessed schoolwork, and instead focus exclusively on formative feedback, both immediate and in the short to medium-term. This intervention was based on assessment for learning, as promoted by 'Inside the Black box' (Black and Wiliam 2003). Indeed, it was an in-service training course on formative assessment techniques by the authors of that pamphlet which prompted the experimental evaluation. The success of formative assessment techniques in raising the achievement of students has been demonstrated by research suggesting an effect size of between 0.4 and 0.7. Rather than introduce the practice across the entire school, the school wanted to pilot it in one year-group, parallel to a wider series of staff training sessions, to find out what difference the intervention made in terms of pupil progress towards Key Stage 3 (up to age 14), and to understand how the pupils reacted to the changed form of assessment. The researchers wanted to see what happens when complex interventions move from a research setting inhabited by pioneers and enthusiasts to wider practice (Smith and Gorard 2005).

The school's Year 7 (12-year-olds) consisted of four mixed ability teaching groups with 26 pupils each. They were judged 'mixed ability' on the basis of prior attainment, teacher recommendation from primary school, and friendship group-ings. One group was chosen randomly for the pilot intervention, and the other three formed the control group. Note that, contrary to common practice, the treat-ment and control groups do not have to be equal or even near equal in size. Up to a certain limit (perhaps three times as many, as in this example) adding cases to the control adds to the overall power of the study. It is usually the control that is larger, because this adds power for so little research cost. There is no extra work on the intervention, and so no need to check fidelity to treatment for all control cases, and where the outcome measure is generated as a matter of course (like Key Stage 3 assessments in a school) there may be no extra expense involved at all. If the intervention effect size were 0.5 of a standard deviation or more, then an indi-vidual sample size of 100 is indicated assuming we want 80% chance of detecting the effect at 5% significance level. Because the pupils are clustered, this suggests that the sample size of 104 is probably underpowered, especially with only 26 cases in the treatment arm (for more on what this means, and why it may not matter, see Chapter Twelve). As will be seen, it is probably irrelevant here anyway.

The staff involved in teaching the treatment group were given appropriate in-house training, cascaded from the training given to the school leaders by the creators of the intervention. The treatment group did not receive any summative marks or grades for any work at all for one year (even where these were gener-ated for other purposes). Instead, their teachers agreed to provide more careful, individual formative feedback of the kind that makes the assessment process also a learning process. The data collected included prior Key Stage 2 teacher assess-ments and test levels in the core subjects, as well as scores on standardised tests such as the Cognitive Ability Test (CAT) and Progress in English (PiE). The school provided a list of the pupils eligible for and taking free school meals, a standard measure of poverty. A questionnaire was administered to all groups with 100% response rate, covering pupil motivation, attitudes towards school, and a range of family background variables. This data formed a context for linear regression mod-elling of the outcomes. The groups were well matched in all respects at the outset. The chief outcomes were year-end pupil National Curriculum levels awarded by the class teachers on the basis of assessments undertaken throughout the school year. Small group interviews were carried out with pupils in the treatment group, to gain an understanding of their experiences of this intervention. In standard notation the design looked like this:

```
N        O        X        O

N        O                 O
```

I have used 'N' here because although the treatment class was selected randomly as a unit, the number of clusters is too small to be considered a true cluster-randomised trial. And the classes were those naturally created by the school without concern for this study.

Surprisingly, the control group had better end-of-year scores in English and Maths, and equivalent scores in Science. Given that there was little in the prior background or prior attainment of the two groups to explain these differences, the control group also made greater value-added progress over the year. A similar pattern was present for the other nine subjects assessed (Smith and Gorard 2005). In fact, almost all of the really high-scoring pupils were in the control group. What went wrong?

It is not likely that the sample size is a problem here, since the difference in favour of the standard approach to giving feedback is so clear (i.e. it is not that the study just missed out on finding the worth of the intervention). The result is not due to a pre-existing difference between the groups, at least not in terms of the known values. There could easily have been some contamination (diffusion) because some teachers taught both the intervention group and others, and they may have deliberately or inadvertently used their formative assessment training with the control classes. But this could not explain the higher attainment of the control group. The pupils certainly did not like the formative assessment, as it was implemented. The majority felt that the teacher comments did not provide them with sufficient information so that they would know how to improve:

'I don't like it when we just have comments. I'd rather marks because you don't know how to beat your score. And I probably end up doing worse than what I am if I have my mark.'

'Well sometimes when you have marks, you have comments anyway. I would rather have both of them.'

'I think that, like, you put all your effort in, like, to write a story and then all you do is get told, like, "oh very good", miss. But if you have marks then you know how good you really did.'

The in-depth work, therefore, suggests that the intervention was implemented poorly by at least some teachers, amounting to little more than the removal of marks from assessed work. Some of the 'formative' comments may have been no more than would traditionally have been given as an adjunct to a mark or grade. The desire of many pupils to receive marks was such that several admitted to trying to work them out. This was particularly so in subjects like maths and languages where pupils admitted to adding up correct spellings in vocabulary tests, for example, in order to work out what marks they had received. In the words of one of their teachers: 'they were gagging for their marks'.

The feasibility of trials

This small study is far from definitive, yet it led to a peer-reviewed article, citations, and a fair amount of debate and press coverage. It could have been done as a one-year student project, and it cost almost nothing to conduct. I think its value lies in giving us an indication of what can happen when a successful scheme is 'rolled out' into wider practice, with perhaps less than committed users. It is quite common for interventions to work better in the pioneering study than in more general practice. This is for a variety of reasons – experimenter and Hawthorne effects, regression towards the mean, motivational factors, and misunderstandings (Chapter Eleven).

Small trials are not expensive because they generally involve no more field work than any other dissertation project. The interventions themselves can be expensive, but these do not have to be funded by the researcher. This distinction, between the cost and challenges of the intervention, and the cost of the evaluation, is crucial in realising how practical it is to run a trial design. There are a large number of interventions waiting to be tested properly in practice, and a plethora of untested interventions already taking place every year in public policy. Causal questions have a special importance in policy research because policy-makers are elected to make informed decisions. In many areas of public policy however, that causal knowledge is inadequate or simply missing. The lack of rigorous evaluations means that policy-making in many areas is not informed by suitable evidence. Relatively few trials have been conducted in any social science area, for example, yet these should be an important part of our safety checking (Torgerson and Torgerson 2008).

9.3 ▌▎ A cluster randomised controlled trial

A somewhat larger study, a true cluster randomised controlled trial (RCT) of the use of a piece of commercial software for the acquisition of reading skills, still took less than one year to complete (Khan and Gorard 2012). And although perfectly feasible for a doctoral or new researcher to conduct with minimal funding, it was at the time the largest trial on this topic in the UK. RCTs are rather easy to conduct, yet make a powerful piece of research with easily warranted conclusions, due to the initial well-established prior design.

A new piece of commercial software, claimed by the publisher to be effective in improving children's reading after just six weeks of classroom use, was compared with standard literacy teaching. Pupil literacy was assessed before and after the trial, via another piece of commercial software testing precisely the kinds of skills covered by the pedagogical software. The sample consisted of nine state-maintained secondary schools that agreed to co-operate with the research, and possessed a minimum level of technology and support, as agreed with the software publishers. The entire Year 7 (grade 6) pupil cohort in each school, 31 classes, was asked to take part. Eight classes had to be dropped because one or both parents withheld permission. The remaining 23 classes had 672 pupils, but seven pupils left naturally before testing, leaving 665 pupils aged 11 and 12. The classes were randomised to treatment (software) or control. The treatment and control groups were very similar in size, and on observed characteristics. Power calculations suggest that this sample is more than adequate to detect a difference in favour of the treatment group of 0.3 standard deviations or more (Chapter Twelve). Both groups were given a computerised pre-test of their existing literacy levels in the first week, and an equivalent post-test after ten weeks. The items tested were directly linked to the material covered in the treatment software activities. The process evaluation and evidence on fidelity to treatment was collected via teacher logs, computer logs of pupil activity, researcher observation, and interviews. The outline design looks like this:

R   O   X   O

R   O   O

At the outset of the trial, the pre-test scores showed that both groups had similar standardised mean scores in literacy. After 10 weeks of software use in literacy lessons the treatment group improved their standardised mean score substantially, just as the software publishers had claimed (Table 9.1). In fact, both the treatment group and the comparison group improved their tested literacy. However, the comparison group improved their literacy scores considerably more than the treatment group, with an overall 'effect' size of −0.37, suggesting that the software approach yields no relative advantage, and may even disadvantage pupils. Therefore, a simple before-and-after design with no control could easily, but falsely, have concluded that the use of commercial software was an especially effective approach to literacy teaching and learning. This illustrates again the danger of conclusions drawn from what constitutes the majority of published work, conducted without suitable comparators.

There is no *prima facie* case here that the improvement for the treatment group was due to the software used. In fact, it would be easier to mount an argument that pupils using the software were disadvantaged. The software package was ineffective in comparison to standard practice. This is an important conclusion, with some wider implications than might first be imagined. The use of software, of a kind that is in very common use across schools in England, was a waste of resource. This could be an important corrective finding for an area of schooling

Table 9.1 Literacy scores for treatment and control groups

Group	Pre-test mean	Post-test mean	Gain score
Treatment	823	863	40
Control	817	886	70

N=665

that has been the focus of intense policy and practice attention. Of course, the actual software used has now been superseded. But there are implications for the use of such software to teach literacy more widely, for the way in which publisher claims are worded, and for the research community in relation to the feasibility of conducting pragmatic trials in school settings. Intriguingly also, the in-depth data collected routinely as part of the trial suggested a high level of widespread satisfaction with the treatment for both teachers and pupils. They believed that it offered a reliable way to help pupils improve their reading skills. All teachers indicated that they would use the same or similar software in the future, and almost all of them said that they would recommend it to other teachers. This shows the very real dangers of relying on studies of perceptions like this for outcome evaluation. Most of the work in social science currently labelled 'qualitative' has this considerable flaw.

Many educational programs have in-built assessment and record-keeping applications. Software publishers then make their marketing research claims based on these records. The problem is that in most of the cases these findings are not based on a comparison with anything else. So, for example, software publishers' claims about the effectiveness of their product should be tempered by a caution that no suitable comparator was used, or perhaps all such claims should only be allowed by advertising standards when a suitable comparator has been used. Otherwise, teachers and educational authorities are in danger of being duped by a claim that is the same in real terms as the kind that is rightly banned in the medical literature. More generally, the results of this study add to the body of research that raises concerns about the effectiveness of technology-based instruction. Given that computers and associated software impose a cost, are frequently updated, and are in widespread use in schools, it is important to have evidence of their impact. The expenditure on ICT may have an impact but not proportionate to the costs. It may have no impact and so be a cost with no benefits. And it may even have deleterious impacts as here. Untested educational initiatives can frequently be harmful for children (Boruch et al. 2002). Rigorous intervention studies with suitable controls have found little or no positive impact from the use of technology-based instruction compared to standard or traditional practice. A number of studies and systematic reviews have found that software packages had no effect on reading or other achievement (Dynarski et al. 2007).

But in isolation such studies do not reveal the true scale of wasted opportunities and possible harm done. In general, marketing teams in the UK offer software to schools on a trial basis. During the trial they show how pupils are making progress by using the in-built assessment process (without an appropriate comparator). Teachers can then see pupil progress over learning activities and may be persuaded to purchase. Once teachers have bought the software they tend to use the convenient in-built assessment process regularly. This makes all those involved part of a reinforcing cycle. The software publishers make money. Teachers have a record of progress made by pupils, for their own and others' satisfaction. Pupils generally enjoy working on computers and playing with different technology applications. Parents will be pleased to see a record of their child's progress. Local and national government is content that their funding of technology initiatives is justified, and schools are persuaded to spend that funding on technology products, making money for the companies to develop new products. It seems that everybody wins, but perhaps actually everybody loses. This is how important robust research design is. Design is our protection against being misled like this by poor evaluation, inflated marketing claims, and the endemic but largely futile research about 'perceptions'.

9.4 ▮▮ Practicalities of experiments

Even larger and more rigorous trials have been undertaken in the social sciences, successfully and with potentially very important results. For example, trials have suggested that psychotherapeutic interventions among men who abuse their partners are largely ineffective (Babcock et al. 2004), community based advocacy programmes for abused women are modestly effective (Sullivan and Bybee 1999), cognitive-behavioural training significantly increases the employment prospects of the long-term unemployed (Proudfoot et al. 1997), and free provision of daycare facilities increases participation in work by mothers (Toroyan et al. 2003). It is possible to undertake large RCTs that are relevant both to policy and practice in almost any setting or field.

The research fieldwork involved in a trial is no greater than for many other designs and so the cost is heavily dependent on the nature and quantity of data collected. In real-world settings, a lot of the data may be collected automatically anyway – re-offending rates, hospital clear-up rates, school qualifications, inspection results and so on. Of course, an intervention can be very costly but this cost is often not usually borne by the researchers. Interventions take place all of the time in all countries and all fields of public policy. Evaluating them properly would cost little more, and could save so much in terms of identifying wasteful and even harmful interventions.

An experimental design is intended to assess the impact of the treatment on the treated by comparing them to the matched group(s) of untreated. This impact will be the same as the average impact of the treatment for the population of both groups, if the groups are otherwise identical. Thus, making the groups identical (or as near as possible) by having them large and randomised, is a more ethical way of uncovering the average effect for the population than using the entire population (and so exposing more cases to possible risk). It is also more ethical to find out whether interventions work and have side-effects before rolling them out in an uncontrolled way. Monitoring them scrupulously to learn the most from these interventions adds very little, proportionately, to their cost.

In the interventions that do occur, it is routine to pilot them or try them out in selected units or areas before rollout. This means that some cases are knowingly excluded from the new treatment from the outset. Such partial coverage happens routinely with no ethical objection, until or unless someone suggests that the pilot and rollout should be systematic. For some reason, selecting cases at random, so that the impact of the intervention can be safely estimated, is considered unethical. Selecting cases on an *ad hoc* basis, so that the impact of the intervention is confounded with problems of unmatched treatment and control groups, is somehow preferred. This is nonsense. A trial should only be conducted or proposed when there is equipoise. This means that if we know that the treatment does or does not work then a trial is not needed. If we have no idea whether it works then a trial would be inappropriate. A smaller pilot or exploratory study should be preferred instead (Chapter Two). So, a trial should only take place when the intervention shows promise but its effect is not certain. In this situation of equipoise, it cannot be deemed unethical to deny the treatment to the control group. Of course, if it becomes clear during the trial that harm is befalling one or more groups, then the trial must cease. And this is more likely to be noticed if the intervention is being evaluated rigorously.

Unfortunately, for researchers, there is often pressure to implement a public policy intervention with all potential participants, leaving us with no feasible comparator. However, such policies or changes in practice are often constrained to be rolled out over a prolonged period of time due to limited resources/expertise. Instead of rolling out in an *ad hoc* manner, an excellent alternative is to implement the changes in a controlled rolling programme, with units or areas receiving the intervention in a random order. This is sometimes called the 'stepped wedge design'. Then all areas are re-tested as each new wave of interventions occurs. The difference in scores correlated with the absence or maturity of the intervention in that unit can provide a good estimate of the overall impact of the change. It does have the added cost that all areas or units need to provide a pre-test score or observation, but it is otherwise a good alternative to randomisation.

Another way of ensuring that an intervention can be evaluated while not denying the treatment to all cases is to use a 'waiting-list' design. Here, every case is offered the treatment or intervention, but each will be randomly allocated to receive it straight away or after a delay. It is important to sign up all cases which accept this condition at the outset before the allocation is made to groups. In the literacy software trial above, all participating schools were offered the software and training as long as they agreed to wait a term if selected to do so. The same analysis of progress after ten weeks was still possible, but no group is favoured long term by receiving a treatment at the expense of the other. However, the results of that trial make the point quite clearly that we must not assume that denial of the treatment is always or ever a bad thing. The waiting list design is ethical and easy to use. It has two possible drawbacks. It limits the length of time that we have to compare the effect of treatment versus non-treatment. For example, in a smoking cessation trial, an outcome of interest would be levels of smoking several years later. This becomes a problem if both groups have received the intervention by then. The extended time also means that there may be more opportunities for contamination/diffusion and dropout (Chapter Eleven).

An even simpler idea is a crossover trial design. Where the treatment is not a one-off thing (an example would be an ongoing course of medicine such as blood pressure pills), then one group can receive the treatment and the other group a fake or placebo treatment. Then the groups can be reversed for the same time period. In this way, both groups receive the treatment equally but it is still possible, as with the stepped wedge design, to calculate the impact of the genuine intervention. The biggest limitation here is developing a social science intervention that has the same characteristics as a drug regime to contain a chronic medical condition. An incentive payment scheme (for attending job interviews or training perhaps) has the characteristic of being ongoing. But it is hard to envisage a placebo for it. Perhaps all participants could be told that they would receive a random amount of incentive payment, including nothing. Then half could be randomised to receive nothing or considerably less than average for the first period of the study. Another variant is to run two trials at once, with each treatment group acting as the control for the other trial. Of course, this means finding two interventions that are unlikely to interact or interfere with each other in any way. But the design does have the benefit for morale and recruitment that *all* cases are deemed treatment cases. A condition of receiving the treatment in one trial is being a control for the other one. Experiments are genuinely feasible, perhaps limited only by our ingenuity in overcoming potential barriers.

9.5 ╎╎ Conducting good experiments

If experiments are to be conducted then it is important not to waste the opportunity. They ought to be as high quality as possible. How do we achieve this? Perhaps the best place to start is with an ideal study. If all we were concerned with was how to answer a causal research question then how would we plan our study? Having planned, we can then consider the barriers we face in conducting this ideal study, and either solve the problems and make compromises or decide that the study is not possible. Either way the result will likely be better than starting with a compromise, because we will either be more daring and ambitious, or we will not undertake pointless research that could not possibly answer the research question (all too common I am afraid).

Clearly, given the condition of equipoise (above), we will want the study to be as large as possible. The larger it is the more secure the findings will be, all other things being equal. However, we may have concerns about exposing too many cases to any unknown side-effects of the intervention, or we may have to limit the scale of the intervention for resource reasons. In this situation, where the cost is clearly greater for one group than another, we can increase the size of the other group. For example, if we are concerned about the side-effects of the intervention, that puts no restriction on the size of the control group. Similarly, if the intervention is quite costly we can increase the size of the study at little cost by increasing the control group. This increase in size will increase the 'power' of the study even though the extra cases play no part other than by providing a more robust counterfactual.

However many cases are in the trial, there is usually some drop out, where cases change their mind, or people move districts. In some examples, such as cluster randomised controlled trials, it is even possible for cases to change legitimately from the experimental to the control group, or *vice versa*. A patient may change doctors on clinical grounds, or a child may change schools, for example. Where they do, it is worth trying to follow them up even if only to provide data for the post-test. You could include them in the analysis, which then becomes an 'intention to treat' analysis. You have to decide what it is precisely that you are testing. Pragmatically, you could say that you are testing only the impact of the *availability* of the intervention. In real-life, after rollout, people will change schools and doctors etc., and so the most realistic estimate of the impact could be in terms of which group the cases were initially intended to be in. If you can get data on the drop out cases, it is therefore worth including them in the analysis even if they did not receive the correct, or indeed any, treatment.

A similar idea concerns fidelity to treatment. Cases can ignore, subvert or abuse an intervention being evaluated, but then they could also do the same once it has been rolled out into wider practice. Treating such problems as part of the intervention in real-life provides a more realistic assessment than trying to tidy everything away (see exercises below). This is important and economic, since some interventions have been found to work well in efficacy trials, delivered by enthusiastic users with ample resources (see Smith and Gorard 2005 above). Yet they can be ineffective when implemented more widely, and the researchers have not necessarily known why (Fukkink 2002). The pragmatic approach sacrifices some standardisation for realism, and means that the natural variability in delivery that occurs between practitioners/users must be recorded and monitored by in-depth means as well as by more traditional outcome measures (Campbell et al. 2000). Trials are most likely to be successful if they involve both an outcome which is the average effect of intervention, and in-depth observation showing how this effect occurs (the process evaluation). This enhances transportability at little cost to causal claims since what is being tested is a template (intention to treat), while the in-depth data provides evidence on fidelity to treatment, so enhancing explanation. And without in-depth data drawn from the same study, it is not clear what can be learnt from an unsuccessful intervention (other than that it does not work). Evaluations are most likely to be fruitful if they involve both observation and measurement.

It is also important that the intervention itself is mature and clear, with a distinct possibility of success. This means that it should have been developed over a series of prior phases such as pilot and feasibility studies (Chapter Two). It should have been implemented in full, at least at small scale, and tested for acceptability to providers and the target audience. This will also provide an estimate of its effect size before a full and more definitive trial, and test the trial procedures, such as the definition of the alternative treatment. The precise outcome measures or criteria for success and failure must be spelt out in advance. This is much more convincing (the stage magician again!). Some well-conducted evaluations have looked at the impact of flawed interventions that could never work, or would be of no value or too costly, or that would never be adopted by practitioners, making them unethical and a waste of effort. A well-conducted trial of a poor intervention cannot overcome such problems.

9.6 ‖ Conclusion

There are many further designs for experiments, perhaps most notably the factorial designs, allowing more than several interventions at once, and interactions between them (Edwards 1972). But they do not alter the basic principles outlined in this chapter. I will end the chapter by drawing attention both to the importance of conducting more and better trials in social science, and to the fact that trials are just one part of the complete research cycle (Chapter Two).

The major claim made for the use of experimental designs (Fisher 1935) is their ability, used correctly, to uncover and test causal mechanisms (Badger et al. 2000). This is not a moot point, since the difference between experimental and other forms of evidence can be crucial. It can save lives (Roberts 2000). However, the general lack of relevant RCTs means that social science policies and practices affecting a wide range of issues are not currently underpinned by suitably rigorous evidence. The US Congress's Committee on Education and the Work Force, for example, has been 'concerned about the wide dissemination of flawed, untested educational initiatives that can be detrimental' (Boruch and Mosteller 2002, p.1). This *lacuna* can have worldwide consequences. The economic and financial derivatives that led to the crash of 2008/9 were not understood by experts, who did not know how they worked or what their possible consequences were. The derivatives had not been properly trialled, and they are not alone in this. Think of the introduction of the most recent changes to the tax laws in your own country, or new guidelines for social workers. No one has any idea whether these things really work. So much takes place worldwide that is just a gamble on a hunch that it is quite scary to consider.

When subjected to a definitive trial by experiment, many common interventions and treatments actually show no effect, identifying resources wasted on policies and practices. Both of the studies discussed in this chapter illustrate the more general difficulty of finding anything in policy or practice that works or indeed that is not actually harmful. In fact, there is a strong inverse relation between the level of experimental control in an evaluation and the likelihood of something being judged effective (Gomm 2004). This is an indictment of so much sloppy and poorly-designed work that so conveniently and dangerously finds in favour of the prevailing theory or policy fashion. Because we are generally so poor at evaluating interventions, we have little skill in picking real winners. There are many examples of interventions that have been widely disseminated on the basis that they are driven by good intentions, seem plausible and are unlikely to do any harm, yet when they have been rigorously evaluated have been found to be ineffective or positively harmful. Psychology debriefing as an intervention for post-traumatic stress disorder in trauma survivors apparently does not help (Bisson et al. 1997). Culling badgers in response to incident bovine TB has been found to increase the occurrence of TB (Donnelly et al. 2003). The 'Scared Straight' programme, which aimed to deter delinquent children from a life of crime, was well-received and widely-implemented. Unfortunately, it was found to increase delinquency rates (Petrosino et al. 2000). A Bike-Ed training programme to reduce bicycle accidents among children was associated with an increased risk of injury (Carlin et al. 1998). Without such knowledge from trial designs people would suffer unnecessarily.

Perhaps this lack of success with interventions is also partly why there is considerable resistance to the idea of the use of experimental evidence. Social work was one of the areas where natural experiments were pioneered but, when these seldom showed any positive impact from social work policies, social workers rejected the method itself rather than the ineffective practices (Torgerson and Torgerson 2001). Those with vested interests in other current social science beliefs and theories may, similarly, consider they have little to gain from definitive trials, showing themselves to be shockingly complacent about the risks to others (Chapter Thirteen). Too many researchers just do not seem to care about their supposed research – the point made in Chapter One.

An RCT design is not any kind of magic bullet. Trials by themselves are unlikely to lead to an understanding of detailed causal mechanisms (Morrison 2001). Identifying the key drivers (or causes) underlying such research often relies on further work, or on the judgement of the user (US Department of Education 2008). Causal description explains the consequences of an intervention, whereas causal explanation is based on understanding why those consequences follow. This is why the cycle of research matters, and why designs for interventions are only one (key) part of it.

⇌ Exercises on interventions

1 A study looking at the causes of unemployment takes place in an area in which it is traditionally hard to find a job. As part of the study, an intervention is developed to enhance the job prospects of those currently unemployed. Everyone registered for

unemployment in that area is deemed part of the study, and these cases are individually randomised either to receive the treatment now or when the study is completed. It
is a waiting-list design. Taking part now or later is a condition of continuing to receive
welfare benefits, and so participation is 100%. This is a very powerful study. The group
receiving the intervention turn out to be far more likely to get a job over the next two
years, with an effect size of 0.5 of a standard deviation difference between the two
groups (Chapter Twelve). The researchers calculate the cost of the intervention (providing training etc.) and compare it with the gains to the economy and reduction in
welfare payments. They conclude that the intervention is cost-effective, and demand
that it is rolled out more widely to benefit the unemployed and society more generally.
Can you think of a good reason why their estimate of the cost-benefits may be heavily
biased?

2   This chapter contains an extended example of a trial of a piece of literacy software,
which found that the control group receiving traditional teaching improved faster than
the group working with the software. The research concluded that using the software
was no more effective than other methods of teaching, and that the manufacturer's
claims for effectiveness were wrong. Applying the warrant principle, think of as many
ways as you can in which the result might not be valid. And then think of how the
experimental design could control for each of them.

3   Select a research report or paper in your own area of interest that uses an active
research design. Summarise the design in notation, specifying the number of groups,
their method of allocation, the pre-tests and post-tests where they occur, and the
position of the intervention in sequence. Note also any additional features to protect
against bias. Perhaps do this in pairs and compare your summaries.

≡ Notes on exercises on interventions

1   As with any study there are a number of possible threats to validity, and the researchers may have made a mistake at any stage. There may be some demoralisation among
those not selected for the treatment, and this might affect their chances of a job in
the short term. The randomisation process might have been subverted in some way
by a well-meaning person trying to put those most likely to benefit in the treatment
group. Nevertheless, this is a powerful research design with 100% participation. The
biggest problem may be one of degrees of freedom. Looked at in purely local terms
there are a finite number of job-seekers and a finite number of job opportunities over
two years. If the treatment does enhance the chances of those taking part then it must
also decrease the chances of those not taking part. Every job taken by someone after
the intervention is a job no longer available for anyone else. An unintended consequence of improving the situation for one group is reduction of the chances for others.
This means that the overall impact of the intervention may really be considerably less
than the 0.5 estimated by the study. It could be closer to zero, since the process is
close to zero-sum in nature. Such unintended and possibly harmful consequences of
an intervention are important factors to take into account. This is part of the reason
for conducting an in-depth process evaluation as part of a trial. It is why beneficial
short-term outcomes alone are not sufficient to justify a treatment. But the focus of
our concern is usually on the participants. Non-participants in the treatment tend to
be regarded as unchanged by the process. As this example shows, this assumption is
not valid, and the impact of the treatment on the non-treated must be factored into

the results. This is a key practical and ethical issue (Chapter Thirteen). Note that this issue is not a problem stemming from the specific design, or even from the conduct of research. It happens anyway for any intervention or change. Those given training to help them find jobs would automatically disadvantage those given training later even if no research was conducted to evaluate the impact. This is worth emphasising because a lot of opposition to trials is based on a complete misunderstanding of the ethics involved.

2 Here are a few obvious examples of areas that any sceptical reader of the study might need convincing about (Chapter Eleven). The literacy levels of pupils were assessed pre- and post- using a commercial package, and the trial result depends heavily on the validity of this test. If this did not test the learning outcomes fairly, then the trial conclusion is in doubt. The researchers conducted lengthy face validity checks, comparing the material in the tests with that in the exercises, and found a good match. They analysed the results for eight individual tests (such as spelling) as well as for the overall scores reported, and the same difference occurred for all. The test was computer-based and so should not disadvantage the treatment group more used to handling such material on the computer (rather the reverse). Perhaps more importantly for a pragmatic trial, the software publisher accepted the test as valid before the start (good practice that reduces 'wriggle-room' for later).

Schools were only permitted to be part of the trial if they met a manufacturer specified threshold for the quality and quantity of their hardware. All schools had ICT support, and all teachers were given training at the start of the trial. Nevertheless, delivery of teaching via software relies on ICT and if this goes wrong then the planned teaching suffers. In fact, this happened in one class (Khan and Gorard 2012). I would say though that this cannot explain the worse performance overall for the ICT treatment group, for three reasons. It was only one class, and the overall difference between groups was more than this. The teacher can anyway continue traditional teaching while any ICT problems are fixed. And more generally, this is one of the hazards of using any ICT-based solution. It should not be 'cleaned' away to enhance the apparent effect of the treatment, any more than poor teaching of the control would be ignored on the basis that it 'should not happen'.

The sample of 23 classes with 665 pupils could be considered quite small, and so perhaps did not have the 'power' to demonstrate the advantages of the software. However, this is not really an issue of power. It is not that the treatment group did slightly better but that we cannot be sure whether the difference is statistically 'significant' (Chapter Twelve). The treatment group actually did substantially worse. The sample size is larger than most studies of this type, and is an order of magnitude higher than the samples used by the publisher to test the software initially.

Schools had classes in both the treatment and control conditions, and this can lead to diffusion whereby treatment pupils share their new approach with control pupils, so reducing the apparent effect size of the treatment. This is a standard concern in cluster randomised trials using teaching groups. However, the treatment was based on content presented using the technology; was not made available in the system to other pupils (login name and password-protected); and it is unlikely that the treatment pupils would remember the details of the activities or discuss them in detail during free time. It is not like passing over a pill, or lending a textbook. Contamination is still possible, but this could not explain the substantially lower level of progress made by the treatment group.

3 I hope that by this stage of the book you are becoming proficient at encapsulating the key features of any design in notation. Make sure that the design you have summarised is truly an experimental one. It needs an intervention (X) that applies to only some

of the sub-groups. Common additional features to protect the study against bias or threats to validity include the use of a placebo or false treatment for the control group (equivalent to a sugar pill in a drug trial), blinding whereby the participants and even the researchers do not know which group they are in, and following up all cases that drop out of the study for any reason to try and find out why. More examples and explanations appear in Chapter Eleven.

☰ Suggested reading

Torgerson, D. and Torgerson, C. (2008) *Designing Randomised Trials*. Basingstoke: Palgrave.

4

More Advanced Considerations

TEN
Further designs for evaluation

SUMMARY

- Sometimes a true experimental design is not possible, even where the research question is clearly causal. In this situation a range of other designs is available.
- Even where an experiment is not possible, considering the design for an 'ideal' experiment can still be useful.
- Alternatives include regression modelling such as Granger models, and 'natural' experiments based on interrupted times series, regression discontinuity, and instrumental variables.
- One of the chapter exercises also illustrates the difference in difference approach.
- Each is intended to offer a flexible and useful alternative to experimental designs, but each also has limitations in use. Granger causation relies on an assumption that will never be met in practice, and other natural experiments depend on an artificial matching process that is only as good as the known variables.
- Design-based studies offer an entirely different approach to active research designs. They are applied, iterative, and working towards a trial. Without such a trial they lack rigour.
- With all of these somewhat weaker designs, it is sensible to try several in the same study. If the results agree this adds strength to the research claims. If the results disagree, this prevents being misled by using only one approach.

10.1 ||| Alternatives to trials

Sometimes a randomised controlled trial is not possible, or is at least not thought possible, even when the research question is clearly causal (Pötter and Blossfeld 2001). The alternatives to 'active' laboratory and naturalistic experiments are 'passive' approaches to research. The key difference is that in the former design, the researcher introduces a change into an environment and monitors subsequent events for the potential impact of that change. In the latter design the researcher simply monitors events and attempts to track back to a cause *post hoc* – a much more difficult task both conceptually and technically (in terms of compensatory statistical analysis, for example). Ironically, it is not always easier to judge with the benefit of hindsight.

Nevertheless, the model of an experiment can still be of assistance, even in passive designs. We can use the natural experiment model. A passive approach can use the naturally occurring interventions going on around us all of the time. The subsequent monitoring phase can be attached to an intervention that is not controlled by the researcher, but using the same analytical methods as for an experiment, sometimes long after the intervention. A historian can arrange their data from long past in the format of a natural experiment (after the event) just as easily as any other social scientist using secondary data. They can easily use many of the ideas in this chapter, such as interrupted time series, for example. It is peculiar that this appears to happen so seldom. Natural experiments are going on around us all of the time, when interventions occur as part of the policy process. If one local health authority changes its practice in some way then this authority can be construed as the experimental group, with the remaining authorities as controls, in a natural experiment. In fact, much social science research is of this type – retrospectively trying to explain differences between two groups. All of these designs are inferior in terms of validity to a true experimental design but can be much more practical. Knowing how an experiment works is important because it enables us to see how far a natural experiment is from that 'ideal'. But it also alerts us to the need for things like comparison or control groups, and it is alarming how often researchers attempt to make comparisons over time and place on the basis of *one* set of observations (and even more alarmingly are believed and cited favourably by others). It also alerts us to the need for a transparent written protocol, so that our findings could be replicated, like those of a real experiment.

The chief problem with all alternatives is that they do not always have the same power and lack of bias as a randomised controlled trial. They generally need a lot more cases to be convincing. This chapter continues by looking at instrumental variables, interrupted time series, regression discontinuity, and design-based approaches, all of which can mimic the power of RCTs to some extent. First though, the chapter looks in more detail at probably the most common approach to studying causation – interpretation of multivariate regression models.

10.2 ‖ Using statistical modelling

Currently the most common alternative to the kind of rigorous field trials and laboratory experiments discussed in Chapter Nine is not really a design at all. It is statistical modelling with increasingly complex mathematical models, datasets and software. The belief is that, working with passive designs either to collect or use existing data, it is possible to overcome their deficiencies in identifying causes via sophisticated analysis.

One basis for this argument, in econometrics at least, is the Granger model of causation. If we have perfect information about every possible variable in the universe, then we can create a statistical model of it. Then if we eliminate one variable of our choice from this model, and if the value of a second specified variable does not alter, then we have proved that the first variable cannot be the cause of the second (Hendry and Mizon 1999). Similarly, if the second variable is affected then the first variable must be the cause, or an 'inus' cause at least (Chapter Five). Structural equation modelling is one approach that allows models based on non-experimental evidence to be rejected as inconsistent or to be tentatively retained as an explanation (Maruyama 1998). Such 'mental experiments' can be used to help determine plausible directions of causation in our explanations (Miles and Shevlin 2001).

The argument works, but only in theory as a philosophical point. If we knew every possible variable and its value in the whole universe then we would probably not need to undertake this kind of social science. Anyway, we are nowhere close to this 'ideal' situation. As soon as even one variable is missing from the model, the argument fails. We cannot convert the ideal to a probabilistic argument since we have no idea how important that missing variable could be, or how many are missing. No regression coefficient can be interpreted as causal until the list of all possible confounds has been exhausted (Pratt and Schlaifer 1988; Sobel 1998). But there is a 'potentially inexhaustible list of potentially confounding variables' (Pan and Frank 2003, p. 23).

All models therefore suffer from omitted variable bias, to a very considerable extent. Perhaps because of the traditions of different relevant disciplines such as psychology and sociology and their sub-divisions and themes, studies tend to examine variables in isolation. Omitted variable bias generally makes variables that are known appear more important than they should be in a Granger universe of information. It can make proxy variables appear as causes. For example, a regression model might find a strong association between parental education and children's social class. But this does not mean that parental education causes their child's social class. It might only be because the model did not include parental social class. If parental social class is added to the model, then the role of parental education will lessen and might disappear completely. Here, the initial omission of parental social class is converting parental education into a proxy for class, and could mislead an unwary analyst. This is a problem for all forms of statistical modelling. Without perfect information, the whole argument for Granger causation fails, because the role of any predictor can then be exaggerated by the absence of one or more key predictors. In the opposite of a Granger perfect universe, where there are no predictors, almost any variable inserted into a model will 'soak up' some of the variation in the outcome. The more variables are omitted the more likely it is that any other predictor tried will be found to 'explain' some variation. A simple model with one outcome variable (individual social class), and a number of predictor variables (including the number of caffeine drinks per day, for example) can yield an R^2 of 1 even if the actual values of all variables are merely random numbers (Gorard 2006a).

The technique of regression analysis was developed for use in the context of mechanics where variables and the (Newtonian) equations linking them were known, where the nature of errors in measurements was clearer, and most importantly there was plenty of opportunity to compare models with reality (Freedman 2005). This is an important consideration when looking at research reports in psychology claiming that a construct like 'self-esteem' is a good predictor of attainment at school, but which gives the specific construct an open space by not controlling for pupil and family background, prior attainment and so on. In the same way that social class and ethnicity are correlated, self-esteem and prior attainment could be correlated. It is possible therefore that self-esteem as a predictor of subsequent attainment is acting merely as a proxy for prior attainment (itself the cause of some of the self-esteem). Nothing in a passive statistical model, however complex it is made, can overcome such omitted variable bias. And the same applies to any combination or number of predictors. Sampling theory cannot help with omitted variable bias, as there is no reason to believe that any uninvolved variable values are randomly related to cases (Gennetian et al. 2008).

Non-experimental methods can therefore never rule out the possibility of reverse causality in any pathway (Kline 1998). Consequently, establishing a correlation, however sophisticated, between two variables is not sufficient to establish a causal relationship. 'It is impossible to tell which of two variables came first, so defending a causal relationship between them is precarious (Shadish et al. 2002). In summary, regression is not any kind of test of causation. It is, more like a graph or table, as a way of presenting the data and seeking or displaying possible multivariate patterns within it. No form of regression can overcome deficiencies of design, and this includes path analysis, structural equation modelling, hierarchical linear modelling, and logistic regression. Any good design may then involve regression modelling as a form of analysis, but it is the design not the regression that does the heavy work of making research claims plausible (or not). Looked at the other way, if the design is right then such complex modelling is often redundant anyway, at least in a causal study. This illustrates again the importance of research design. So what can be done to design a robust study where a true experiment is not possible?

10.3 ∥ Regression discontinuity

Given the right conditions, there is a way of creating a matched comparison group for a natural experiment or quasi-experiment that is as near to unbiased as randomisation is (Cook and Gorard 2007). This is the regression discontinuity design. It can be used when there is a known variable that determines whether a case is given an intervention or not. Perhaps, if the variable is below a certain figure or threshold then the treatment is given, otherwise not. This threshold can then be used to help estimate the true impact of the treatment, since cases on either side of the cut-off will be so similar they form natural comparators for each other. The design would be:

C   O   (X)   O

C   O   O

Once you start thinking about it, the number of examples abound. A lot of welfare benefits are handled like this. A person or family might have to earn less than a certain threshold to be eligible. In the UK, free school meals are decided in this way. Any child coming from a family which lives below an official poverty line are entitled to free meals. Even attendance at school in the UK and many other countries is determined in this way. Children born up to 31 August in any calendar year attend school one year earlier than children born from 1 September onwards in the same calendar year. Glasses are available on the National Health for people who score worse than a certain threshold in a sight test. Blood pressure pills are prescribed for people whose average blood pressure is over a certain threshold. How does identifying a situation like this help?

Imagine that there was a link between the average parental income of a family and the number of occasions when a child from that family was absent from school, for any reason. Figure 10.1 presents an idealised regression line, showing the link between these variables. In reality, the regression line would have more scatter, and may even show a curved pattern. Generally, however, higher income is linked to lower absences in this example. What would happen if families with incomes below 10,000 per year were the target of an intervention that might influence school attendance? Perhaps the treatment is as simple as paying poor parents for the school attendance of their children. If the treatment had no effect then we would expect the outcomes to still look like Figure 10.1.

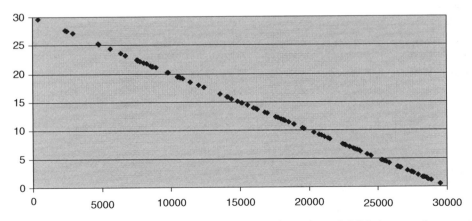

Figure 10.1   Annual parental earned income (x) and number of child absences from school (y)

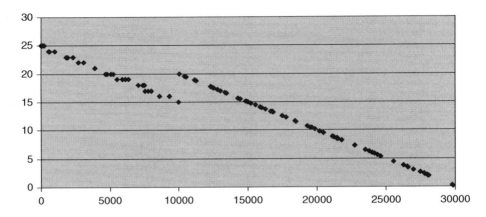

Figure 10.2 Annual parental earned income (x) and number of child absences from school (y), after intervention

However, if the treatment were effective it can only affect people with an income below 10,000, because no one else receives the treatment. This means that the right side of Figure 10.1 should be undisturbed, but the regression line below 10,000 should be disturbed if the treatment is effective. It should have a 'discontinuity' like that in Figure 10.2. Here there is still a link between family income and absences, but it is clearly a different relationship on either side of the 10,000 threshold. This would show that the treatment had been effective. There is a 'regression discontinuity'.

Regression discontinuity can be used, as above, when an experiment is not possible. Or it can be used to create experimental groups, by use of a cut-off value, in an active design. Regression discontinuity is appropriate when targeting a programme to those who most need it, and looking at those who just miss out. We can say there is no treatment effect if there is no discontinuity in the regression line at the cut-off point (as in Figure 10.1). So the conclusion drawn is not only about those just on either side of the cut-off, but is also about the full set of values in a linear or near-linear relationship. In other situations where there is no clear cut-off point, regression discontinuity cannot be used, which is partly why it is so rare. When it is possible it is almost as good as an experiment, but suffers from all of the same threats to its validity, such as regression to the mean.

10.4 ▮▮ Interrupted time series

A related idea, that can be used when there is no direct manipulation of the treatment variable, is an interrupted time series. This is another natural or quasi-experimental approach. Measures are taken for a sample or a series of samples from the same population several times before and after a manipulated event or a naturally occurring event. If this intervening event has an effect then it should be noticeable as an 'interruption' in the series of data points. The interruption could be a decline, a sharp rise or even a plateau – as long as it interrupts the longer term trend of the data. The 'analysis' is usually a visual inspection, and how easy it is to see an interruption depends largely on how dependent each data point is on the last one (Hartmann et al. 1980). Otherwise, a range of numeric analytical techniques is available. This approach is better at ruling out an effect than demonstrating one. An example illustrates this point.

When up-front tuition fees were first introduced for university students in Wales, there was concern whether this would reduce the number of people willing to go on to higher education. One way of looking at the impact of fees is to examine the trend in home student admissions, before and after the new policy became effective. There was a gradual year-on-year increase in the number of Welsh domiciled students attending university in the UK between 1995/96 and 2002/03 (Figure 10.3). The only year that saw a fall in the number of Welsh domiciled students was 1999/00. This was a year after the introduction of up-front tuition fees, and may be a direct response to students who, in 1998/99, were deciding whether to go to University or not. This may have led to a sharper than normal rise. However, if the introduction of up-front tuition fees was a disincentive to those students, it did not deter increased participation for subsequent years.

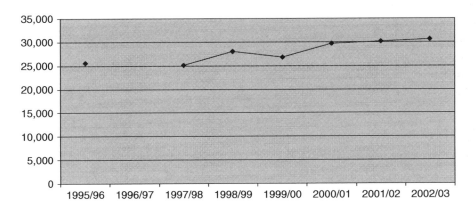

Figure 10.3 Number of Welsh-domiciled first degree undergraduates in their first year in higher education

Source: Taylor and Gorard (2005)
Note: data missing for 1996/97

10.5 ║ Instrumental variables

Propensity score matching was discussed in Chapter Seven as a possible way of creating fair comparator groups in a passive design where a controlled experiment is not possible. An approach that sounds similar involves finding and using an 'instrumental variable', which under certain conditions might generate unbiased causal inferences (Cronbach 1982; Morris 2008). It was originally devised as a way of correcting some problems in the regression modelling of causation (see start of this chapter). One of these problems is that the predicted variable in a regression model might actually be the cause or part cause of any predictor variable (since the regression is only an association). Suppose we wanted to know about the impact of pricing on market demand. We could create a regression model with demand as the outcome, and price plus some other contextual variables as predictors. But while it is clear that price could influence demand, demand could also lead to changes of pricing. There is potential mutual causation (Chapter Five). If it were true, however, that another variable was linked to pricing but not to demand then we could use this as an 'instrument' to help clarify the position. An example, in an agricultural market, could be the quality of the growing season. This might lead to annual fluctuations in price unrelated to demand, except via price, and this overlap (or co-variation between quality and price, and price and demand) leads to an estimate of the pure influence of price. So, putting this instrumental variable of 'quality' as a predictor in the regression can be used to provide that estimate.

This approach can be used where a group of cases have been selected non-randomly (clinically perhaps) to receive an intervention, and the only set of cases for comparison consists of all those who did not receive the intervention. The instrument referred to in the name of the technique is a known variable that is patterned in terms of those receiving or not receiving an intervention, but it must not be patterned in terms of the outcomes. Cases who did receive the intervention and some that did not could be matched in terms of the instrumental variable to provide an estimate of the impact of the intervention on those who received it. An example of an instrument in a study of the effect of a training course could be the residential distance of people from where the training is provided. This might be clearly related to whether people take part in a training course, but unrelated to their results (assuming that they are not more likely to drop out of training if further away). This last point illustrates a drawback of the instrumental variable (IV) approach. It can be very hard to find an appropriate instrumental variable. Even so, economists have used IV analysis for evaluation in a number of areas, with some success (Hoxby 2000; Angrist and Krueger 2001), and the approach is being used, or is claimed to be used, more frequently in other areas of social science (Gottfried 2010). However, the overall logic is not completely convincing, and this design must be considered a far weaker form of causal test than a trial.

10.6 ‖ Combined designs

The approaches discussed in the book so far do not have to be used in isolation. It is perfectly proper to mix designs and approaches. For example, if you are not sure that regression discontinuity is going to lead to an unbiased result then you could use it alongside an instrumental variable approach or propensity scoring as well to create several sets of matched pairs. If all approaches lead to the same substantive answer, about whether an intervention is effective, then you can be somewhat surer and your account to readers will be more convincing. If, on the other hand, the approaches lead to an ambiguous result, so that whether the intervention seems effective depends on the precise method of selecting a counterfactual group, then it would be unwise to proceed with this intervention for the present. Your research report must explain the ambiguity. This combined approach can be extended as good practice to most other areas of research and design, including analysis (Gorard with Taylor 2004).

10.7 ‖ Design-based approaches

The chapter concludes by discussing a set of related active approaches to research that are the subject of some debate. These approaches include action research and design studies (or design experiments), all referred to here as design-based approaches. They fit well with the research cycle (Chapter Two), as both approaches can be seen as a way of developing an intervention and so working towards a trial.

In originally proposing action research, Lewin (1946, p. 38) saw it as 'a spiral of steps, each of which is composed of a circle of planning, action and fact-finding about the action'. Above all, he saw it as practical, set in a real-life context and involving practitioners and users from the outset. But in no way did this suggest that the rigour of the research should be less than scientific, rather the reverse – for 'above all, it will have to include laboratory and field experiments in social change' (p. 36). The basic idea of this action research is that actions (interventions) are evaluated formatively in context. Evaluation involves both uncovering the more general rules linking actions and their consequences, and also 'diagnosing' the specific character of the situation at hand. This means checking for changes in consequences (effects of the action) over and above what might otherwise have been expected, learning what seems to work best and what the barriers are, modifying the action for the next step in the cycle, and starting again. See, for example, Munn-Giddings et al. (2005) on developing an intervention to overcoming mental distress at work.

All of this is very like the programme cycle of research in Chapter Two, and is similar to more recent ideas about the impact of social science, involvement of users, Mode 2 social science, and working in Pasteur's quadrant (Gorard with Taylor 2004). It is also similar to the UK Medical Research Council (MRC) model for complex interventions. Unfortunately, other commentators have used Lewin's title of 'action research' to describe their own approaches, which are nothing like this. They eschew the robust science called for by Lewin, and take on only the idea of participatory reflective progressive problem solving (e.g. McNiff and Whitehead 2002). There is no definitive testing of the actions, and the work has become by tradition solely or almost entirely 'qualitative' in nature. So, if someone describes their design as action research, remember to enquire whether it is in the original Lewin mould, or simply using the same name in a rather confusing manner.

More recently, a proposal has been made to look at what happens in design science or engineering (as opposed to natural science) and use this as one model for social science (Urlich and Eppinger 2000). Researchers in social science have long borrowed techniques from other disciplines. Some use laboratory methods derived from psychology, others use ethnography, survey methods, and so on. In 1992, Ann Brown, a psychologist, looked to the field of design and engineering for inspiration on how to conduct experimental research in classrooms. She called her formulation – a hybrid cycle of prototyping, field-testing, and laboratory study – 'design experimentation'. In the past decade, that original notion of the design experiment has been transmuted.

Some researchers claim to be doing design experiments by simply modifying multiple interventions continuously and documenting the process (often via video recordings), but it is not clear that this behaviour is very different to the purely qualitative distortion of the action research model already mentioned. In their ideal form, design experiments would go beyond action research. In the original formulation, Brown (1992) assumed that work would iterate between laboratory and classroom, capturing the advantages of both. Typically, action research now only takes place within the real-world setting. McNiff and Whitehead (2002) would not consider researching in a laboratory, for example!

Design studies are a reasonably new but underdeveloped way of preparing an intervention. Whereas the natural sciences have been concerned with whether things work and how they may be explained, design sciences such as artificial intelligence or aeronautics are more concerned with producing and improving artefacts, and establishing how they behave under different conditions. The emphasis is on a general solution that can be 'transported' to any policy/practice environment where users would be encouraged to determine the contextualised final product (Cobb et al. 2003). In a design study, currently accepted theory is used to develop an intervention that is tested, modified, re-tested and re-designed in both ideal and real settings, until a version is developed that both achieves the aims required, and allows reflection on the processes involved in attaining those aims. Studies can therefore use, rather than discard, an ineffective design as the starting point for the next phase of the design process. The changes that are necessary to move from an ineffective to an effective design can illuminate the sources of the original design's failure. However, adopting this approach is not a straightforward matter, and comes at a cost in terms of causal strength. Design studies often monitor several dependent variables, revise the procedures while live, allow participants to interact, involve users and participants in the design, and generate copious amounts and types of data (Middleton et al. 2008).

⇌ Exercises on further designs

1 Card and Krueger (1994) used an approach called 'difference in difference' to mimic a true experiment. They wanted to look at changes in patterns of employment in the fast-food industry in New Jersey after the introduction of a new minimum wage. Does a minimum wage cost people jobs in such traditionally volatile occupations, or does it protect them? They could have looked at the before and after figures for employment in New Jersey, but these could be influenced by other changes happening at the same time as the new minimum wage. They had no comparators available in New Jersey, because the legislation affected all sectors. So they selected Pennsylvania as a close and somewhat similar region where the legislation did not apply but where similar economic changes might take place over time. Their comparison was then of the difference in employment pre- and post- the minimum wage in New Jersey with the difference in employment over the same time period in Pennsylvania. This is the difference in the difference. Of course it looks a lot like a pre- and post-test trial (Chapter Nine), and in notation form it would be:

N   O   [X]   O

N   O   O

In what important respects does a difference in difference (or DID) design differ from a true experiment?

2 A typical statistical study might use data from a cross-sectional design, select a variable as an outcome and then use other variables as 'predictors' to explain variation in the outcome via some form of regression analysis. As noted above, where this is done in much the same way as drawing a graph, to illustrate interesting relationships between variables, this is entirely appropriate. It is an exploratory approach that can help create suggestions for a causal model. A lack of association between a predictor and the outcome suggests that the predictor variable cannot be the cause of the outcome. But the reverse does not hold. Why not?

3 Two colleagues are studying the same field, looking at whether the introduction of freedom of speech legislation in a country helps to create innovations of thought. Innovation is assessed by the number of patents registered by people in each country per year. The presence or absence of freedom of speech legislation (or equivalent long-established practice, as in the UK) is defined by a United Nations register. These are certainly not ideal measures, but let us assume that they have some validity for present purposes. One colleague uses a case-matching approach, finding pairs of countries with one having freedom of speech and one not. The pairs are matched as closely as possible on

all known variables (except number of patents registered per year). This creates two groups whose only known difference is the freedom of speech legislation, which can then be compared in terms of the number of patents. The other colleague uses regression modelling to try and predict (or explain) the number of patents per country using all known variables, including whether there is freedom of speech legislation. The reasoning here is that if there is a substantial non-zero coefficient for the legislation, all other things having been accounted for, then the legislation must be linked to innovations. Which approach is better and why? Put another way, if the colleagues come to differing conclusions, who is more likely to be correct?

⇶ Notes on exercises on further designs

1 This difference in difference design varies from a true experiment in many crucial respects. Most notably, there is neither randomisation to groups nor individual matching of cases. Pennsylvania might be a good comparator for New Jersey but there will be many differences between them, both known and unknown. There are obvious threats and areas for confusion and bias. Volatile labour and even some employers may move between the two areas in reaction to the minimum wage law. The law itself could be the outcome of economic success (something that becomes affordable), rather than its cause. A lower or markedly higher initial position in either area could create a regression towards the mean. The approach used is probably slightly safer than a simple before-and-after design, but in itself it does not approximate anything like a true experiment.

2 Studies typically use correlations or regression coefficients as a measure of the effect size in the relationship between a potential cause and a potential effect. If this effect size is zero or near zero then it follows that the relationship cannot be causal. There must be an association for a cause to be identified (Chapter Five). So such studies are reasonably efficient at deciding what is *not* a cause. This is the standard falsification approach (Chapter Four). However, if the effect size is substantially greater or less than zero, this does not mean that the predictor variable is the cause of the outcome variable. The same strength relationship would also appear if the predictor were considered the outcome. This is what an association means, and is unchanged by converting a correlation to a regression model. There is also a distinct possibility that both variables could be being influenced by a third variable that is not in the study. There is really only one way to tell, and that is to do an experiment or a close approximation to an experiment.

3 I do not feel that either approach is intrinsically better. It is unlikely that they will produce very different results. The matching approach is a closer simulation of an experimental design than the regression model. But it has several defects. If the number of countries with and without freedom of speech legislation is different, then the pairing design necessarily involves dropping some data instances from further consideration (the unpaired cases). This is inefficient, whereas the modelling retains all cases. Any matching process is usually imperfect, and compromises have to be made in the pairing process about the priority of specific variables. On the other hand, any cases with any variables with missing values have to be dropped from the regression, or a series of (usually unrealistic) compromises have to be made to estimate what the missing data could be. Both approaches are subject to omitted variable bias, of the kind that randomisation overcomes automatically. The matching design is sometimes called a

kind of 'case control' whereas the regression model is a kind of 'internal control'. My proposal would be that, given the data available, both approaches should be tried and compared. If the results agree, this is some small confirmation, and if they disagree, this is a warning about the safety of the results.

≡ Suggested reading

Cook, T. and Gorard, S. (2007) 'What counts and what should count as evidence', pp. 33–49 in OECD (eds) *Evidence in Education: Linking Research and Policy*. Paris: OECD.

ELEVEN
Challenges for validity

SUMMARY

- The 'validity' of any findings refers to their real-life applicability and to their robustness when examined sceptically. In a sense, making valid research claims is what this whole book is about.
- Perhaps the most obvious source of doubt for any study is a problem with the data, such as an error in measurement. Less obvious, and not usually remarked on in methods resources, is that the design of a study can be a strong influence on how important such an error becomes.
- The simplest design of two near-equivalents is usually the best. So, a post-test only experiment reduces the complications of initial errors, for example, in comparison to a pre- and post-test design.
- Researchers can deliberately or unintentionally influence their study at all stages. Protection against this includes sub-contracting stages, being open and clear about protocols, and caring more about getting the right answer than a specific answer.
- Distancing the researcher from the results is not related to, and does not need to influence, the important issue of rapport with research participants.
- Attrition and non-response are major threats, in any design and with any type of data. An intention-to-treat analysis overcomes some problems.
- A sensitivity analysis estimates how little of the missing data would have to differ to alter the research findings.
- One of the exercises is about the problems of participant resentment, and the usually neglected issue of the impact of a treatment on the non-treated.

11.1 |¦| Introduction

This chapter is about protecting study designs from mistaken conclusions due to bias, or challenges to their validity. Most research methods resources divide validity into a number of domains, such as internal and external. Internal validity refers to the strength of the design itself, external to the generalisability or realism of the findings. Sometimes the two domains are felt to be in tension, as in the claim that tightly controlled experiments allow us to be surer about less. Shadish et al. (2002) add to these two domains of validity, statistical (concerned with the validity of correlations and similar) and construct validity (concerned with sampling and complex indices). I prefer not to make such distinctions here. They can become confusing, needlessly complex and sometimes get mixed up with issues of reliability (which is concerned only with methods of data and analysis). I prefer to consider validity, or the absence of errors, to be about how convincing a claimed result is for a sceptical reader. Of course, if the claim is about widespread applicability we may use slightly different criteria to judge it than if the claim is about certainty of the findings, but then we may use different criteria for a wide range of claims. Underlying all of these criteria is the warrant principle (Chapter Four): if the claim is not actually correct then how else can we explain the evidence presented for it? This chapter presents a range of generic alternative explanations for any results, based on chinks in the research design. It also presents a number of approaches and craft tips to deal with these 'threats'. See also Campbell and Stanley (1963) and Cook and Campbell (1979). Many threats to validity and ways to protect against them have been covered fully in Chapters Seven to Ten. This chapter concentrates on further ideas and tips, some of which have so far been completely ignored in methods resources.

11.2 ‖ Bugs and other data errors

The first threat you may face to your findings, especially if they are numeric, is that your research calculations may be wrong. I do not mean, only, that you may have made a mistake. A problem with careless and apparently random mistakes in research is that they are not necessarily random. Where it has been possible to test, it has been shown that when typing in results, and even adding up totals by hand, researchers tend to make mistakes that unwittingly favour their own preference for the results or their best prediction of the results (Adair 1973). The same problem applies to coding in-depth data. There are a number of ways to avoid this. First, of course, is the attitude for researchers promoted throughout this book. Care passionately about your research in the sense of wanting to get the right answer, but avoid caring too much about what that answer is. Another low cost protection is to ensure that your datasets are publicly available, so that others can repeat your analysis. If someone discovers a simple error, be glad that it was discovered, not defensive. We all make errors sometimes. It is how we respond to their discovery by ourselves, or by others, that really defines us as researchers. Another possibility is not to enter the data yourself but to employ someone else to do it, with you spot-checking their work for quality. In fact, using independent people can be a good idea in many areas of a study from picking a sample, through allocating cases to groups, to running the final analysis. Of course, you have to be sure that the other people are as good and as careful as you are. If resources are low, you can achieve the same outcome by swapping with someone else. For example, if two doctoral (PhD) researcher colleagues have both done interviews for their study it could be better for each to do the coding of the interviews for each other. Coding interviews is even more susceptible to researcher bias than entering a column of figures. Chapter Nine explained how many studies would be best conducted 'blind' meaning that the researcher does not know which group any participant is in, and the participant does not know either (this would be 'double-blind'). Perhaps we should say that studies are better quadruple-blind, so that the person entering the data does also not know which groups cases are in, and nor does the person running the analysis. All can be revealed at the end. For example, the analyst can work out that one group has a higher mean score than another, but will not know until an envelope is opened which group is the treatment and which the control. These are the kinds of imaginative things we should do if we want the safest and most convincing research results.

What is more interesting is that errors in calculations occur even where we as researchers have made no mistake at all. There are a range of possibilities here. One is that software is notorious for being marketed before it has been fully tested. The producers treat the customers as their testers. So, for example, there have been versions of IBM SPSS in which the results obtained for a calculation via the menu interface are different from the results obtained using the syntax procedure, and the results from SAS have been different again (Li and Lomax 2011). One protection is only to use older versions of software. These will either have had their bugs ironed out, or at least the bugs will be known about. SPSS is one of the oldest pieces of widely-used software in existence, and I first used it in 1977 (on punch cards, via syntax of course). This makes it one of the safest. We should also insist that software is better tested before marketing. The stream of modifications and error patches that follow the purchase of new software is partly an indictment of poor testing.

Even when working as intended, calculators and computers do not store all numbers accurately. This is due to the change in number base and the finite number of binary digits used to store all numbers in binary floating-point format. The simple decimal fraction 0.1, for example, cannot be exactly represented in the binary numbering system used by computers and calculators, however much memory is allocated to it. Thus, representing 0.1 in one byte (8 bits) would lead to an error of over 6% even in an otherwise perfect measurement. All numbers are generally stored in floating-point form, involving a fractional mantissa and a binary exponent. Thus, the problem of representational errors can happen with any figure, whether it is an integer in denary (base 10) or not. However many bits are allocated by a computer to storage of a number, there will be, by definition, an infinite number of denary values that cannot be stored precisely. Increased accuracy decreases these representational errors, but cannot eliminate them. If complete accuracy is important to you then this is definitely worth double-checking.

More important in most studies is the level of measurement error in any of the numbers involved. By measurement error I mean discrepancies between what we achieve as a measure and what we are trying to measure, including the impact of missing data and cases. It is a good idea always to estimate the likely discrepancy between your achieved data and what it could be in an ideal world. You may be shocked at how far apart these can be. In many areas of social science we cannot even begin to estimate this discrepancy since we have nothing to calibrate our 'measures' with (Gorard 2010a). For example, if we use a proprietary test to assess the mental well-being of someone, then how can we assess the measurement error? We only have the test result. At the very least, such considerations should stop you quoting your results to n decimal places! And it means that we cannot be sure that small and even medium-sized differences between many measurements are meaningful (Chapter Twelve).

Any real-life value might be observed or measured without complete accuracy. This incomplete accuracy applies to physical measurements such as height and weight, to estimates such as sales forecasts, and to other social values such as scores on psychological and educational tests. All are liable to small, or even substantial, measurement errors. There is no reason at all to assume that such measurement errors are random in nature, or that they will tend to cancel each other out when aggregated. These are over and above any random errors, or any random sampling variation. A clear example of measurement error might stem from a ruler that was slightly too short, and so always tended to over-estimate the distance it was used to measure. This is not a random error. There may also be random errors in operating this ruler, or in recording the scores generated from it. But these would be additional to the underlying bias, which would remain even after a large number of similar measurements had been aggregated.

Even more important for most studies, but almost completely un-remarked upon in research methods texts, is the ensuing problem of error propagation. However the initial errors creep in – from missing cases, missing data, discrepancies in measurement, and errors in data entry or storage – it is *certain* that any resulting dataset will contain errors. None of these sources of error is random, and none can be dealt with by using sampling theory and its derivatives. It should then be obvious that any calculations done with this dataset will contain errors, and that the ensuing results will therefore also contain errors. Yet this is not widely acknowledged. In fact it is ignored in methods texts, which all seem to assume that the answer you get from calculations performed with your measurements will be completely accurate. You should be aware from what I have said that your calculations will almost never be completely accurate. But perhaps this does not matter, because you might assume that if the discrepancies start small then they will end up small. This reassuring view of research is completely wrong. As already stated, in many studies we genuinely have no idea how inaccurate our measures are at the start. But in most studies we can at least track any assumed error through to the results. Doing so in your own study will surprise you.

In some calculations the 'effect' size could never really be large enough to overcome doubts about the measurement error. These are called ill-conditioned calculations.

Consider measuring the height of a child once, and then again two weeks later. Each measurement will be in error to some extent, but the error relative to the height of the child will be small (1cm in 1m perhaps). This level of error is useable for everyday purposes (if the child's height had to be written on an official document, or to buy clothes in their absence). But if the two measurements are used to calculate how much the child has grown over two weeks, then this involves subtracting one height from a very similar height, so that the child's actual height is all but eliminated in the answer. The maximum errors are also added in each measurement (since it is not known if the error is positive or negative in each measurement). This means that the maximum error in the result is larger in absolute terms than in either initial measurement. But this new larger error applies to a number (the apparent difference in heights) that is also much smaller than either initial measurement. The error relative to the height 'residual' will therefore have grown enormously. Imagine that the child was measured as 1m tall on the first occasion but we accept that this might represent a true height of 1m plus or minus 1cm (99cm to 101cm). Imagine that on the second occasion, the child was measured as 1.01m which might represent a true height of 1.01m plus or minus 1cm (1m to 1.02m). The child appears to have grown 1cm but the true picture may actually be anything from losing around 1cm (100-101) in height to gaining 3cm (102-99). Using these data alone, an analyst can genuinely have no idea whether the child has grown, shrunk or stayed the same. A 1% error in each initial measurement has propagated to a 200% maximum relative error in the result (200% since the true value could be twice as far from the apparent answer of 1cm as the size of the answer itself). This is so even though heights are quite easy to measure (certainly in comparison to many social science concepts). The initial measurement error has 'propagated' to such an extent that the answer will be misleading in practice.

If we have two measurements with their initial measurement errors, and subtract one from the other, then the answer is also in error by some amount. Since we do not know whether either of the original measurements was too large or too small (positively or negatively in error) we must assume the worst. The worst case is that one measurement was too large and one too small, which means that our subtracted result includes the sum of these errors, while the subtraction has reduced the size of the apparent answer. This means that the maximum relative error in our result is considerably larger than in the initial measurements. This is clearer in the following example. Imagine that our initial measurements were 1,000 and 990, but that both were only 90% accurate, having a maximum relative error of 10% each. This means that the first number should actually lie between 900 and 1,100. The second could be anywhere from 891 to 1,089. When we subtract our two measures we get 10, but the true answer might be anywhere from −189 (900–1089) to +209 (1100–891). Put as a relative error, our computed answer of 10 could be as much as 199 away from the true answer, so the maximum relative error in the result is 199/10 or 1,990%. The simple act of subtraction has converted a 10% initial measurement error into a possible error of 1,990% in the answer. This means, of course, that the answer is useless for all practical purposes.

This is a simple example of ill-conditioning. It goes on all of the time in our calculations, usually unconsidered and so undetected. What are the implications of this for design?

As a general rule, fewer and simpler calculations make the propagation of initial errors easier to track, and less likely to occur. Compare, for example, the post-test only and the pre- and post-test experimental designs (Chapter Nine). In the first, the basic outcome measure is the difference in the mean scores for the treatment and control groups. In the second, the basic outcome measure is the difference in the gain scores for the treatment and control groups, where the gain score is the difference between the pre-test and post-test scores for each group. In the post-test only design, two similar estimated scores (the means for each group) are subtracted to create an answer that is considerably smaller yet contains the error component of both initial scores. This means that the maximum relative error will propagate, sometimes very considerably as in the example above, even where the initial errors are within reasonable bounds. The situation is worse for the pre- and post-test design however. First the pre- and post-test scores are subtracted for each individual. This again creates an answer that is considerably smaller yet contains the error component of both initial scores. These error-ridden gain scores are then averaged, and then the whole process happens again. The two very similar gain scores are subtracted to create a difference that is now very much smaller than any of the initial scores, but the maximum error components of each are still added into the computed result. We have no reason to assume that averaging the individual gain scores cancels out all or even any of the initial error. Remember that these are biases and systematic rather than random errors.

This result has been confirmed both by algebraic proof and by repeated simulation using the same datasets with known initial errors, as if derived from different initial designs (Gorard 2012b). In each simulation, the simpler design gave the result with the least error. In one example, the pre- and post-test design propagated an initial measurement error of 10% to an error of around 7,000% in the answer. Clearly, larger samples and more accurate measures capable of objective calibration can help, as can avoiding having a large number of measures in any study. Of course, such considerations also have implications for the use of significance tests, and the power calculations often based on them (Chapter Twelve). These apparently precise statistical computations are based on mathematical probabilities assuming that there is no measurement error involved. Imagine what a 7,000% relative error does to this assumption, and the steps that follow from it!

So, although error propagation is a problem for any real-life situation where computations are conducted with measures that are less than 100% accurate, it is less of a problem for the *simplest* designs where less computation is needed. All other things being equal, a post-test only design should be preferred to a pre- and post-test design for this reason. For the same reason, anything that can be done in planning the study (design) to avoid complex *post hoc* dredging of data will tend to improve the accuracy of the results.

11.3 ¦¦ Other threats

The problem of error propagation is properly a design issue, because the design affects the validity of the result. Many other threats to validity, such as non-random errors in entering data, are not intrinsically design issues because they can appear in any design (and using any kind of data). Several examples of these threats are summarised here, and further details can be found via the references and suggested further reading. In general, identification of any threats to validity comes from consideration of the warrant principle in relation to any research study. What follows are some of the general areas in which these threats might occur.

The researcher effect

The researcher can not only unwittingly skew the results of research once data has been collected, they can influence the research process from start to finish. This needs to be controlled for in the design, if possible, and made visible in the reporting of results. Researchers can inhibit or unwittingly demand certain responses, they can bias detection where observations favourable to some outcomes are more likely to be noted, and they can sabotage a study either through ignorance or sympathy for a participant. This researcher effect appeared most famously in the story of Clever Hans, the horse that could do arithmetic, tapping its hoof the correct number of times for the answer to any sum. In fact, Hans could not count but sensed the expectation in the audience or researchers when the correct answer was reached, and knew to stop at that point. If the researcher or audience did not know the answer themselves, then Hans could not 'count'. Social science often involves people both as researchers and participants. The opportunities for just such an effect, like misconstruing trying to please the researcher as a real result, or reacting favourably or unfavourably to an accent, appearance, or person's age, are manifold. Sometimes just conducting the research is enough to produce a change, or potentially misleading result, because people and organisations react to being researched (perhaps in the same way in which things are tidied up before a scheduled inspection). Again, this idea is famously encapsulated by one study – of the Hawthorne factory, where an increase in lighting increased production temporarily, and then a decrease in lighting increased production again. Almost any intervention or change could bring about a temporary change in outcome, and this can be guarded against by having data from some time before the intervention and for some considerable time afterwards.

Sub-contracting parts of the research to people with no vested interest in the outcome can help protect against the researcher effect. The sub-contracted role could be as varied as allocating cases to groups, or deciding whether an extract of data matches a pre-defined code, and running the eventual analysis. Sometimes this can be done by co-operating with a colleague, so that there is no financial implication for either study. Some aspects of the study can be automated, such as collecting some forms of data, or controlling aspects of a laboratory protocol. Some aspects can be blinded so that the researcher does not know which sub-group each case belongs to when collecting data from them. In order to protect this group identity from the case and the researcher, a *placebo* can be provided in which everyone appears to undergo the same treatment even though some of the treatment is phoney or empty (equivalent to a sugar pill in a drug trial). Other ways of minimising researcher bias include getting more than one account of any observation, by using several people as observers and looking at the inter-rater reliability of all measurements taken, or by a combination of methods wherein the findings are checked against evidence from other sources. All of these are useful, and many can be used in combination. Perhaps the single most important protection is to make sure that the complete research protocol is published, so that any study can be replicated, and that the primary dataset is publicly available for others to analyse.

It is important to realise that trying to separate the influence of the researcher from the collection and analysis of data in such ways is very different from issues of rapport. When dealing with people as participants in social science research, it is generally important to establish a relationship of trust, to encourage confidence, and to ensure that this confidence is justified. There are many useful resources on the craft tips for conducting interactive and participatory research. But this still means that the coding can be checked by a third party, and that the interviewer can conduct the interview without necessarily knowing which sub-group the interviewee is in, or how and why that case was selected. And the dataset can still be made public (with appropriate protection for anonymity).

Attrition of cases

There is a distinction between non-response and participant dropout. If a study defines a population, and tries to use data for the whole population, then any missing cases are like non-response. Similarly, if a sample is selected from the population but some of the cases in the sample do not take part (either they refuse or cannot be contacted) then this is non-response. Both examples would affect our ability to make general statements about the nature of the population on the basis of the data we collected. This is an issue of generalisability. We cannot assume that the missing cases (or data) are in any way a random sub-set of the population. In fact, it is safer to assume that they are not random (they may be more transient, less literate, not online, and so on). This means that there are no valid technical methods for replacing these cases or overcoming the deficiencies caused by their absence. Replacing them with other cases who do participate will lead to bias, since these replacements are less likely to have those characteristics leading to non-response in the first place. If we assume that non-respondents are somehow like the respondents, and so we use existing data to create the non-existent cases (or missing data), then this also leads to bias, because the study then over-represents those with the participants' characteristics. Some statistical and other methods resources will try and offer methods to deal with this problem, but examine them carefully. They will be a variant of one of the methods already mentioned – replacing cases or crafting the missing data from existing data.

The only really convincing way to handle such a generalisation, if you really want to make a generalisation, is to consider how different the missing cases would have to be for the result you found to be incorrect. This is a kind of sensitivity analysis. Imagine that you select a sample of 100 cases, but 10 do not participate in your study. You find that 50 of the 90 cases agree with a certain statement in a survey (that bankers' bonuses should be curtailed, to return to an earlier example). This means that a majority of your achieved sample of 90 agreed with the statement. If you report this precisely you are making a safe research claim. But how safe is it to report that a majority of the population agree with the statement? This issue is addressed further in Chapter Twelve, but note here that if all 10 of the missing cases would have disagreed with the statement, then the majority would not have agreed. Reporting like this highlights only the biggest, strongest and safest results, of the kind that would survive a skewed or stratified response from those whose response is unknown. However, it is also perfectly proper to note the non-response and then not attempt to generalise further, but to conduct analyses only with the achieved sample (or completed cases for a population).

The latter is what generally happens in experimental designs (Chapter Nine). The 'population' for the experiment (or similar design) consists only of those cases agreeing to take part. It is these cases only that the result will be generalised to in the first instance. Of course, the cases invited to take part may have been selected also to represent a wider population, in which case the next level of generalisation proceeds as above (and consent bias then becomes a key concern). If the cases agreeing to participate form the population, there is then no issue of non-response. Instead, we are concerned primarily with cases dropping out from the study after agreement – also termed 'attrition' or 'mortality'. This is a special problem in studies with a longitudinal element, since people may change residential areas, jobs or family circumstances; they may fall ill, emigrate or even die. It also surfaces in experimental designs where one group (often the treatment group) is seen as more desirable to be in than another. And as with non-response, it is likely that those cases less likely to continue with a study are systematically different from the rest (perhaps in terms of motivation, leisure time, geographic mobility and so on). Drop out means bias, or at least the strong possibility of bias.

Both non-response and drop out should be kept to a minimum by whatever means (making participation as easy as possible), but they will still occur. A number of approaches are feasible even so. Many are considered in Chapter Nine, such as *placebo* treatments, crossover and similar designs that mean all cases are in some kind of treatment group. In cluster designs, it is advisable to sign all cases up individually before allocating clusters to treatments. Participants should be made aware from the outset of the difference between being in the study and being part of any intervention. This means that if they walk away from the intervention (or control) they realise that their input to the study will still be valuable. The data can and probably should be analysed on an intention-to-treat basis, so that even drop out cases can be included.

11.5 ⊪ Conclusion

Care and attention to possible biases and confounds is part of good warranting of research claims. Such care is usually obvious in a research report, and is part of what it takes to be convinced and convincing about a research-based conclusion. Most methods resources focus on the threats to validity that occur within experimental designs and similar studies. This is because this area is well-theorised, and because the rigour and control of some experimental studies is so great that it is important for their consumers to realise that there may still be flaws in the warrant. Nevertheless, the careful design of experiments both makes their analysis easy and deals with a multitude of threats to their validity. They are intrinsically less likely to mislead through bias, selectivity and confounds than most other designs. The threats to validity can occur in *all* designs, and using any method of data collection and analysis. They are not worse in experimental approaches. They are generally better.

⊑ Exercises on validity

1   A large team of sales-persons are divided by their bosses into two groups at random. These groups will be used to test the effectiveness of a new motivational package given to one group only. After using the package for three months, the sales figures for both groups will be compared. The company bosses expect, on the basis of success elsewhere, that the motivational package will significantly boost sales for those using it.

   a   What are some of the key threats to the validity of the findings of such a study, as it has been described?
   b   In what relatively simple ways could the company protect the study from these threats?
   c   Could these attempts to protect the study from bias introduce new biases as well? If so, how?

2 Issues of validity for experiments have been discussed in some detail here. Consider how the kinds of issues raised in this chapter emerge in other research designs. Perhaps discuss these in a group and keep a record of your observations.
3 Find a research article in your area of interest that purports to evaluate an intervention. Look at the design, and check how many of the threats to validity the research is designed to be protected from. How does it protect from some? And which threats is it still open to?

⇇ Notes on exercises on validity

1 a There are several potential problems here. Salespeople often operate on commission. If the motivational package is actually successful it may lead to more sales for the treatment at the expense of the control. It may be that sales are not infinitely expandable and that each sale gained by one group represents a possible sale lost to the other. This would exaggerate the apparent effect of the treatment (see also Chapter Nine). Even if this does not happen, the control group may imagine that it will. They could be demoralised, which would exaggerate the apparent effect of the treatment, or they could react to prevent it, so reducing the apparent effect of the treatment. Worse, the demoralisation might mean that there is increased dropout or non-cooperation from the control group. Why should they cooperate with a study that may damage their livelihoods?

 b The company could explain that, for the duration of the study, the average commission of both groups will be kept artificially the same. This might prevent demoralisation of the control group.

 c But doing this might then cause problems for the treatment group who have to do the extra training, work hard to gain extra sales, and then see their commission shared with those who did not 'earn' it. This might again lead to a reduction in the apparent effect of the treatment. There will be other threats and other possible solutions with side-effects. The battle against bias is never won.

2 It is important to keep recalling that issues about validity and bias apply to all research designs. Experimental and near-experimental approaches have been better theorised than other designs. Perhaps there is also an element of those who use other designs in preference to experiments not wanting to open the can of worms that a straight comparison of validity would reveal. Of the issues in the chapter, it should be obvious that measurement errors and any errors in data collection, recording and storage are applicable to all designs. Similarly initial errors will 'propagate' in some way with any kind of data and any kind of coding or analysis. The researcher bias (misreading results in favour of a particular conclusion), and the researcher reactivity bias (inadvertently encouraging participants to say a particular thing in interviews or asking leading questions in a survey) are also clearly applicable to any design. In fact, such biases will probably be more influential in designs without strict randomisation and so on. As ever, the problems can be minimised by caring about the quality of the research answer rather than what the answer is, by having independent researchers check key steps in the study, and by making your data openly available for re-analysis by others.

3 Does the study use blinding – of the researcher, or participants? Does it have a *placebo* treatment group? Is allocation to groups done strictly and/or independently? How much dropout is there? And are the missing cases followed up for an intention-to-treat

analysis? Does the study use independent data collectors to protect participants from undue influence? Is the full data set available somewhere for inspection? And how many of these issues does the paper even report?

☰ Suggested reading

Chapter Eight in Gorard, S. (2003) *Quantitative Methods in Social Science: The Role of Numbers Nade Easy*. London: Continuum.

TWELVE

How big is a difference, and related matters

SUMMARY

- In judging whether a perceived difference between two measurements or observations is worthy of further investigation, a number of factors need to be considered.
- These factors include the relative size of the difference, its variability between sub-groups, and its substantive, economic or theoretical importance if accepted.
- Many of the same factors using the same kind of logic apply to judgements in the analysis of other kinds of data, and in looking at any pattern or trend.
- There is a range of standard effect sizes, sometimes complementary but mostly for use with different contexts or types of data.
- These include the absolute difference in the scores divided by their sum; the absolute difference divided by their standard or mean deviation; odds ratios for categorical variables; and the percentage of variation in common or explained.
- If a study has random variation in sampling, then it is possible to consider random sampling variation as one of the possible explanations for any difference. Once such sampling variation has been rejected as a likely explanation, then the question becomes whether the difference is worthy of further notice.
- If a study does not involve random sampling variation then this stage should be skipped, and analysis proceeds directly to the question of whether the difference is worthy of further notice.
- Measurement errors, non-response and case drop out must also be taken into account, usually in a hypothetical analysis to judge the possible impact or missing or erroneous data. As in Chapter Eleven, the propagation of errors should be a major concern.
- In the end, any decision is a judgement, and must be explained and justified to others as such.

12.1 ⅼ⫶ Introduction

This chapter is about deciding how big a difference between two measurements has to be before we accept that this is an important and genuine difference. Why is this an issue for research design? Partly because specifying differences of interest is good preparation for a study. Partly it is of interest because a lot of the book so far has depended on judgements about differences over time, or between places, sub-groups or treatment arms. Partly it is because we need some understanding of the issues in this chapter to make and understand warranted claims. Much of the focus of the chapter is on differences between two or more measurements. However, it is also about the related matters of patterns and trends or differences in any datasets. Given that there is rarely a simple or technical answer to the question about differences, the underlying logic of the decision is the same in a variety of analytical situations.

As presaged by the discussion in Chapters Six and Seven, there is no easy answer to how big a difference between two groups has to be for it to be taken seriously, whether for policy, practice or theory. For example, in measuring the average heights of two groups of adults, a difference of a fraction of a millimetre will probably be ignored. Everyone can imagine that such a small difference, relative to the average height of an adult, could be the result of a tiny error in one measurement, or a minor variation caused by the method of sampling, or in the identification of the two groups. In a physics experiment, on the other hand, even a difference this small could be of great importance, perhaps because it is larger relative to the things being measured, or because the measurements are more precise, or the sample is millions of times larger. The context and the meaning of the numbers involved combine with estimates of measurement precision, the study's power of discrimination, the scale and variability of the measurement, and the sample size, to help a researcher make a judgement about whether a difference matters. So, on the one hand, there is no technical and easy way of saying that an observed difference in the data is important, or not. On the other hand, we all routinely make such sophisticated judgements all of the time, almost without noticing. We are naturally quite good at it.

Consider this analogy. You are in a supermarket (chain A) trying to buy an item – perhaps a number of tins of soup. You see the price and are aware that another local supermarket (chain B) is offering the same item for 4c less each. Which of the two supermarkets is selling this item for the lowest price? I suspect that sounds like an easy and rather silly question. It is a silly question. Supermarket B is offering the tin of soup for 4c less, and that is the lowest price of the two. Yet I have had researchers, both new and highly experienced, asking for my help to decide on similar questions very regularly. Perhaps they have used an attitude scale and found that the men respondents had an average score of 3.7 and the women an average of 3.8. Clearly, the score for women is higher.

But the researcher asks me if it is 'really' bigger. And I say, helpfully, yes it is really bigger, as long as you measured, transcribed, recorded and analysed the individual scores correctly. The researcher usually, and wrongly, brushes these caveats aside as unimportant to them. What the researcher seems to want to ask is a combination of two very different questions. They want to know whether this apparent difference between the attitudes of men and women would also be true of some larger population of men and women. That is, they want to generalise their finding, using statistical inference. And they also want to know the really crucial thing, which is whether this difference of 0.1 is worth pursuing, substantively, practically, or scientifically.

The supermarket analogy can help here. It shows that the first generalisation question is often not very important. If you want one tin, then it is not relevant whether chain A supermarkets generally charge 4c more than chain B's for this soup. You know that this branch of supermarket A charges 4c more than supermarket B. This is all the information you need to make your decision. And if the two chains have a standard pricing policy then you know that all will have the same price for this item, barring mistakes. Or if the tin is dented and appears on a shelf devoted to reduced cost items, then you know that the price will generally be even higher elsewhere. In each of these situations and many others, the generalisation answer is trivial in the sense that it makes no practical difference to you. And even if you do want to consider the difference for entire chains of supermarkets, you are still then stuck with the second question about whether the difference is big enough to matter.

The key issue is therefore the second one – is the saving of 4c sufficient to make you go to the other supermarket instead? The answer to this crucial question depends on such a lot of different factors that there is no definite answer for all people. Yet each of us will come up with the right answer for ourselves quickly and easily, in practice. For example, if you wanted to buy a large number of tins of soup then the total saving could be large, and this might influence the decision in favour of going to the cheaper supermarket. If the other supermarket is a long way away, or you are short of time, this might influence the decision in favour of sticking with the more expensive supermarket. If your resources are large relative to a 4c saving, or 4c is minimal in relation to the cost of the tin, you may be more likely not to change supermarkets. So it is perfectly proper that different people will come to different rational decisions, and there is no simple technical way of deciding. Yet, in reality, the decision is usually easy to make. We can almost instantly compare scale, quality, convenience, value-for-money and other factors, and then synthesise the results and decide what to do. The same is true with data analysis. It is really quite easy. What makes it harder than 'real-life' is that as a researcher you must also explain fully to others, via a research report, why you decided to ignore or pursue the difference you found.

So there are a number of factors to consider when examining a possible difference. There is the direction, the scale (size of difference relative to the scores themselves), the variability of the scores and their relative value for sub-groups of cases, the costs and benefits of getting the decision wrong in either direction, and the substantive and theoretical importance of the decision. That is a lot to take into account in one decision. The discussion so far has been about differences between groups or cases. This can be important, but lack of difference can be just as interesting as difference in a finding. The same idea about judging differences and explaining your judgement to others also applies to uncovering trends, or indeed any pattern in your data. This chapter presents a number of useful techniques to help you judge whether a pattern or difference in your data is worth pursuing, and whether it might also apply to a larger number of cases than in your study.

12.2 ||| A range of 'effect' sizes

Whether you are interested in a difference between two or more groups, or a pattern or trend, perhaps the most important thing to establish first is its strength or scale. This is referred to as its 'effect' size, which is not a good name because it implies an unjustified causal relationship. Just remember that an effect size does not necessarily imply that the difference or pattern is an effect of any known cause (yet). The effect size needs to be standardised in some way to take account of the context and units of measurement – a difference of 1cm may be large in the growth of a person, but less so as the difference in length between two car journeys, for example. This is well-known and understood in everyday situations. A score of 51 to 49 in basketball denotes a close game. A score of 3 to 1 in football (soccer) represents a reasonably comfortable victory margin. However, this distinction is regularly ignored in the more confusing environment of research, when it could be quite easily dealt with by looking at the differences in terms of proportions. For example, we could look at the differences in sports scores in terms of the total scores. Thus, a 3:1 football score shows a 50% victory margin, calculated as the difference in scores divided by the sum of the scores, or $(3-1)/(3+1)$, or 0.5. The basketball score, on the other hand, could be represented as a 2% victory margin, or $(51-49)/(51+49)$, or 0.02. This simple conversion of the raw-score difference tells us what we should already know, which is that the football margin of victory is greater, but it does so in a formal and standardised way that can be used to guard against inadvertent misjudgement in the matter.

    This 'achievement gap', calculated as the difference between two scores divided by their sum, is a perfectly proper way to represent an effect size, when there are only two sets of scores, as here. It is closely related to a range of other useful effect sizes, and indices of inequality (Gorard and Taylor 2002). A point that must be grasped early on is that there are a number of similar approaches, each of which may have relative merits in certain situations; none is perfect, and it is only convention that any one is more common than any other. All sensible approaches should lead to the same substantive finding, of the direction and probably the scale of the difference. If a finding depends on which precise version of effect size is used, then this is not safe or convincing. And all approaches still require judgement on the part of the analyst (see below). Not using any standardising procedure for effect sizes has led many commentators into error and misunderstanding – about the apparent underachievement of boys at school, for example (Gorard et al. 2001a).

A useful standardising summary when dealing with tallies of categorical data is the odds ratio. Table 12.1 shows some figures for an organisation, employing both men and women, of whom a minority have been promoted this year. It is not immediately clear whether men or women were more likely to be promoted, and by how much. It would be even harder to compare this difference between the promotion chances of the sexes with those in another smaller company (Table 12.2). Which company has the best odds of promotion, and how do these vary between men and women? Which company is the 'fairest', just on the basis of this data, between promotions for men and women?

The odds ratio is the ratio of the odds of an event occurring for one group compared to the odds for a second group. In Table 12.1 the odds of a man being promoted this year are 92:185 or just about 50%. The odds of a woman being promoted are 35:130 or just under 27%. It is clear from the example that the odds of promotion for men are higher than for women in the larger company. The odds *ratio* is (92/185)/(35/130) or 1.85. The odds ratio is standardised and has an everyday meaning. This example shows that men in the larger company are almost twice as likely to get promoted as women.

In Table 12.2, the odds of a man being promoted this year are 80:64 or about 125%. The odds of a woman being promoted are 54:78 or 69%. The odds ratio is (80/64)/(54/78) or 1.81%. The odds ratios are about the same in both companies,

Table 12.1 Male and female promotions this year, larger company

	Men	Women	Total
Promoted	92	35	127
Not promoted	185	130	315
Total	277	165	442

Table 12.2 Male and female promotions this year, smaller company

	Men	Women	Total
Promoted	80	54	134
Not promoted	64	78	142
Total	144	132	276

and neither is clearly the fairest in this sense. The smaller company offered better chances of promotion for both sexes, but the relative chance of promotion for a woman in comparison to a man was about the same as in the larger company.

If we label the four key tables' cells from left to right by rows, so a = men, promoted; b = women, promoted; c = men, not promoted; and d = women, not promoted, then the odds ratio is (a/c)/(b/d). Alternatively this can be expressed as (a.d/b.c). It has the advantage of being comparable across similar tables with different size values and distributions. However, it is unbounded between 0 and infinity, and it is confusing for beginners that values less than 1 are on a different scale to values greater than 1. So, 0.5 is equivalent in scale to 2, 0.1 is equivalent to 10, and so on. Neither of these characteristics is convenient. An alternative, but less common, approach is to use the determinant of a two by two table. This is (a.d–b.c), using the same notation for cells. The 'risk ratio' is more commonly used for trial designs. If we exchange men and women for treatment and control groups in such a design, and promotion becomes success or failure in some outcomes, then the 'risk' ratio is (a/(a+c))/(b/(b+d)). In Table 12.1 this would be (92/277)/(35/165) or 1.57. In Table 12.2 the risk ratio would be (80/144)/(54/132) or 1.36. Again this suggests that the situation in both datasets is similar, but here the data in Table 12.1 appears slightly more stratified. The risk ratio is closely related to the Gorard Segregation Index for measuring stratification across larger tables with any number of cells, while the odds ratio is more closely related to the Dissimilarity Index that similarly extends its reach to any number of cells (Gorard 2009).

There are a number of other summary and related effect sizes that mostly spring from epidemiology and health sciences, such as the risk reduction factor. Probably the most versatile and easy to comprehend is the number needed to treat (NNT). In medical treatment, NNT is the mean number of people who need to take the treatment for one person to benefit (to be cured, report alleviation or whatever). Or strictly it is that number who benefit compared to a control receiving no treatment. Of course, we would like this to be one, so that every person treated benefits (and no one in the control does!). But in reality this will not happen, and NNT will be greater than one, sometimes considerably greater. NNT can be adapted to consider unintended harmful consequences as well, and NNT can be extended in social science to situations beyond health (although we probably want to think of a new name for it). Almost any intervention, such as new incentives for bankers, new rules for social workers, or a new training course for architects, can be the treatment.

These approaches are all good at standardising 'effect' sizes by overcoming differences in scale, and to some extent the distribution. Just as important is to handle the variability with any set of numbers. We might be able to describe the mean difference between two sets of numbers as scientifically trivial if the numbers themselves show considerable variation over time or place (volatility). Or, put the other way around, a mean difference of a certain scale between two sets of numbers is more convincing if the numbers themselves have a low standard or mean deviation. The standard deviation is the most commonly used measure of variation, defined as the square root of: the sum of the squares of all deviations from the mean, divided by the number of measurements. This is a somewhat strange metric for everyday use, and the reasons for its widespread use in most basic measurement situations are unclear (Gorard 2006a). A simpler alternative is the absolute mean deviation, which is defined as the average of all absolute deviations from the mean. The major disadvantage of the mean deviation is that it is not in widespread use. As with so many alternatives, both give a very similar substantive result, except where the standard deviation (SD) is strongly influenced by extreme outlying scores.

There are a number of variations on the standard effect size for the difference between the means of two groups. Probably the most common is Cohen's d. This is defined as the difference between means divided by their standard deviation. This yields an effect in terms of a multiple of standard deviations (how many SD distant are the means of the two groups?). This is clever, because it deals with both scale and variability at once. A slight ambiguity concerns which mean this standard deviation relates to. Cohen claimed it could be the SD of either group, but that it could also be the pooled SD for both groups combined. The latter seems to make more sense. And of course, the mean deviation could be used instead. A variant of this is Glass's delta, defined as the difference between means divided by the SD for the control group alone, who are deemed to represent the wider population more than the treatment group. As with so many choices presented in this book, all options and several other variants make some sense, and if a result depends on precisely which version of effect size is used then it is probably not worth pursuing anyway.

Sometimes we are concerned not so much with a difference as a pattern or trend. Again, there are a number of 'effect' sizes available for use. Most have as their basis the proportion of the variation between two sets of numbers that is common, or the proportion of variation in one set of scores 'explained' by consistent variation in another set. A good example is the square of the Pearson's R value calculated as a correlation coefficient. R^2 is an estimate of the common variation between two sets of scores – also known as the coefficient of determination. R^2 of +1 (or –1) means that any variation in one set is exactly matched by variation in the other. So, either the two sets are actually scores of the same thing, as would happen with a series of temperatures measured using the Centigrade and Fahrenheit scales, or one score is somehow an analogue of the other, such as the angle of a speedometer compared to the speed of a vehicle. R^2 of 0 suggests no linear relationship between the two sets of scores at all. As with all effect sizes, there are assumptions here about the kind of numbers involved (they must be real numbers), and about their inter-relationship (R^2 cannot assess a relationship between two variables that is non-linear when cross-plotted). In the same way, Cohen's d and related effect sizes are for use with real numbers, and were devised for two sets of scores each with a near-normal (bell-shaped when plotted) distribution.

Less technically, we can look at the stability of a difference over time and place, or of a trend over time. What we might accept as a small difference of no great importance should be considered very differently if it appears annually for example. A growth in unemployment of 0.1% in a month may be written off as the normal volatility of numbers. A growth of 0.1% for 20 successive months not only adds up to 2% growth, but would be more interesting because it happens so regularly. This issue is picked up again at the end of the chapter.

Once a standard effect size has been calculated it can be compared to the cost, if known, of creating that effect. For example, we may have a good idea of the total cost of implementing an intervention with n cases in a field trial. We could divide the cost by n to obtain the cost of the programme per participant, and then compare the effect size with that cost to produce the unit cost of improving the situation for one case by one standard deviation (of the outcome score). This is a useful approach. It might overestimate the costs when or if the intervention is rolled out into wider practice, because the unit cost might be higher for the trial. On the other hand a trial is conducted only with the willing, so the early cost might be lower. This approach could also try to bring in other costs, and indirect benefits or dangers. The advantage for those 'treated' may have deleterious consequences for those not participating in the trial. Or there may be value-added. A cost-benefit analysis is not straightforward, but it is good practice once an effect has been reasonably well-established (towards the end of the cycle in Chapter Two).

Before looking in more detail at the key question of how large, cheap or stable an effect size has to be before we decide to pursue it, I must deal first with the considerable problem presented by the red-herring of statistical significance testing.

12.3 ▍ The relevance of random sampling variation

The chapter started by listing the relative size of any difference, its variability between sub-groups, and its substantive, economic or theoretical importance, as some of the criteria to use in judging differences (or patterns or trends). Yet most studies I have encountered in systematic reviews consider *none* of these issues. Those labelled 'qualitative' by their authors usually consider none of these issues, give the reader no information on which to make their own judgements, and present or make public very little of the data. Yet, these studies continue to make bold claims about patterns and differences without much justification that I can see. The remaining studies involve numbers and most of these also consider none of the key issues. Instead they focus on the less important topic of random sampling variation. Of course, if a study has random variation in the sampling procedure, then it makes sense to check for sampling variation as one of the possible explanations for any difference. But this is additional to the points made in this chapter so far. It should not be done *instead* of considering the other factors like scale, cost and substantive importance.

When I have conducted reviews, I found that studies involving numbers usually presented only a small part of the necessary analysis. What they did was to consider how likely it was that any difference arose solely through the randomisation process (randomisation of allocation in a multi-group study, or of random selection for a survey). They approached the issue of random sampling variation via sampling theory and used its derivatives such as standard errors, confidence intervals, and significance testing (both stand-alone and as part of modelling). The calculation of sampling probabilities is grounded in various assumptions, such as a random or randomised sample and complete measurement of all cases in the selected sample (de Vaus 2002). There are many examples of misuse of the method such as widespread acceptance of p-values based on non-probability samples, or dredging datasets via multiple use of a technique whose probability calculations are predicated on one-off use (Wright 2003). Many, perhaps even most, such studies I have seen completely misuse these sampling theory derivatives. I have encountered significance tests with birth cohort studies and other population data, with non-random samples, and with samples deigned to be random but in fact not so because of very poor response rates or high dropout. Almost all such studies then further misused the sampling theory derivatives in the sense that they presented the significance test outcomes as though they could handle measurement error and the other issues in this chapter. In fact, of course, such tests only address sampling variation. And if sampling variation is ruled out as an explanation of the difference in scores between two groups, then the analyst still has to consider all of the other possible explanations before deciding that the result is substantively important. Social science could make an overnight improvement simply by deciding to use sampling theory only where it is relevant (in a tiny minority of studies).

There is also a logical problem in the use of sampling theory derivatives, even when used correctly and for their correct purpose (Gorard 2010c). The procedure for a significance test (or use of standard error or confidence interval) is essentially a probabilistic version of the classic argument by falsification, or *modus tollendo tollens*. The question facing analysts is whether a difference between two (or more) sets of scores in their sample(s) would also be found in the population from which the sample was taken (Siegel 1956). Mathematically this is a bit like drawing six red and four blue balls from a bag of 1,000 red and blue balls, and trying to decide from this sample of 10 how many red and how many blue balls there were in the bag. This is impossible to judge. A much easier question is – if there were in fact 500 red and 500 blue balls in the bag, how likely is it to draw six red balls in a sample of 10? Here, the number of balls of each colour is known initially, and the calculation is a relatively trivial probability exercise. This kind of calculation is what statisticians *actually* do with significance tests. If they assume that there is in fact no difference in the population between two sets of scores, it is a simple matter of calculation to work out how likely it is that they will encounter a difference at least as large as the one they found in any random sample of a given size from that population. But why should they or anyone else want to know this probability? What they want is the probability that there actually is a difference between two groups in the population. But this is an entirely different probability (see Chapter Four).

The problem with significance testing arises because analysts do not know the actual distribution for the population, and do not actually want to know the probability they have calculated. They are using one kind of calculation (about the sample, or how likely it is to draw six red balls) incorrectly as though it could answer a completely different kind of question (about the population, or what the six red balls tell us about what is left in the bag). Simple logic shows that this is incorrect (Shadish et al. 2002). A low probability of the difference observed in the sample, given no difference in the population, does not mean that there is a high probability of a difference in the population. In fact, these two things are contradictions of each other. The two probabilities in isolation are not calculable from each other, and the probability for the population can only be estimated from the probability for the sample by the application of Bayes' theorem, and knowledge of a third probability (the unconditional probability of there being no difference in the population at the outset). In real-life this unconditional probability is not known, and so the whole probabilistic *modus tollens* argument fails. A low probability for the sample could be associated with a high, middling or low probability for the population, and therefore each says almost nothing about the other in isolation. Rolling a two followed by a three with one die is less likely than the 0.05 probability used in significance testing, but provides no evidence at all that the die is biased. Sadly, we seem to have a psychological flaw, making us ignore prior probability when new data appears, so that the new data simply replaces what we knew rather than modifying it appropriately (Tversky and Kahneman 1974).

There are therefore considerable problems with the sampling theory approach to judging differences and patterns – whether it is used properly or not. The approach encourages the separation of social science and statistics, leading to nonsensical statistical claims. Statisticians have 'a regrettable tendency' (Senn and Julious 2009, p. 3205) to regard the meaning and quality of measurements as the province of others. This leads to problems in publications and in the teaching of numeric methods to each generation of researchers. Students generally show widespread misunderstanding of the meaning of numeric results (McAlevey and Sullivan 2010), and are no better having completed a statistics course. This is usually because their teachers know no better anyway. Common mistakes are in the interpretation of p-values as being the probability of any hypothesis being true, or the belief that the true value of a measure must lie within its confidence interval, or has a specific probability of lying within that confidence interval. Even after peer review, there are clear errors in reporting such things in many papers (Henson et al. 2010). There is little attention to the important issues of the meaning of numbers, the impact of non-response, or the accuracy of measurements. Published papers rarely use effect sizes, the reported analysis is usually over-reliant on software default settings, there is often an insufficient sample-to-variable ratio, and causal statements are misused to describe associations (which takes us back to the early part of this book). Above all, the subjective nature of statistical decisions is rarely understood or explained. In these senses, a lot of social science is currently what Park (2000) called 'Voodoo science'.

In summary then, statistical testing is often inappropriate, and is always insufficient to help decide whether one set of measures is markedly greater than another. Yet analysts want precisely that ability to judge the probability of the nil null hypothesis, and so they pretend that this is what they have calculated, and so-called methods experts and resources connive in promulgating this widespread error, such as:

> [Statistical significance is] the likelihood that a real difference or relationship between two sets of data has been found. (Somekh and Lewin 2005, p. 224)

This is plain wrong. Yet, unfortunately it is an accurate description of what too many social scientists think their p-values mean. This widespread error could be part of the reason why social science statistical results so often lead to non-effective treatments and 'vanishing breakthroughs' (Harlow et al. 1997). This needs to change. There is no point in having a robust research design, and then using a logically flawed approach to analysis. Researchers are entitled to report the probability of getting the data they did, assuming that their nil null hypothesis is true, as long as they report it as such correctly. But, I repeat, why would they or anyone want to know that probability? As soon as authors start reporting it correctly, hopefully they will realise the error. We must insist that they do report it fully and correctly, because it is part of the warrant (Chapter Four). As a first step, we should insist on no more significance tests with non-probability samples, including population data, convenience, opportunity or incomplete samples, or any data with measurement error or missing values. This wipes out most current uses immediately, making analyses easier and more robust at the same time.

12.4 ‖ Conclusion – so how big is a difference?

It is clear that, for any dataset, dividing the cases into two sub-groups will rarely yield exactly the same scores on all measures for both groups (Meehl 1967). It is unlikely *a priori* that the school pupils sitting on the left-hand side of a classroom will have exactly the same average height as those sitting on the right. Their parents are unlikely to report drinking exactly the same average number of cups of tea every day, and so on. A difference in scores or observations may, therefore, have no useful meaning at all. Whether a difference is more than this, and is actually substantial and worthy of note, can depend on a number of factors. It depends on the size of the difference in relation to the scale in which the difference occurs (an observed difference of two centimetres may be important in comparing the heights of two people, but not in comparing flight distances between Europe and Australia). It depends on the variability of all of the scores. It is harder to establish a clear difference between two sets of scores that have high levels of intrinsic variation than between scores in which each member of each group produces the same score as all other members of that group. The noteworthiness of a difference may also depend upon the benefits and dangers of missing a difference if it exists, or of assuming a difference if it does not (Cox 2001).

All of these issues of scale, variability and cost are relevant even if the scores are measured precisely. But in reality, scores are seldom measured precisely, and measures like self-esteem, aspiration, occupational class and ethnicity will be subject to a very high level of measurement error. Measurement error is nearly always a bias in the scores (i.e. it is not random). People who do not respond to questions accurately (or at all) cannot be assumed to be similar to those who do. Children for whom a school has no prior attainment data, or no knowledge of eligibility for free schools, cannot be assumed to be the same as everyone else. A ruler that is too short and so over-estimates heights will tend to do so again and again, uncompensated by any kind of random under-estimates to match it. Even human (operator) error has been shown to be non-random, in such apparently neutral tasks as entering data into a computer. So knowledge of the likely sources of error in any score, and an estimate of the range of measurement errors, is an additional and crucial part of deciding whether a difference between groups is big enough (to justify a substantive claim). The harder it is to measure something, the larger the errors in measurement will tend to be, and so the larger the difference would have to be, to be considered substantial.

As illustrated in the book and the chapter exercises, one way of approaching all of these potential issues together is to consider how much any score or set of scores would have needed to differ for there to be no observed difference, and then compare this level of difference with the natural variation and with the scale of measurement error. This involves judgement, but is also a tough test. As a heuristic, a difference that is worth working with will usually be clear and obvious from a fairly simple inspection of the data. If we have to dredge deeply for any 'effect', then it is probably 'pathological' to believe that anything useful will come out of it. We cannot specify the minimum size needed for an effect, nor can we use standardised tables of the meanings of effect sizes (Gorard 2006b). Those tables showing an effect size of 0.2 as 'small' and 0.8 as 'big' and so on are a guide only. But we can say with some conviction that, in our present state of knowledge in social science, the harder it is to find the effect the harder it will be to find a use for the knowledge so generated. It is probably unethical to continue to use public money pursuing some of the more pathological findings of social science. We need to focus our limited social science funding on effects that are big, sustained or have a high benefit:cost ratio.

⪦ Exercises on differences and patterns

1 A research project reports a survey of 1,033 members of a sports club, asking them about the strategic direction of the club. A total of 473 members responded. The survey involved 20 questions each making a statement or proposal for action, and asking respondents to state whether they: strongly agree; agree; disagree; or strongly disagree with each. There are also a few background questions, including how long the respondent had been a member of the club. On one substantive question, the research reports a clear relationship between length of club membership and level of agreement. The agreement levels were converted to scores of 1 for strongly disagree, 2 for disagree, 3 for agree, and 4 for strongly agree. These scores were used with months of membership to calculate a Pearson's R correlation coefficient of 0.31, which was described as significant at the 0.05 level.

a What is the published effect size here?
b What does significant at the 0.05 level mean here?
c From the outline description, suggest three ways in which the effect size and p-value might be misleading?

2 A new study has conducted 500 home-based structured interviews with householders. There were 300 middle-class families (according to their responses) and 200 working-class. Because of refusals, 1,200 homes were approached to gain these 500 responses.

a What is the response rate in this study?
b How different from this 60:40 distribution of the classes would the non-responding families have to be for there to be actually more working-class families in the initial 1,200?
c Assume that the study does not attempt to generalise, but is only concerned with the achieved sample of 500. Imagine also that the process of deciding on who is middle- or working-class leads to around 10% mis-classifications in each direction. The study reports that middle-class respondents are more likely own a car (200 of them) compared to working-class (of whom only 100 had a car). How safe is this claim, considering the cases in the study?

3 Select a research paper or report in your own area of interest that involves in-depth data from interviews. Decide if the paper provides enough information on the strength or prevalence of any patterns or differences it reports. From what is reported, can you make your own estimate of the strength or prevalence of any reported patterns or differences?

⪦ Notes on exercises on differences and patterns

1 a The apparent effect size would be 0.31 squared, or just under 10% of the variance.
   b Reporting this effect size as 'significant at the 0.05 level' means the following: hypothetically, if the same question were asked of a series of random samples of club

members, of the same size as the sample in the study, and if there was no relationship between the response and length of membership, then a correlation at least as strong as this would be found less than one time in 20. It does *not* mean anything like: there is only a 1 in 20 chance of there being no relationship. The calculation assumes there is no relationship from the outset.

c I hope you can see lots of problems here. The sample is not random, so the whole process of calculating a p-value has been done in error. There is not really even a sample, but an incomplete census of the members of one club (less than 46% response rate). There is also a suggestion that many significance tests have been run and this one picked out because it is 'significant'. So, even if the sample had been a random sample, the p-value would still have been misleading because it is based on an assumption that only one test is being run. Roll six dice and you are likely to get at least one six. This means nothing. Run twenty significance tests and you are likely to get at least one p-value less than 0.05. This also means nothing. Finally, are you happy that the agreement scale is a real number that can be correlated with the length of membership? A real number system has equal intervals between points on the scale. Can the difference here between 1 (strongly disagree) and 2 (disagree) really be the same as the difference in meaning between 2 (disagree) and 3 (agree)? I do not think so. In fact, I think this whole study (while not at all unusual in the literature) is shockingly poor.

2 a The response rate, as far as we can tell, is 500/1200 or 42%. This is quite poor, but higher than in quite a lot of published studies. It means that we can really tell very little about the population. It means that we cannot do any sampling theory statistics, such as significance tests, since these assume full response.

b In the achieved sample there are more middle-class families (300/500). If all cases approached (1,200) had taken part, the minimum number of families needed for there to be a majority of working-class families would have been 601. This means that if 401 or more of the 700 non-responding families were working-class then working-class would (and should) have been a majority. So the study has to argue that there is no reason to suppose that the missing cases were this much more likely (57% in total) to be working-class. If, on the other hand, we can think of a reason why working-class families would be less likely to take part in a household interview then we might want to reject the study findings (in this respect). Note that this is not a technical issue, nor even a statistical one as that term is usually intended. There is nothing that random sampling theory can do to help.

c This gets a bit complex to envisage even though there are only two variables to consider (class and car ownership). This difficulty of conceptualisation may be part of the reason why error theory and error propagation is largely ignored even in other resources devoted to research design. A 10% mis-classification rate is perfectly realistic when converting interview responses into a rather subjective category system such as occupational class. There are 300 middle-class and 200 working-class respondents. If 10% of each are in the wrong category, then 30 apparently middle-class families are working-class and 20 apparently working-class families are really middle-class. Thus, there should have been 290 middle-class and 210 working-class families. This 10% mis-classification alone does not substantially affect the proportions of each class. A 10% initial error leads to a relatively small error in the result. This is acceptable, and quite normal both in social science and beyond. However, the situation is not as simple as that.

We do not know how many car owners were in each of the mis-classified groups. Originally, it seemed that 66% of the middle-class (200/300) and only 50% of the working-class (100/200) owned cars. This seems a sound basis to declare a difference. But if all of the mis-classified middle-class (30) owned cars and none of the mis-classified working-class did (20) then the difference disappears. There are now 170/290 or 63% car owners in the middle-class, and 130/210 or 62% in the working-class. The apparently substantial difference has disappeared at a stroke! This may seem extreme, but the principle of looking at how safe any results are if there are errors in the initial data is a good one. Of course, it gets a lot more complicated in most real studies. Even in this simplified example, we have ignored so far the possibility that there is also some mis-classification in reporting car ownership as well. Imagine building that into the calculation, and then imagine how to track the propagation of errors and their possible implications in a multivariate analysis. Simple is good, in design, in logic, and in calculations.

3 It is alarming that many papers and research reports do not provide much detail about the data involved. This is perhaps especially the case for work involving in-depth data where no numbers are attached to the claims. Notice that this does not prevent the authors claiming the existence of things like patterns and differences. It just means that the readers can have no real idea of the prevalence of any pattern or trend. Instead of explicit numbers, vague terms like 'many', 'some' and 'most' are used. The dataset is seldom available. And the data examples quoted are unclear. Are they average examples, ideal, the best expressed or even the most extreme for that 'code'? Usually, from what is reported, I have no way of making my own estimate of the strength or prevalence of any reported patterns or differences. Surely this has to change if we demand it, or at least if we just ignore any research that does not provide this very basic information. A lot of this chapter has been about numeric data. It is important to recall that the difficulties and problems are almost certainly worse, if somewhat harder to demonstrate, with non-numeric data.

⇶ Suggested reading

Gorard, S. (2010) 'All evidence is equal: the flaw in statistical reasoning', *Oxford Review of Education*, 36(1): 63–77.

THIRTEEN

A second principle of ethics

SUMMARY

- Much of the writing about ethical issues in research, and the legislation and oversight that goes with it, concerns the principle of not harming the research participants.
- This chapter considers, in addition, the perspective of people who do not take part in the research, but who may fund it or be affected by its results.
- From this perspective the quality of the research conclusions, as aided by a robust design, is paramount.
- It is therefore unethical to conduct poor research, and make unwarranted research claims.

13.1 ▌▏ Introduction

This chapter looks at the ethics of research design. Most resources dealing with the ethics of social science research tend to focus on detailed aspects of research behaviour that could be subsumed under one principle. This principle is – do not harm the participants in research. The same principle underlies most of the codes of practice published by professional and academic research organisations, such at the British Sociological Association. There are good reasons for these codes, based partly on a reaction to work conducted in the mid-twentieth century in which research participants were subjected to stress, made to behave out of character, or given treatments that they had not agreed to. It is also important to consider the researchers and research assistants as participants in the study and what possible damage may be caused to them.

There is a range of well-known and widely reported methods for ensuring that researchers cannot do what they did in the bad old days. These include oversight by

independent ethical committees, transparency of research procedure and protocols, formal agreement to participate, clarification that participants are able to
withdraw from a study, anonymity of participants in research reports, monitored
destruction of sensitive data after use, and many others. Perhaps more importantly, these rules for research are really an indication that times have changed.
Researchers generally do not seem to want to cause harm to their participants,
if they ever did. And why would they? A growing proportion of social science
research uses pre-existing data and evidence, and much of the rest uses data that
is or could have been generated anyway. An example of the former could be a
re-analysis of official figures on obesity in the UK, broken down by age and area
of residence, considered before and after a new policy push to reduce obesity. An
example of the latter could be the testing of a new method of teaching fractions
in school to 11-year-olds. This kind of change goes on all of the time in schools,
where teachers adopt new curricula, new textbooks or return from an in-service
development course. Treating such a change as research does not make it less or
more ethical. It is part of professional practice.

However, there are a number of further ethical issues that are not so well covered in traditional methods texts or professional codes of practice. These are the
main focus of this chapter.

13.2 ▮▮ Conflicts of interest

An example of such an issue is the idea of a 'conflict of interest'. It is clear
in health sciences that a pharmaceutical company which has spent millions
of pounds developing a new drug or medicine will have a conflict of interest
when that drug is evaluated for effectiveness, cost-effectiveness and possible
side-effects. Although any bias on the part of the company may be completely
inadvertent, bias can still arise. It is much better that the people evaluating the
drug before licensing it for wider use do not stand to gain or lose on the basis
of what the result is. The evaluator's concern, indeed their passion, must be to
find the best answer to the questions about effectiveness. Therefore they should
care about the research, but not about what the research finds. If the research
finds that the drug works, that is good because then a new medicine is available. If the research finds that the drug is hazardous to health, then that is good
because the study has saved a large number of potential users from harm. But
what is true here is also true for all forms of social science research in whatever
area the research is. The job of the researcher is to answer the research questions
as safely and securely as possible, with concern for the quality of the findings
and conclusions, but with no concern for what the findings actually are. There
is an immediate conflict of interest whenever the researcher cares what the
findings are.

In some areas this is clear, as there is a close analogy to drug evaluation. For example, software manufacturers who evaluate the effectiveness of their products for use in hospitals, offices, or school classrooms have a conflict of interest. Chapter Nine included an example of software manufacturers advertising a product's effectiveness on the basis of a before-and-after score with no comparator. This is a clearly invalid design for the kinds of claims made 'on the tin'. Whether this is due to incompetence or something more culpable, it seems obvious that such claims ought to be tested independently. The same situation arises when social science researchers have developed a product – such as software for data analysis, or a method of teaching – and are also the ones to test it out. Wherever money follows to the researcher from the precise nature of the research findings (as opposed to their quality), there is a conflict of interest. However, sometimes this conflict can be quite subtle or surprising.

I was once awarded a research contract with colleagues to summarise the patterns of under-achievement of boys at school in Wales, and then to use existing and new research to find out the reasons for this under-achievement. The contract was based on an understandable concern about 'failing' boys. I worked on a wonderful set of figures representing all schools, subjects and phases of education. I found quite convincingly that failing boys were not the issue, and that the notion of under-achievement did not work to explain the apparent over-representation of girls at high levels of qualification in some subjects (Gorard et al. 2001a). The problem for the research team was that the funder then decided not to proceed. Why would they waste money on a review of evidence and new research to try and explain a pattern that I had shown did not exist? But these later stages of the research were what the bulk of the research funding was for. We lost out. This kind of situation, where later funding is contingent on the results of earlier research, can easily set up a conflict of interest. If I had somehow allowed my re-analysis to show the problem that the funders feared, we would have very probably received considerably more funding.

A very similar situation can arise when dealing with almost any funder for two or more distinct projects. A lot of funders have a significant interest in the actual results of research, whatever they might say, and even where any conflict is inadvertent. They may have a client group, such as people living in poverty, or a declared aim, such as to promote religion. It is natural therefore that researchers who tell a good story about people in poverty or who 'find' evidence of the benefits of religion will be more likely to obtain repeat funding. Some high profile researchers have said to me that if they found evidence unfavourable to the bias of their funders then they would suppress it. Most do not see a problem with this, because they are concerned with the same issue as the funders. For example, one professor told me that he would always suppress any good news about the underachievement of boys from Black minority ethnic groups because otherwise there was a danger that political and funding attention would move elsewhere. This tips the balance from being a conflict of interest in research to just not being research at all. What such people are doing is using the allure of social science research, such as it is, to act as agents for a political agenda. It is dishonest and possibly harmful to the very groups they claim to be trying to help. Even where the problem is not as blatant as this, funders increasingly make it hard for researchers to publish findings without their permission. And permission sometimes comes with considerable pressure to modify the research report.

The UK has had two admirable ways of trying to protect researchers from the kind of conflict of interest that arises with funders. One is a system of generic research councils who award funds for research after peer review of proposals. The most relevant one for social science is the Economic and Social Research Council (ESRC). The money comes from the government via the taxpayer, but the actual awards to researchers are almost entirely independent of the government. The system is not perfect but it is better than the government, charities' or pressure groups' handling of research funding. The second and even more important mechanism for ensuring freedom of speech for researchers is the block grant to research-active universities. Approximately every six years, all universities with academic researchers are required to submit examples of research and a report of what has been achieved with the block grant paid by the government, via the higher education funding council for their home country. This assessment exercise, now called the Research Excellence Framework (REF), determines how much each university receives as a recurrent research grant for the next six years. Again the system has been far from perfect. For example, several of the researchers whose work I have shown previously to contain elementary but crucial errors, such as not being able to total their figures correctly, or to construct a valid syllogism, have subsequently been selected to be on a panel who make the assessment of research quality! *Quis custodiet ipsos custodes*? Nevertheless, it is almost impossible to overstate the potential benefit of this funding system for social science, because it largely removes the issue of conflicts of interest. It allows researchers to speak truth to power, at least more so than if it did not exist. Both of these routes are under pressure because of funding cuts, and increased political interference. It is also true that most academics I have come across resent the peer-review of both ESRC and REF, and misunderstand the power that it gives us to work without (so much) fear of a conflict of interest.

13.3 ‖ The forgotten principle of ethics

I have discussed conflicts of interest (COIs) at length because they are important, and generally not well covered in traditional resources on ethics. COIs are important because they can endanger the quality of research, and this leads to a consideration of those key stakeholders in social science research other than the researchers, the participants, and the funders. Social science is largely paid for by the general public. The public are taxpayers and charity-givers, who provide the money that actually pays for most public research and for academic salaries. Where social science is relevant to real-life it is also the general public who are affected by its results. Research that leads to a new sentencing policy in courts, a new way of allocating places at schools, or new guidelines on taking children into care, could make a difference to society. Yet there is no mention of the people in this society in standard texts on ethics, although they are clearly the majority of those affected. They are the people for whom the research is done, and who are paying for it to be done. How would the ethics of research look to them?

I think that they would want research to be relevant and realistic, but above all they would want it to be of the highest quality possible. I have previously used extended examples of real projects to illustrate this point (e.g. Gorard 2002c). All research runs some kind of risk. An intervention may not work well, and so disadvantage those it was intended to help. An observation may influence that which it is meant to be observing, perhaps making it less efficient in delivering a service. Simply conducting research takes time for all concerned – participants and researchers. Therefore it has an opportunity cost in terms of both time and resource. However, these risks and downsides should not prevent research from taking place – as long as the research is worth the risk. This seems obvious. Poor or shoddy research runs these risks for no possibility of gain. It is therefore automatically unethical. It follows that only high quality research, leading to warranted and evidenced conclusions, can ever be truly ethical. But this is seldom made explicit in any discussion of research ethics. Pointless research remains pointless however 'ethically' it appears to be conducted. I propose this as a second key principle, after the first principle of not seeking to harm anyone involved in the research itself. Or perhaps it merely extends the first principle to a wider group. Thus, we should not harm anyone connected with the research – researchers, participants, those paying for it, and those who might be affected by its results. This means that there should be considerable ethical pressure on all researchers to use the most robust research design available for their questions. Using an inappropriate design or no design at all, as is currently so common in the existing social science literature, is just as unethical as research that sought to harm its participants. Perhaps more so. In fact, such poor research does harm the participants by wasting their time, and the rest of us by wasting our money. Many researchers do not seem to know right from wrong here, and misuse money – money that should be for real research – for some other purpose that I cannot quite fathom.

⫤ Exercises on ethical issues

1 Surely it cannot be ethical to deny an intervention to the cases in the control group of an experiment? If the intervention is effective, then the control group is being disadvantaged even though they have agreed to participate in the research. Discuss.

2 Is it ethical to randomise cases to treatments and control even where this is the most rigorous approach to answering the research question? Surely randomising people's lives is just wrong? Discuss.

3 In longitudinal work it is essential to follow individual cases over time. It would obviously be efficient for data collection to use the same 'identifier' for each case in the study and all of their relevant records. For example, their lifelong health, education, employment, tax, benefit, criminal and other records could all have the same identifying key code so that they could be easily matched by researchers. Is such a universal and lifetime identifier ethical? Discuss.

⚏ Notes on exercises on ethical issues

1 Although the argument that denying an intervention to a control group is unethical has some apparent force at first sight, I think this is an illusion. People are receiving, and not receiving interventions, all of the time. Governments and other bodies conduct pilot schemes to try out ideas, and these involve an intervention for some parts of the country but not others. This happens routinely, and without objection on ethical grounds. Practitioners such as teachers can decide to try a new way of teaching or to select a new textbook. Their students will receive what amounts to an intervention. Other students, even in the same school, will not. Again this happens routinely, and without objection. Making a pilot scheme or a new practice part of a rigorous evaluation means we will have a better idea of whether the intervention works. This makes the intervention more ethical if anything. It is also true that an evaluation should be conducted only when there is a good case that the intervention works but the outcome is not certain. An evaluation can help decide if the intervention works better than what it replaces, and also see if there are any unintended consequences. Until this is clear it is as likely that the group who do not receive the intervention have the advantage as it is that they are being deprived of anything. Of course, if an evaluation shows early on that the intervention is very damaging then it must stop.

Additionally, there are a large number of ways of making allocation of the intervention fairer. A waiting-list design offers the intervention to the treatment group as standard, but also offers it to the control group after a wait (and assuming it is not shown to be harmful). Thus, all participants receive the intervention but not all at once. Again, this is routine in non-experimental situations and no one complains.

2 It is important to separate the issue of randomisation from issues concerning the intervention itself. It is intriguing that commentators generally accept the allocation of an intervention to only a sub-set of possible cases as long as the allocation appears *ad hoc* in some way. An example might be a government pilot scheme only tried out in one city. But as soon as the allocation is described as random, some people object. If this objection is not because of denial of the intervention, which happens anyway without random allocation, what is the problem? In a randomised controlled trial, the participants must be signed up before allocation and they must agree to accept being in either treatment or control. If they do not agree, they are not part of the study. It may be inconvenient to lose possible participants like this, but it is scientifically sounder, and it solves the ethical issue.

3 In one respect my response here would be similar to the concern about randomisation. If individuals have agreed to participate in a longitudinal study, and they are aware

that this means a linkage between all of their state records, then this is probably all right. Participants would need to have the right to withdraw, and so have their records unlinked again. And there would need to be special provision for agreement about new-born babies, as used in the very valuable birth cohort studies. However, there have been attempts to link such records more generally, not necessarily for research purposes, in a general public database. This would be very useful for researchers, but ethically my response would be rather different. At present, such a life-time linkage of differ-ent records at an identifiable individual level is banned by law in many countries. It is banned to protect civil liberties. I think this is probably correct, because providing data for a database involves a kind of contract, even if it is not made formal. Personal data is provided for a specified purpose. The use of such data for another purpose, even where it is anonymous, raises ethical issues that have not yet been resolved (Grinyer 2009).

≡ Suggested reading

Gorard, S. (2002) 'Ethics and equity: pursuing the perspective of non-participants', *Social Research Update*, 39: 1–4.

5

Conclusion

FOURTEEN

Revisiting the need for robust design

SUMMARY

- Consideration of prior design improves research and everyone gains, from the people taking part to the people paying for it.
- The design selected must be suitable for the research questions being addressed, taking account of the elements of design.
- It is worth considering an even more robust design than you originally believe to be possible. This keeps researchers aware of the limitations of what they can do.
- Even so, we need to work to overcome resistance to the robust evaluation of social science ideas.
- When preparing a grant application, reviewers value clarity, explicit design, and warranted conclusions.
- Design is the chance to get things right from the start. It makes everything easier from then on.

14.1 ₪ Introduction

A consideration of design is a valuable preliminary part of high quality research. If research did not matter, then we should not do it and taxpayers should not fund it. Assuming research does matter, then we must do it well, and this means a robust approach to research design from the outset, making research conclusions convincing to a sceptical audience.

I sometimes hear a purported counter-argument to the use of design in research that goes something like this. Research design (logic, rigour, or even specific designs like RCTs) is all very well in the natural sciences where things are predictable and easy to control, but the social sciences are inherently much more complex. We cannot match groups, for example, because there are so many unknown variables – people are not like molecules. This view is nonsense and should be addressed as such wherever it is encountered. It fails as an argument at all levels. It is certainly not true that only the most able students select these supposedly complex social sciences once given the option, whereas most students flock to chemistry because it is so easy. True RCTs are anyway seldom used in science bench-work. They are more suitable for areas like agriculture from where they sprang, and public policy where they have been developed. Above all, the argument fails because the complexity of social science is an argument *for* design not against it. For example, the process of randomisation takes care of unknown differences between the groups, however many differences there are, and however variable people are. It is, therefore, even more valuable in a social science context.

14.2 ▮▮ How to choose a design?

There are a large number of possible designs. How do we select the most appropriate design for any study? Where they cover study design at all, traditional methods resources tend to start with off-the-shelf designs, whereas this book has been built up from the principles and elements of design. Combining these elements in different ways leads to the majority of off-the-shelf designs, and a range of possible new ones. I believe this is a far more flexible approach to understanding and using design. In the same way that research questions can evolve as a project unfolds, so can its design(s). The structure of a standard design is not intended to be restrictive, since designs can be easily used in combination; nor is it assumed that any off-the-shelf existing design is always or ever appropriate. Instead, consideration of design at the outset is intended to stimulate early awareness of the pitfalls and opportunities that will present themselves, simplify subsequent analysis, and so aid solidly warranted conclusions.

It is hard to summarise all possible research designs in a neat package, because of the number of elements and dimensions to consider. One attempt, in two dimensions, is portrayed in Table 14.1. Here, the element of timing forms the columns, representing in turn a design with no time element, a repeated cross-section, and tracking the same cases over time. How cases are allocated to sub-groups forms the rows, representing a design with no sub-groups, unmatched sub-groups and either matched or randomised groups. More variation, and so more rows and columns are possible even with just these two elements, and that is without considering the method of selecting cases. As might be expected, the rows and columns with no comparator and no time element have only a few simple entries, whereas the last cell of the table has more alternatives. There is not much that can be done with a snapshot design and no comparator, for example.

Table 14.1 lists 'case study' as a possible design here, but this is not really much of a design; rather it is an indication of scale, a very small scale. In fact, it is almost the absence of design, represented by:

N   O

Since design is so often ignored in social science, the case study is an easy escape route for anyone pressed to specify a design. This most common type of 'design' in social science involves no treatment, no allocation to groups, and no consideration of time. It is this design that makes it the hardest for a researcher to warrant any claims. There can be no comparison between groups or over time or place, because if such comparisons are valid the design would come from a different row or column. As soon as a case study has more than one group or several time periods, it is no longer simply one case study. Some commentators might opine that a case study is somehow special as it involves in-depth research with one case, but in doing so they are over-stepping the boundaries of design into methods of data collection. A longitudinal study, a field trial and a comparative study can be in-depth. Research design is independent of such considerations. But much more exciting work can be done with explicit comparators, a time element, and an intervention than can be done with a single case. Obviously.

Table 14.1 also reinforces the idea that a cross-sectional comparative claim needs an explicit comparator group. A claim of change over time needs a time element. In addition, a convincing causal claim needs an intervention, either one controlled by the researcher (a standard RCT) or simply piggy-backed by the researcher (a natural experiment). Without such an active intervention the design is passive and reliant on what turns up. It is a kind of fishing expedition. Such considerations also show how this table, or something like it, could be used to help a newer researcher, or someone unused to thinking about design, to decide on a design appropriate to their research questions. If a research question is comparative then the first row of Table 14.1 must be ignored. If a research question is about change then the first column of Table 14.1 must be ignored. If a research question is causal in nature, then everything not in bold can probably be ignored.

A simple question like 'Do girls do better than boys as school?' is already more interesting than could be addressed by a case study. It is comparative *and*

Table 14.1 One classification of standard designs: interaction of variations in timing with allocation to groups

	Snapshot	*Repeated snapshot*	*Longitudinal*
No comparator	Case study	Trend study	Panel/cohort study, before-and-after
Heterogeneous groups	Comparative/cross-sectional	Trend study	Panel/cohort study
Attempted homogeneous groups	–	Trend study	Panel/cohort study, **RCT, natural experiment**

Note: items in bold involve a specified intervention.

cross-sectional. A question like 'Is the attainment gap between boys and girls at school growing over time for each cohort?' would be comparative, about change, and non-causal. The groups – boys and girls – are heterogeneous, and so the middle cell of Table 14.1 contains an appropriate design listed as 'trend study'. Of course other designs can be created that would also be appropriate, but you could not go wrong with a repeated cross-sectional approach here. If the question was instead 'Does the attainment gap between boys and girls at school increase as they get older?', then this is again comparative, about change and non-causal. But it is longitudinal, not about repeated cross-sections (Chapter Eight). I hope you can see the difference. Therefore, a panel or cohort design would be one appropriate design. As a final example here, the research question 'Why do girls do better than boys at school?' is a causal comparative one (Chapter Five). I do not think it can be answered simply with any of the designs in Table 14.1, because it involves a programme of work rather than just one study. It is, if you like, an incomplete research question because it represents a problem rather than a puzzle (Chapter Three). It could be addressed in an exploratory way first, to generate possible explanations for the gap in attainment. Panel studies, cross-sectional approaches, plus modelling and theoretical work could all help. The real causal puzzle questions would then be more specific, like 'Is the gap in attainment between boys and girls caused by the nature of the assessments used?' A series of these questions can then be addressed to find the most convincing determinants of the gap. Because these studies would require interventions, such as changing the nature of school assessments, they should be natural experiments, or preferably RCTs (Chapter Nine).

The designs listed in Table 14.1 are not exhaustive, and could vary depending on a number of factors such as the method of sampling and allocation to groups (Chapters Six and Seven). Recall, a quasi-experiment would have an experimental design, and would normally have attempted homogeneous comparison groups, but the cases would not be randomised to groups, perhaps because the researcher has no or little control over the process. None of the designs listed in the table are iterative in the way that design-based approaches are (Chapter Ten), and as the model in Chapter Two demands. The rows and columns could also be very different elements. One dimension could be whether the research is intended to be exploratory, explanatory, or both together. Another dimension could be whether the study involves a controlled intervention, an uncontrolled one, or no intervention at all. And as suggested in Chapter Eight, we could also add 'place' as an explicit element in some way. Perhaps as a final exercise, you might try improving on or rearranging Table 14.1 in light of these suggestions.

One way of deciding on a design, in an exercise that I often use with my colleagues and students, is to imagine that you really cared about finding out the answer to your research question. People often say they care, but then betray that they do not by the way they then (mis-)conduct their research. The exercise is to think of your question, and imagine that you are someone like Louis XIV of

France. You are rich, all-powerful, a god-on-earth, and apparently without scruple (Louis reportedly took neonates away from their mothers, and kept them in isolation to see what the original human language was). But you are also genuinely curious to find the correct answer to a research question. So if the only thing that mattered to you in the world was doing the study well, without concern for time, resource, cost, ethics and so on, how would you do it? Thinking like this is free, and harms no one. We can think the unthinkable by imagining what a perfect design would be like for our area of investigation. Then we can try and get as close as possible to that ideal, given the inevitable limitations on what we can do in reality. Thinking like this has two main advantages. It encourages ambition and so high quality research, and it provides us with a ready-made log of all of the compromises we had to make from the ideal plan. This keeps us humble in our claims. For example knowing the format and power of RCTs for an evaluation gives us a template against which to measure what we might do instead, and even helps us to design what we do better. This is partly why everyone needs to learn about a range of designs even if they never intend to use them. We need to work to overcome the inertia about, and resistance to, trials and their often simpler equivalents like regression discontinuity. One way of doing this is to give more prominence to the second principle of ethics (Chapter Thirteen).

14.3 ▮▮ Preparing a research proposal

What are the lessons from this book for developing a research proposal, ranging from a postgraduate application to a first research grant? I have been a reviewer of research grant applications for around 30 international funding bodies, and am a grants awarding panel member for the UK ESRC, and for the US Institute of Education Science. What do we look at when assessing an application for research funding? As explained in Chapter Four, the first essential thing is clarity. If I cannot understand a proposal then I cannot recommend funding it. It is as simple as that. So do not send in your proposal full of lengthy sentences and obscure words. Such 'academicese' will not fool most reviewers. Write in plain language for a wide audience.

Second, you are asking for money to conduct research, so your focus from the outset must be on what that money is for. Sending in a wonderful conceptual background and a full review of literature might prove that you have done some good work and thinking in the past. But that cannot be a reason to ask for funding for the future. So do not make the mistake of spending the first three pages of a six page application on the build up to your new idea. A grant application is not a suspense novel. Of course, it can be important to portray your sound knowledge of the existing area for your new study, but it is best to do this succinctly at the outset, or in passing. Come to the point quickly.

There must be explicit and answerable research questions (Chapter Three). The proposal should almost always be to solve a research puzzle, of the kind that needs only the application of resources to solve. There should be a proposed design, or a mixture of design elements in a design-based approach. Reading a research proposal without a design section, or where the author is confused and has described methods as design, means I am reading a proposal without a plan. Funding bodies are not in favour of funding research with no plan. For most proposals, especially at the outset, the approach *cannot* be 'trust me, I am an expert'. The same applies to the methods. While the description of sampling and data collection methods is often adequate, the detail on analysis is often perfunctory. I do not really want to know what software you intend to use for analysis. But I do want to know how you will synthesise different parts of the data, how you will select codes, encourage reliability and validity, create models and so on. The design and methods are the key elements of an application for funding. They are what the bulk of the funding is going to be spent on. They must fit the research questions, and there must be a clear line of logic from questions, through design and methods, to the kinds of conclusions you want to draw. If this is not clear, or it is clear but clearly not correct, then the project will generally not be funded.

Finally, do not try to *teach* the reviewer elementary things, about research methods for example. In your proposal you can say how many interviews you want to be funded to conduct and why these are appropriate. You must not tell the reviewer what an interview is, and how it differs from a survey, or what the relative merits of the two are. And do not do this with anything else as basic as interviews. State which predictors you might use in your regression model, not what a regression model is. The reviewers already know, or should know, everything you know about methods in general. Their interest is in what precisely you propose to do.

14.4 ▌▌ A final plea

I end the book by repeating my plea. A good design can fail because of poor or inappropriate data. But a poor design remains poor however good your data is, and whatever type it is. A poor design, including no design at all, means that you will not be able to draw the kinds of conclusions you want to. Unfortunately, in this situation you may still be tempted to try to draw unwarranted conclusions, which encourages dishonest appraisal of facts, and disrespect for the research process. It means that your time, and the time of everyone involved in or reading about the research, has been largely wasted.

The message of this book can be summarised in two quotations from Rosenbaum (2002, p.368):

> Care in design and implementation will be rewarded with useful and clear study conclusions.

and

> Elaborate analytical methods will not salvage poor design or implementation of a study.

The same two ideas were put even more lucidly, and more cleverly if you pardon his exaggeration, in one aphorism by the nuclear physicist Ernest Rutherford:

> If your experiment needs statistics, you ought to have done a better experiment.

Both authors present the essence of the message of this book: preparation before conducting research, and making allowance at the start for the kinds of claims you will want to make afterwards, will generate better research. It really will. It will also generate results that are easier to analyse, and research conclusions that are more firmly warranted. They will also be easier to communicate to a wide audience. This is really all that research design is. It is the researcher's friend because it makes research easier. It is in the interests of the general public who might be affected by the implication of social or policy research, because it makes research better. It is the research funder's ally because it makes the research they are paying for both better and easier to use. A focus on research design means that everybody wins – except, of course, anyone with a vested interest in the existing generally poor level of social science research.

References

Abbot, A. (1998) 'The causal devolution', *Sociological Methods and Research*, 27(2): 148–81.

Adair, J. (1973) *The Human Subject*. Boston: Little, Brown and Co.

Altman, D. and Bland, M. (2005) 'Treatment allocation by minimization', *British Medical Journal*. 330: 843–44.

Angrist, J. and Krueger, A. (2001) 'Instrumental Variables and the Search for Identification: From Supply and Demand to Natural Experiments', *Journal of Economic Perspectives*, 15(4): 69–85.

Arjas, E. (2001) 'Causal analysis and statistics: a social sciences perspective', *European Sociological Review*, 17(1): 59–64.

Babcock, J., Green, C. and Robie, C. (2004) 'Does batterers' treatment work? A meta-analytic review of domestic violence treatment', *Clinical Psychology Review*, 23: 1023–53.

Badger, D., Nursten, J., Williams, P. and Woodward, M. (2000) 'Should all literature reviews be systematic?', *Evaluation and Research in Education*, 14(3&4): 220–30.

Bernard, R. (2000) *Social Research Methods: Qualitative and Quantitative Approaches*. London: SAGE.

Berry, W. (1984) *Nonrecursive Causal Models*. London: SAGE.

Bhaskar, R. (1994) *Plato Etc.: The Problems of Philosophy and Their Resolution*. London: Verso.

Bisson, J., Jenkins, P., Alexander, J. and Bannister, C. (1997) 'Randomised controlled trial of psychological debriefing for victims of acute burn trauma', *British Journal of Psychiatry*, 171(1): 78–81.

Black, P. and Wiliam, D. (2003) 'In praise of educational research: formative assessment', *British Educational Research Journal*, 29(5): 623–38.

Blalock, H. (1964) *Causal Inferences in Nonexperimental Research*. Chapel Hill: University of North Carolina Press.

Bland, M. (2003) *Cluster Randomised Trials in the Medical Literature*. Available at: http://epi.klinikum.uni-muenster.de/StatMethMed/2003/Freiburg/Folien/MartinBland.pdf, accessed 25/4/06.

Blumer, H. (1954) 'What is wrong with social theory?' *American Sociological Review*, 18: 3–10.

Booth, W., Colomb, G. and Williams, J. (1995) *The Craft of Research*, Chicago: University of Chicago Press.

Boruch, R. and Mosteller, F. (2002) 'Overview and new directions', in F. Mosteller and R. Boruch (eds) *Evidence Matters: Randomized Trials in Education Research*. Washington: Brookings Institution Press.

Boruch, R., De Moya, R. and Snyder, B. (2002) 'The importance of randomised field trials in education and related areas', pp. 50–79, in F. Mosteller and R. Boruch (eds) *Evidence Matters: Randomised Trials in Education Research*. Washington: Brookings Institution Press.

Bradford-Hill, A. (1966) 'The environment and disease: Association or causation?' *Proceedings of the Royal Society of Medicine*, 58: 285.

Brighton, M. (2000) 'Making our measurements count', *Evaluation and Research in Education*, 14(3&4): 124–35.

Brignell, J. (2000) *Sorry, Wrong Number! The Abuse of Measurement*. European Science and Environment Forum.

Brown, A. (1992) 'Design experiments: Theoretical and methodological challenges in creating complex interventions in classroom settings', *Journal of the Learning Sciences*, 2(2): 141–78.

Bryson, A., Dorsett, R. and Purdon, S. (2002) *The Use of Propensity Score Matching in the Evaluation of Active Labour Market Policies*. Policy Studies Institute, Working Paper 4. Available at: http://eprints.lse.ac.uk/4993/1/The_use_of_propensity_score_matching_in_the_evaluation_of_active_labour_market_policies.pdf

Bynner, J. and Joshi, H. (2002) 'Equality and opportunity in education: The evidence from the 1958 and the 1970 birth cohort surveys', *Oxford Review of Education*, 28(4): 405–25.

Campbell, D. and Stanley, J. (1963) *Experimental and Quasi-experimental Designs for Research on Teaching*. Boston: Houghton Mifflin.

Campbell, M., Elbourne, D. and Altman, D. (2004) 'CONSORT statement: extension to cluster randomised trials', *British Medical Journal*, 328: 702–08.

Campbell, M., Fitzpatrick, R., Haines, A., Kinmouth, A., Sandercock, P., Spiegelhalter, D. and Tyrer, P. (2000) 'Framework for design and evaluation of complex interventions to improve health', *British Medical Journal*, 321: 694–6.

Campbell, M., Julious, S. and Altman, D. (1995) 'Estimating sample sizes for binary, ordered categorical, and continuous outcomes in two group comparisons', *British Medical Journal*, 311: 1145–8.

Card, D. and Krueger, A. (1994) 'Minimum wages and employment: a case study of the fast-food industry in New Jersey and Pennsylvania', *American Economic Review*, 84(4): 772–93.

Carlin, J., Taylor, P. and Nolan, T. (1998) 'School based bicycle safety education and bicycle injuries in children: A case control study', *Injury Prevention*, 4: 22–7.

Ceglowski, D., Bacigalupa, C. and Peck, E. (2011) 'Aced out: Censorship of qualitative research in the age of "scientifically based research"', *Qualitative Inquiry*, 17(8): 679–86.

Cobb, P., Confrey, J., diSessa, A., Lehrer, R. and Schauble, L. (2003) 'Design experiments in educational research', *Educational Researcher*, 32(1): 9–13.

Cochrane (2012) *Issues Related to the Unit of Analysis*. Available at: http://www.cochrane-net.org/openlearning/html/modA2-4.htm, accessed 20/10/12.

Coe, R. (2010) 'Unobserved but not unimportant: the effects of unmeasured variables on causal attributions', *Effective Education*, 1(2): 101–22.

Cohen, J. (1994) 'The earth is round (p < .05)', *American Psychologist*, 49: 997–1003.

Cook, T. and Campbell, D. (1979) *Quasi-experimentation: Design and Analysis Issues for Field Settings*. Chicago: Rand McNally.

Cook, T. and Gorard, S. (2007) 'What counts and what should count as evidence', pp. 33–49, in OECD (eds) *Evidence in Education: Linking Research and Policy*. Paris: OECD.

Cooper, H. and Hedges, L. (1994) *The Handbook of Research Synthesis*. New York: Russell SAGE.

Corbi, J. and Prades, J. (2000) *Minds, Causes, and Mechanisms*. Oxford: Blackwell.

Coventry, A. (2008) *Hume's Theory of Causation*. London: Continuum.

Cox, D. (2001) 'Another comment on the role of statistical methods', *British Medical Journal*, 322: 231.

Creswell, J. and Plano Clark, V. (2007) *Designing and Conducting Mixed Methods Research*. London: SAGE.

Croll, P. (2009) 'Educational participation post-16: A longitudinal analysis of intentions and outcomes', *British Journal of Educational Studies*, 57(4): 400–16.

Cronbach, L. (1982) *Designing Evaluations of Educational and Social Programs*. San Francisco: Jossey-Bass.

Davis, J. (1994) 'What's wrong with sociology?', *Sociological Forum*, 9(2): 179–97.

Dawes, R. (2001) *Everyday Irrationality*. Oxford: Westview Press.

de Groot, C., Mulder, C., Das, M. and Manting, D. (2011) 'Life events and the gap between intention to move and actual mobility', *Environment and Planning A*, 43(1): 48–66.

de Vaus, D. (2001) *Research Design in Social Research*. London: SAGE.

de Vaus, D. (2002) *Analyzing Social Science Data: 50 Key Problems in Data Analysis*. London: SAGE.

Dehejia, R., Wahba, S. and Stanley, M. (2002) 'Propensity score-matching methods for non-experimental causal studies', *The Review of Economics and Statistics*, 84(1):151–61.

Dixon-Woods, M., Fitzpatrick, R. and Roberts, K. (1999) 'Including qualitative research in systematic reviews', *Journal of Evaluation in Clinical Practice*, 7: 125–33.

Donnelly, C., Woodroffe, R., Cox, D., Bourne, J, Gettinby, G., Le Fevre, A., McInerney, J. and Morrison, W. . (2003) 'Impact of localized badger culling on tuberculosis incidence in British cattle', *NATURE*, 426: 834–37.

Dowe, P. and Noordhof, P. (2004) 'Introduction', pp. 1–11, in P. Dowe and P. Noordhof (eds) *Cause and Chance*. London: Routledge.

Dubin, R. (1978) *Theory Building*. New York: Macmillan Press.

Dynarski, M., Agodini, R., Heaviside, S., Novak, T., Carey, N., Campuzano, L., et al. (2007) *Effectiveness of Reading and Mathematics Software Products: Findings from the First Pupil Cohort*, (Publication No. 2007-4005), Washington, DC: U.S, Department of Education, Institute of Education Sciences. Available at: http:// ies.ed.gov/ncee/pdf/20074005.pdf

Edwards, A. (1972) *Experimental Design in Psychological Research*, 4th edn. New York: Holt, Rinehart and Winston.

Egger, M., Smith, G. and Phillips, A. (1997) 'Meta-analysis: Principles and procedures', *British Medical Journal*, 315: 1533–41.

Emmet, D. (1984) *The Effectiveness of Causes*. London: Macmillan Press.

Erzberger, C. and Prein, G. (1997) 'Triangulation: Validity and empirically-based hypothesis construction', *Quality and Quantity*, 31: 141–54.

Fehring, H. and Bessant, J. (2009) 'Life course research design for transitional labour market research', *Journal of Education and Work*, 22(2): 81–90.

Festinger, L. and Carlsmith, J. (1959) 'Cognitive consequences of forced compliance', *Journal of Abnormal and Social Psychology*, 58: 203–10.

Feyerabend, P. (1993) *Against Method*. London: Verso.

Fisher, R. (1935) *The Design of Experiments*. Edinburgh: Oliver and Boyd.

Fiske, E. and Ladd, H. (2000) *When Schools Compete: A Cautionary Tale*. Washington DC: Brookings Institution Press.

Freedman, D. (2005) 'Linear statistical models for causation: A critical review', in B. Everitt and D. Howell (eds) *Encyclopedia of Statistics in Behavioral Science*. London: Wiley.

Fukkink, R. (2002) 'Effects of instruction in deriving word meaning from context and incidental word learning', *L1 – Educational Studies in Language and Literature*, 2: 37–57.

Funk, P. and Gathmann, C. (2011) 'Does direct democracy reduce the size of government? New evidence from historical data, 1890–2000', *The Economic Journal*, 121(557): 1252–80.

Gambetta, D. (1987) *Were They Pushed or Did They Jump? Individual Decision Mechanisms in Education*. London: Cambridge University Press.

Garrison, R. (1993) 'Mises and his methods', pp. 102–17, in J. Herbener (ed.) *The Meaning of Ludwig von Mises: Contributions in Economics, Sociology, Epistemology, and Political Philosophy*. Boston: Kluwer Academic Publishers.

Gennetian, L., Magnuson, K. and Morris, P. (2008) 'From statistical associations to causation: What developmentalists can learn from instrumental variables techniques coupled with experimental data', *Developmental Psychology*, 44(2): 381–94.

Gigerenzer, G. (2002) *Reckoning with Risk*. London: Penguin.

Glass, G., McGaw, B. and Smith, M. (1981) *Meta-analysis in Social Research*. Beverley Hills, CA: SAGE.

Glymour, C., Scheines, R., Spirtes, P. and Kelly, K. (1987) *Discovering Causal Structure*. Orlando: Academic Press.

Goldthorpe, J. (2001) 'Causation, statistics, and sociology', *European Sociological Review*, 17,(1): 1–20.

Gomm, R. (2004*) Social Research Methodology: A Critical Introduction*. Basingstoke: Palgrave Macmillan.

Goodman, N. (1973) *Fact, Fiction and Forecast*. New York: Bobs-Merrill.

Gorard, S. (2002a) 'Fostering scepticism: The importance of warranting claims', *Evaluation and Research in Education*, 16(3): 136–49.

Gorard, S. (2002b) 'The role of causal models in education as a social science?', *Evaluation and Research in Education*, 16(1): 51–65.

Gorard, S. (2002c) 'Ethics and equity: Pursuing the perspective of non-participants', *Social Research Update*, 39: 1–4.

Gorard, S. (2003) *Quantitative Methods in Social Science: The Role of Numbers Made Easy*. London: Continuum.

Gorard, S. (2004a) 'Scepticism or clericalism? Theory as a barrier to combining methods', *Journal of Educational Enquiry*, 5(1): 1–21.

Gorard, S. (2004b) 'Three abuses of "theory": An engagement with Nash', *Journal of Educational Enquiry*, 5(2): 19–29.

Gorard, S. (2006a) *Using Everyday Numbers Effectively in Research: Not a Book About Statistics*. London: Continuum.

Gorard, S. (2006b) 'Towards a judgement-based statistical analysis', *British Journal of Sociology of Education*, 27(1): 67–80.

Gorard, S. (2007) 'The dubious benefits of multi-level modelling', *International Journal of Research and Method in Education*, 30(2): 221–36.

Gorard, S. (2008a) 'Research impact is not always a good thing: a re-consideration of rates of "social mobility' in Britain", *British Journal of Sociology of Education*, 29(3): 317–24.

Gorard, S. (2008b) 'Who is missing from higher education?', *Cambridge Journal of Education*, 38(3): 421–37.

Gorard, S. (2009) 'Does the index of segregation matter? The composition of secondary schools in England since 1996', *British Educational Research Journal*, 35(4): 639–52.

Gorard, S. (2010a) 'Measuring is more than assigning numbers', pp. 389–408, in G. Walford, E. Tucker and M. Viswanathan (eds) *Sage Handbook of Measurement*. Los Angeles: SAGE.

Gorard, S. (2010b) 'Serious doubts about school effectiveness', *British Educational Research Journal*, 36(5): 735–66.

Gorard, S. (2010c) 'All evidence is equal: The flaw in statistical reasoning', *Oxford Review of Education*, 36(1): 63–77.

Gorard, S. (2011) 'Now you see it, now you don't: School effectiveness as conjuring?', *Research in Education*, 86: 39–45.

Gorard, S. (2012a) 'The increasing availability of official datasets: Methods, opportunities, and limitations for studies of education', *British Journal of Educational Studies*, 60(1): 77–92.

Gorard, S. (2012b) 'The propagation of errors in experimental data analysis: a comparison of pre- and post-test designs', *International Journal of Research and Methods in Education*. Available at: http://dx.doi.org/10.1080/1743727X.2012.741117

Gorard, S. and Cheng S.C. (2011) 'Pupil clustering in English secondary schools: One pattern or several?', *International Journal of Research and Method in Education*, 34(3): 327–39.

Gorard, S. and Cook, T. (2007) 'Where does good evidence come from?', *International Journal of Research and Method in Education*, 30(3): 307–23.

Gorard, S. and Fitz, J. (2006) 'What counts as evidence in the school choice debate?', *British Educational Research Journal*, 32(6):797–816.

Gorard, S. and Rees, G. (2002) *Creating a Learning Society?* Bristol: The Policy Press.

Gorard, S. and Roberts, K. (2004) 'What kind of creature is a design experiment?', *British Educational Research Journal*, 30(3): 577–90.

Gorard, S. and Taylor, C. (2002) 'What is segregation? A comparison of measures in terms of strong and weak compositional invariance', *Sociology*, 36(4): 875–95.

Gorard, S. with Taylor, C. (2004) *Combining Methods in Educational and Social Research*. London: Open University Press.

Gorard, S., Fitz, J. and Taylor, C. (2001b) 'School choice impacts: What do we know?', *Educational Researcher*, 30(7): 18–23.

Gorard, S., Rees, G. and Salisbury, J. (2001a) 'The differential attainment of boys and girls at school: Investigating the patterns and their determinants', *British Educational Research Journal*, 27(2): 125–39.

Gorard, S., Rees, G. and Selwyn, N. (2002) 'The "conveyor belt effect": A re-assessment of the impact of National Targets for Lifelong Learning', *Oxford Review of Education*, 28(1): 75–89.

Gorard, S., See, B.H. and Davies, P. (2011) *Do Attitudes and Aspirations Matter in Education? A Review of the Research Evidence.* Saarbrucken: Lambert Academic Publishing.

Gorard, S., Taylor, C. and Fitz, J. (2003) *Schools, Markets and Choice Policies*. London: RoutledgeFalmer.

Gorard, S. with Adnett, N., May, H., Slack, K., Smith, E. and Thomas, L. (2007) *Overcoming Barriers to HE*. Stoke-on-Trent: Trentham Books.

Gottfried, M. (2010) 'Evaluating the relationship between student attendance and achievement in Urban and Middle school: An Instrumental Variables approach', *American Educational Research Journal*, 47(2): 434–65.

Green, J., Nelson, G., Martin, A. and Marsh, H. (2006) 'The causal ordering of self-concept and academic motivation and its effect on academic achievement', *International Education Journal*, 7(4): 534–46.

Grinyer, A. (2009) 'The ethics of secondary analysis and further use of qualitative data', *Social Research Update*, 56, 4 pages.

Hagenaars, J. (1990) *Categorical Longitudinal Data: Log-linear, Panel, Trend and Cohort Analysis*. London: SAGE.

Hakim, C. (1982) *Secondary Analysis in Social Research: A Guide to Data Sources and Methods with Examples*. London: Allen and Unwin.

Hakim, C. (2000) *Research Design*. London: Routledge.

Harlow, L., Mulaik, S. and Steiger, J. (1997) *What If There Were No Significance Tests?* Marwah, NJ: Lawrence Erlbaum.

Hartmann, D., Gottman, J., Jones, R., Gardner, W., Kazdin, A. and Vaught, R. (1980) 'Interrupted time-series analysis and its application to behavioral data', *Journal of Applied Behavior Analysis*, 13: 543–59.

Hemming, K., Girling, A., Sith, A., Marsh, J. and Lilford, R. (2011) 'Sample size calculation for cluster randomised controlled trials with a fixed number of clusters', *BMC Medical Research Methodology*, 11: 102–09.

Hendry, D. and Mizon, G. (1999) 'The pervasiveness of Granger causality in econometrics', in R. Engle and H. White (eds) *Cointegration, Causality, and Forecasting: A Festschrift in Honour of Clive W.J. Granger*. Oxford: Oxford University Press.

Henson, R., Hull, D. and Williams, C. (2010) 'Methodology in our education research culture: Towards a stronger collective quantitative proficiency', *Educational Researcher*, 39(3): 229–40.

Hollis, M. (1994) *The Philosophy of Social Science*. Cambridge: Cambridge University Press.

Hoxby, C. (2000) 'Does competition among public schools benefit students and taxpayers?', *American Economic Review*, 90(5): 1209–38.

Huck, S. and Sandler, H. (1979) *Rival Hypotheses: Alternative Interpretations of Data Based Conclusions*. New York: Harper and Row.

Hume, D. (1962) *On Human Nature and the Understanding*. New York: Collier.

Hutchison, G. (2009) 'Designing your sample efficiently: Clustering effects in education surveys', *Educational Research*, 51(1): 109–26.

Jerrim, J. and Vignoles, A. (2011) *The Use (and Misuse) of Statistics in Understanding Social Mobility: Regression to the Mean and the Cognitive Development of High Ability Children from Disadvantaged Homes*. Department of Quantitative Social Science Working Paper 11–01, London: Institute of Education.

Kano, M., Franke, T., Afifi, A. and Bourque, L. (2008) 'Adequacy of reporting results of school surveys and nonresponse effects', *Educational Researcher*, 37(8): 480–90.

Khan, M. and Gorard, S. (2012) 'A randomised controlled trial of the use of a piece of commercial software for the acquisition of reading skills', *Educational Review*, 64(1): 21–36.

Kline, R. (1998) *Principles and Practices of Structural Equation Modelling*. New York: Guilford.

Kuhn, T. (1970) *The Structure of Scientific Revolutions*. Chicago: University of Chicago Press.

Lewin, K. (1946) 'Action research and minority problems', *Journal of Social Issues*, 2(4): 34–46.

Li, J. and Lomax, R. (2011) 'Analysis of variance: what is your software actually doing?', *The Journal of Experimental Education*, 79(3): 279–94.

Mackie, J. (1974) *The Cement of the Universe*, Oxford: Clarendon Press.

Marsh, H. (1990) 'Causal ordering of academic self-concept and academic achievement: A multiwave, longitudinal panel analysis', *Journal of Educational Psychology*, 82(4): 646–56.

Maruyama, G. (1998) *Basics of Structural Equation Modelling*. London: SAGE.

McAlevey, L. and Sullivan, C. (2010) 'Statistical literacy and sample survey results', *International Journal of Mathematical Education*, 41(7): 911–20.

McKim, V. and Turner, S. (1997) *Causality in Crisis? Statistical Methods and the Search for Causal Knowledge in the Social Sciences*. Indiana: University of Notre Dame Press.

McNiff, J. and Whitehead, J. (2002). *Action Research: Principles and Practice*. London: Routledge Falmer.

Medical Research Council (2000) *A Framework for Development and Evaluation of RCTs for Complex Interventions to Improve Health*. London: MRC.

Meehl, P. (1967) 'Theory-testing in psychology and physics: A methodological paradox', *Philosophy of Science*, 34: 103–15.

Mensah, F. and Kiernan, K. (2010) 'Gender differences in educational attainment: Influences of the family environment', *British Educational Research Journal*, 36(2): 239–60.

Middleton, J., Gorard, S., Taylor, C. and Bannan-Ritland, B. (2008) 'The "compleat" design experiment: from soup to nuts', pp. 21–46, in A. Kelly, R. Lesh, and J. Baek (eds) *Handbook of Design Research Methods in Education: Innovations in Science, Technology, Engineering and Mathematic Learning and Teaching*. New York: Routledge.

Miles, J. and Shevlin, M. (2001) *Applying Regression and Correlation: A Guide for Students and Researchers*. London: SAGE.

Mill, J. (1882) *A System Of Logic, Ratiocinative and Inductive, Being a Connected View of the Principles of Evidence, and the Methods of Scientific Investigation* (8th edn). New York: Harper & Brothers.

Morgan, C. (1903) *Introduction to Comparative Psychology*. London: Walter Scott.

Morris, P. (2008) 'From statistical associations to causation: What developmentalists can learn from Instrumental Variables Techniques coupled with experimental data', *American Psychological Association*, 44(2): 381–94.

Morrison, K. (2001) 'Randomised controlled trials for evidence-based education: some problems in judging "what works"', *Evaluation and Research in Education*, 15(2): 69–83.

Morrison, K. (2009) *Causation in Educational Research*. London: Routledge.

Munn-Giddings, C., Hart, C. and Ramon, S. (2005) 'A participatory approach to the promotion of well-being in the workplace', *International Review of Psychiatry*, 17(5): 409–17.

Pan, W. and Frank. K. (2003) 'A probability index of the robustness of a causal inference', *Journal of Educational and Behavioural Statistics*, 28(4): 315–37.

Park, R. (2000) *Voodoo Science: The Road from Foolishness to Fraud*. Oxford: Oxford University Press.

Pawson, R. (2006) *Evidence-based Policy: A Realist Perspective*. Los Angeles: SAGE.

Pearl, J. (2000) *Causality: Models, Reasoning, and Inference*. Cambridge: Cambridge University Press.

Petrosino, A., Turpin-Petrosino, C. and Finckenauer, J. (2000) 'Programs can have harmful effects! Lessons from experiments of programs such as scared straight', *Crime and Delinquency*, 46(1): 354–79.

Phillips, D. (1999) 'How to play the game: A Popperian approach to the conduct of research', in G. Zecha (ed.) *Critical Rationalism and Educational Discourse*. Amsterdam: Rodopi.

Pocock, S. and Simon, R. (1975) 'Sequential treatment assignment with balancing for prognostic factors in the controlled clinical trial', *Biometrics*, 31: 102–15.

Popper, K. (1959) *The Logic of Scientific Discovery*. London: Routledge.

Pötter, U. and Blossfeld, H. (2001) 'Causal inference from series of events', *European Sociological Review*, 17(1): 21–32.

Pratt, J. and Schlaifer, R. (1988) 'On the interpretation and observation of laws', *Journal of Econometrics*, 39(1–2): 23–52.

Proudfoot, J., Guest, D., Carson, J., Dunn, G. and Gray, J. (1997) 'Effect of cognitive-behavioural training on job-finding among long-term unemployed', *Lancet*, 350: 96–100.

Pruss, A. (2006) *The Principle of Sufficient Reason*. Cambridge: Cambridge University Press.

Puffer, S., Torgerson, D. and Watson, J. (2005) 'Cluster randomized controlled trials', *Journal of Evaluation in Clinical Practice*, 11(5): 479–83.

Roberts, I. (2000) 'Randomised trials or the test of time? The story of human albumin administration', *Evaluation and Research in Education*, 14(3&4): 231–6.

Roberts, K., Dixon-Woods, M., Fitzpatrick, R., Abrams, K., and Jones, D. (2002) 'Factors affecting uptake of childhood immunisation: An example of Bayesian synthesis of qualitative and quantitative evidence', *The Lancet*, 360: 1596–9.

Robinson, D., Levin, J., Thomas, G., Pituch, K. and Vaughn, S. (2007) 'The incidence of "causal" statements in teaching-and-learning research journals', *American Educational Research Journal*, 44(2): 400–13.

Rosenbaum, P. (2002) *Observational Studies*. New York: Springer.

Rosenbaum, P. and Rubin, D. (1983) 'The central role of the propensity score in observational studies for causal effects', *Biometrika*, 70(1): 41–55.

Salmon, W. (1998) *Causality and Explanation*. New York: Oxford University Press.

Selwyn, N., Gorard, S. and Furlong, J. (2006) *Adult Learning in the Digital Age*. London: RoutledgeFalmer.

Senn, S. and Julious, S. (2009) 'Measurement in clinical trials: A neglected issue for statisticians?', *Statistics in Medicine*, 28: 3189–209.

Shadish, W., Cook, T. and Campbell, D. (2002) *Experimental and Quasi-experimental Designs for Generalized Causal Inference*. Belmont: Wadsworth.

Shafer, G. (1996) *The Art of Causal Conjecture*. London: MIT Press.

Siegel, S. (1956) *Nonparametric Statistics for the Behavioural Sciences*. Tokyo: McGraw Hill.

Simpson, E. (1951) 'The interpretation of interaction in contingency tables', *Journal of the Royal Statistical Society*, Series B, 13: 238–51.

Smith, E. and Gorard, S. (2005) '"They don't give us our marks": The role of formative feedback in student progress', *Assessment in Education*, 12(1): 21–38.

Sobel, M. (1998) 'Causal inference in statistical models of the process of socio-economic achievement: A Case Study', *Sociological Methods and Research*, 27(2): 318–48.

Somekh, B. and Lewin, C. (2005) *Research Methods in the Social Sciences*. London: SAGE.

Sullivan, A., Heath, A. and Rothon, C. (2011) 'Equalisation or inflation? Social class and gender differentials in England and Wales', *Oxford Review of Education*, 37(2): 215–40.

Sullivan C. and Bybee, D. (1999) 'Reducing violence using community-based advocacy for women with abusive partners', *Journal of Consultative and Clinical Psychology*, 67: 43–53.

Sword, H. (2009) 'Writing higher education differently: A manifesto on style', *Studies in Higher Education*, 34(3): 319–36.

Taylor, C. and Gorard, S. (2005) 'Participation in higher education: Wales', in *Fair and Flexible Funding: A Welsh Model to Promote Quality and Access in Higher Education*. Cardiff: Welsh Assembly Government.

Thouless, R. (1974) *Straight and Crooked Thinking*. London: Pan.

Tooley, J. with Darby, D. (1998) *Educational Research: A Critique*. London: OFSTED.

Torgerson, C. and Torgerson, D. (2001) 'The need for randomised controlled trials in educational research', *British Journal of Educational Studies*, 49(3): 316–28.

Torgerson, D. and Torgerson, C. (2008) *Designing Randomised Trials*. Basingstoke: Palgrave.

Toroyan, T., Roberts, I., Oakley, A., Laing, G., Mugford, M. and Frost, C. (2003) 'Effectiveness of out-of-home day care for disadvantaged families: Randomised controlled trial', *British Medical Journal*, 327: 906.

Toulmin, S., Rieke, R. and Janik, A. (1979) *An Introduction to Reasoning*. New York: Macmillan.

Tversky, A. and Kahneman, D. (1974) 'Judgment under uncertainty: Heuristics and biases', *Science*, 185(4157): 1124–31.

Ty Wilde, E. and Hollister, R. (2002) *How Close is Close Enough? Testing Nonexperimental Estimates of Impact Against Experimental Estimates of Impact with Education Test Scores as Outcomes*. Institute of Research on Poverty Discussion Paper 1241-02. Available at: www.ssc.wisc.edu/irp/

Urlich, K. and Eppinger, S. (2000) *Product Design and Development*. Boston: Irwin McGraw-Hill.

US Department of Education (2008) *Reducing Behaviour Problems in the Elementary School Classroom*. Institute of Educational Sciences, National Evaluation and Regional Assistance Report, NCEE 2008-012.

Weiss, C. (2002) 'What to do until the random assigner comes', in F. Mosteller and R. Boruch (eds) *Evidence Matters: Randomized Trials in Education Research*. Washington: Brookings Institution.

White, P. (2009) *Developing Research Questions: A Guide for Social Scientists*. London: Palgrave.

Willms, D. and Echols, F. (1992) 'Alert and inert clients: The Scottish experience of parental choice of schools', *Economics of Education Review*, 11(4): 339–50.

Wilson, D. and Lipsey, M. (2001) *Practical Meta-analysis*. Thousand Oaks: SAGE.

Wright, D. (2003) 'Making friends with your data: Improving how statistics are conducted and reported', *British Journal of Educational Psychology*, 73: 123–36.

Yin, R. (2009) *Case Study Research: Design and Methods*. Thousand Oaks: SAGE.

Index

37532631R00131

Made in the USA
San Bernardino, CA
19 August 2016